Also by Judy Collins:

JUDY COLLINS SONGBOOK

TRUST YOUR HEART

An Autobiography

Judy Collins

FAWCETT CREST • NEW YORK

AUTHOR'S NOTE: This book recounts many conversations held over a long period of time and reconstructed from memory. In each instance the substance and tone of these conversations is accurate; the dialogue is as precise as memory permits.

A Fawcett Crest Book
Published by Ballantine Books
Copyright © 1987 by Judy Collins

The author has made every attempt to locate all owners of photographs and to obtain permission to reproduce them. Any errors or omissions are unintentional and corrections will be made in future printings if necessary. Collins family photographs courtesy of Marjorie Byrd Collins Hall and Miriam Starlin. Photographs of Jim Hensen and the Muppets are copyright © 1977 by Hensen Associates, Inc. Reprinted by permission. All rights reserved.

The author gratefully acknowledges permission to quote lyrics from the following songs: "This Land is Your Land," words and music by Woody Guthrie, used by permission of TRO. Copyright © 1956 (renewed 1984), 1958 (renewed 1986), and 1970 by Ludlow Music, Inc., New York, N.Y. "Oh, Had I a Golden Thread," by Pete Seeger, used by permission of Stormking Music, Inc. Copyright © 1959 (and renewed) by Stormking Music, Inc. All rights reserved. "It Isn't Nice," words by Malvina Reynolds, music by Malvina Reynolds and Barbara Dane, used by permission of Schroder Music Co. Copyright © 1964 by Schroder Music Co. (ASCAP). "Someday Soon," by Ian Tyson, Copyright © 1963 by Warner Bros., Inc. All rights reserved. Used by permission. "Hard Loving Loser" ("Hard Lovin' Loser"), by Dick Fariña, Copyright © 1966 by Warner Bros., Inc. All rights reserved. Used by permission. "Just Like Tom Thumb's Blues" ("Tom Thumb's Blues"), by Bob Dylan, Copyright © 1965 by Warner Bros., Inc. All rights reserved. Used by permission.
"Trust Your Heart" by Judy Collins © 1987 by CBS, Inc., and the Wildflowers Company. All other songs by Judy Collins are copyrighted by The Wildflowers Company or by Rocky Mountain National Park Music Co., Inc.

Library of Congress Catalog Card Number: 87-17180

ISBN 0-449-21662-4

First published by Houghton Mifflin Company. Reprinted by permission of Houghton Mifflin Company.

Manufactured in the United States of America

First Ballantine Books Edition: February 1989

Trust Your Heart

In the sky, the phantom moon appears at midday
To join the sun in some forgotten dance;
In their light, our voices tremble with reflections
Of what we know and what we leave to chance;

   The heart can see beyond the sun
   Beyond the turning moon
   And as we look, the heart can teach us
   All we need to learn.

We have dreams, we hold them to the light like diamonds,
Stones of the moon and splinters of the sun;
Some we keep, to light the dark nights on our journey
And shine beyond the days when we have won;

   The heart can see beyond our fears,
   Beyond our fondest schemes,
   And tell us which were made for fools,
   And which are wise men's dreams . . .
   Trust your heart, trust your heart.

Politics is the art of the possible.

Acknowledgments

This book is dedicated to a group of friends who were never strangers and to: Louis Nelson, my friend and my lover; Clark, my son; Holly Collins, my sister; David, Denver, and Michael Collins, my brothers; my mother, Marjorie Byrd Collins Hall; and to the memory of my father, Charles Thomas Collins.

My gratitude and thanks to Nan Talese, my sensitive, caring editor who has added her counsel and friendship to the process. She saw the future in the past and gave me the courage to continue and finish this book; to Signe Warner Watson, Shelly Perron, Luise Erdmann, and Sarah Flynn for their insight and guidance; to Lynn Nesbit, my agent, for her encouragement and perception. Thanks to Joyce Ashley, Gail Buchicchio, Cynthia Macdonald, Alison Mayron, Cousin Lois Collins, Uncle Frank Collins, Great-aunt Violette Collins, Percy and Ruth Booth, Mary Jane (Peterson) McCort, Cousin Lillian Cope, and Jonathan Segal. I want to thank Tad Mosel for his time and his wisdom and Louis Nelson, who listened to me read the book out loud, and gave me attention and insight, even after midnight. To all my friends, who had to tolerate my wandering attention and broken dates during deadlines, my heartfelt thanks for their patience and support.

Preface

Perhaps there is something unnatural about writing an autobiography when you are still only four decades old and counting. But having long been devoted to the process of keeping journals, I am convinced that writing about the same events at different times in one's life leads to seeing the same things quite differently.

Since publishing *Trust Your Heart*, I have often been asked what it was "like" to be at the center of the musical and social change that occurred in the sixties, the years in which I came to prominence as a singer. They were intensively revolutionary, important, and exotic years, poignantly marked with dead friends and longed for by those who weren't there, or feel they missed out anyway. William James is quoted as having said, "live as though you make a difference," and I assume he meant consciously. But in addition to the conscious direction to one's life, I believe there is an inner clarion whose note and tone are only later identified as having been part of a given history.

My interest in politics, in social justice, and in, if you will, revolution, was acquired from my Quaker predecessors, as certainly as were my curiosity and my blue eyes. My efforts were felt in a more public way than some, and as to how it feels to be at the center, I believe that when you are doing what you are called to do, you probably aren't watching.

Today I hear the sixties discussed as if they were some model of dinosaur, extinct, irreplaceable. I was in my early twenties and felt as though I was living in the skin of someone whom I barely knew, whose name was foreign to me, a willful and often lost child. But the creative and political juices of the sixties are not over. There is life in music, pop music, folk music. Suzanne Vega and Carly Simon, Sting and U.2, Paul Simon and Joni Mitchell, Bruce Springsteen, Leonard Cohen and Tracy Chapman all make music with heart and soul, with lyrics of concern and beauty.

Just as there were many social revolutions going on in the sixties, so there are today. Social change is continuous, and it is encouraging to see a great number of performers and individuals involved in efforts to feed the poor, pay attention to the family farmer, and take firm actions against apartheid in South Africa. The commitment to those issues goes on and there is "life after the sixties."

I participated in actions that resulted in great social change: the actions against the war in Vietnam—the voter-registration efforts in the summer of 1964 in Mississippi, *Mississippi Summer*; the beginning of the second wave of feminism—the growing awareness of women's rights, the issues of equal pay for equal work. As I write today, the pay schedule for women at most companies is sixty cents to the dollar for an equal amount of work done by a man. The white minority government of South Africa, practicing apartheid against black South Africans, still rules, and there is still racial, and sexual discrimination in our country. There is work to be done, and it must go on whether in the light of press coverage or not. The sixties may be chronologically over, but the values for which that time stood will never be gone.

After writing the book I am also much more aware of how the loss of custody of my son in 1965 devastated me, emotionally and spiritually. Today I have a beautiful relationship with my son Clark, but I'm sure I couldn't have stood to know then how long it would take to recover emotionally, or that I would never entirely do so. Since the first publication of *Trust Your Heart*, I've received poignant letters from women who have had similar experiences. I am more and more convinced that there is a physical destruction that takes place when a child is removed from the mother against her wishes. Although my son came back to me only three years after my loss of custody, a part of me has never, and I think will never, recover from that wound.

I wanted to say something more about Mark Abramson, one of the people who made a great difference in my musical recording life. He and I produced many records during the years from 1964 to 1971 and he is now a painter, an artist of great quality. His art is strong and unusual, as is his musical taste. My admiration for his insight, musical taste, and ability to take risks, are enormous.

In *Trust Your Heart* I was able to share some of the story of my recovery from the disease of alcoholism. Cracking open the denial with which all my active and previous recovering years had been cloaked was extremely difficult and I was greatly assisted in doing this by the care, concern and integrity of my friend and editor Nan Talese and my friend Tad Mosel. I am more convinced than ever that we must accept and treat alcoholism as a disease. The American Medical Association has taken this stand for many years. Alcoholism is directly or indirectly responsible for a hundred thousand deaths a year in the United States alone, statistically competing with heart disease and cancer. Alcoholism is the documented cause of a high percentage of violent crime, social depravity and family devastation. Without facing its potential for treatment, we have little hope of going to one of the most important sources of healing and help at all levels of society. Alcoholism and chemical addiction are social issues, as important as feminism, equality, world hunger and world peace.

If I hadn't been a singer I've always thought I might have wound up in the Park Service, maybe as a fire lookout somewhere in the Rocky Mountains, maybe as a botanist. I am sure that anywhere I went, and whatever profession I might have chosen, I would have had to express my outrage about the polluted, raped, pillaged planet on which we live. Perhaps my future could have been as a naturalist in the Azores, or writing a book about the terrible plight of the rain forests, and the fact that there are less than half the birds on migration paths since 1939, the year I was born. They say that many of the tropical forests are being felled because of the need for grazing land to raise cattle for the production of hamburgers. It is true that we need an inexpensive, nutritious meal for millions of people, but to do so at the risk of destroying the forests that protect our planet seems a high price; perhaps there is some alternative. Where there is a picket line that protests this, you will probably find me. And you will probably be there yourself, if you bought this book.

This morning I have written in my journal, finished the work on my latest album, my twenty-second, called *Sanity and Grace*, and made a date with Louis Nelson, the man I live with, to go to watch whales next week with Roger Payne. Roger was the marine biologist who first brought me a recording of singing whales in 1969 which I put on an album called *Whales and Nightingales*, letting the whales sing to my accapella version of *Farewell to Tarwaithie*. Going to see the whales reminds me of how interconnected are the issues of nature and social change.

I am a troubadour today, as I was at the beginning, still singing, still flying to places like Baton Rouge and Quebec, meeting up with you in Israel and France and Wyoming. I look for the right song to sing wherever I go; to bring a song to life, to breathe into it the spirit of the present, that is the task of the troubadour. The constant search is to find the song that will live forever in my heart and memory, and in yours.

Judy Collins
New York, New York
August 1988

Maid of Constant Sorrow

Tuesday, January 1, 1985 / New York

It is the first new day of the New Year, and I am here in my studio on the Upper West Side of Manhattan, in the sprawling apartment that is home, thinking of new beginnings, old griefs, buried bones, and the dozen full moons since last January first. The Italian cup on my desk is filled with strong espresso coffee, made from beans ground this morning. The sun is streaming through the windows, and although the temperature outside is in the low teens, it is warm in here; the steam heat works, cranking and slamming against the radiators. The light is brilliant, the rent is low, and the New Year is coming into focus.

From the rooms of this big, airy apartment above the river I hear a trio of voices. The baritone is Louis, the man I love and live with, a Norwegian whose accent gives no hint that he grew up in Queens, New York. The alto, a spray of glass bells chiming, is my sister, Holly Ann. Holly is a weaver, the youngest of my four siblings; her seven-year-old son Kalen's voice is a tenor staccato, bouncing from room to room. Holly and Kalen live in Los Angeles and have spent the holidays with us here in New York. My tall red-headed son, Clark, has gone back to St. Paul, where he lives now. His lean face with its high cheekbones and blue eyes still looks to me at times like the face of my baby, but

Clark is a man, soon to be twenty-six: Capricorn, late bloomer. There were years when our visits were troubled, as our lives were troubled, and our friendship now is a gift more dear for having had its difficulties. For a few days the five of us were together. We walked the Christmas-lit streets of New York, opened presents, closed each other in embraces, and smiled at each other suddenly, without warning. We toasted the New Year last night, and on miniature scraps of blue paper we wrote down the things we wanted most to be relieved of (anger, lust, greed, jealousy, fear, pride, fear again, I wrote) and burned the papers in the Chinese wok. I prayed to have all my fears go up in flames. In the light of the New Year, I am determined to rise from the ashes, like a mythical bird, on new wings.

Yesterday was the last of my twenty-four-year contract with Elektra Records. I have spent more than half my life and made twenty albums with Elektra, some of them gold, all of them full of my life's blood and passion. I have been there longer than most people I know have been married, longer than I was ever with a man, or a city, or a dream. My life with Elektra meant more than it should have. It had come to resemble a romance that goes on long past the time when it should have ended, when just a bittersweet hope keeps it alive. I will bury it, for the love affair is over.

In the spring of 1984, I released *Home Again*, my twentieth album. I travel through the country doing promotion, press, radio, television; but the music business had changed, and so had Elektra.

Last year Bob Krasnow, the new president of Elektra, told me I am not the company's kind of artist anymore. He was sitting in his leather swivel chair behind his white marble desk. On the walls of his office, in a building on Fifth Avenue that towers above St. Patrick's Cathedral, the framed platinum albums and singles reflected the sunlight.

I sank deeper into a designer couch.

"Can you tell me why?" I asked, but he didn't answer. Last year Elektra continued to release records by heavy-rock groups, such as Mötley Crüe, Dokken, and Metal Church, which compete for time on pop radio with groups like Twisted Sister. Perhaps I should dye my hair orange, wear handcuffs, a black-leather studded jacket, and ride into town on a motorcycle singing a punk-rock version of "Both Sides Now."

It reminds me of the story about what Duke Ellington said to Clive Davis, the president to Columbia Records, when Clive was letting the Duke go from Columbia twenty-two years ago.

"We can't keep you here. You don't sell records," said Clive. Tony Bennett was there as well, and Duke Ellington looked from Tony to Clive in wonder. Then he said, "It is our job to make records. It is your job to sell them." Orange hair might be just the thing.

Survival, I know, is to begin again.

Blue glass and stained glass shimmer in the sunlight, shafts of gold spill into the studio through bamboo blinds. On the walls are photographs: Duke Ellington, his head thrown back, a racetrack stadium in the background; Georgia O'Keeffe, with the skull of a mountain sheep above her head; me with Patricia McBride; my son, Clark, when he was nine, his red hair shining in the sun; and my brother Denver John and his children, Joshua Cody and Corrinna Rebecca. Pinned to the bulletin board are a letter from Corita Kent and photographs—one of Rosa Parks with me at Gloria Steinem's fiftieth birthday party, another of some of my relatives posing for a family portrait in St. Louis in 1928, taken just before they headed for the West. The are dressed in their best, old and young faces scrubbed, babies in boots and hats, ladies in big skirts and bonnets, men in their stiff Sunday suits, smiling. They sit primly in front of the camera, on the edge of the frontier.

This room is my own frontier, filled with memories and hopes. The Steinway piano top is stacked with music, my latest song is on the tape recorder. This morning I travel beyond these walls, moving through time, and although I must not stare, I can look back. On my desk is my first diary, begun when I was fifteen, a brown, leatherbound, gold-etched book, its corners bitten off by Koko, our family's cocker spaniel. I open it and read the penciled scrawl, turning the pages that have slipped loose from the binding. There are my high school loves, and the record of my family's life together, the fights and the tears and the smiles. Next to the diary is an oval sepia photograph in a leather frame—the face of my beloved and baffling father, Charles. The sight of him takes me back to my early childhood as nothing else can.

* * *

I was born on May 1, 1939, in Seattle, Washington, the land of crisp apples and rainy days, days meant for meditation and contemplation, a place where, when the sun finally does come out, it blazes with beauty, and your heart leaps at the sight. The year I was born, Roosevelt was president, Sigmund Freud died, FM radio was invented, and Steinbeck received the Pulitizer Prize for *The Grapes of Wrath*. The big movies that year were *Gone with the Wind* and *The Wizard of Oz*; the popular songs were "Over the Rainbow" and "God Bless America." Germany invaded Poland and scientists demonstrated the possibility of splitting the atom. I was named Judith, after the heroine in the Bible who saved her people by cutting off the head of Holofernes, but Daddy usually called me "Brighteyes," or "Dreamboat."

My first memory of my father is watching him on his knees in the bathroom of our home in Seattle. He is running his hands over the white tiles on the floor, searching for pieces of his blue and white glass eyes. They have slipped from his fingers and shattered, splintering and scattering into every corner.

"Goddammit," he mutters, laughing at the same time. "Dreamboat, where are my poor eyes? Gone again."

I am about two and a half, the first of my father's five children. I can run very fast, count to thirty, and carry a tune. I know he cannot see me, with or without his glass eyes. I often felt not that he was blind, but that I was invisible.

"Let me help you look, Daddy," I say.

Down on the floor, both of us on our knees, we retrieve the bigger pieces. Daddy stands up to continue his morning ablutions. He has another pair of eyes, no loss. He raises his eyebrows, the lids raise with them, and I glimpse a landscape of raw-looking flesh on his own useless eyes as he slips the other glass eye into place. In later years his eyes would be made of plastic and would bounce, whole and unbroken, across other tile floors in other houses.

I am as tall as his knees, and I look up to see a taut, handsome Irishman, an optimist, nude this morning except for his shorts. I see that my father is wonderful. There is nothing flabby about him. His face alternates between stretches of smooth skin and knotted cheek muscle. My face is a small, fair version of his own. He is running the fingers of his right hand over the surface of his skin, holding his after-shave in his left hand. The after-shave bottle is white, with a blue ship on it, and he splashes scented water on his shaving cuts, gritting his teeth at the sting of the alcohol bite. His sweet and mellifluous voice pervades the house as he sings, slipping into a freshly laundered white shirt and fixing his tie in a Windsor knot. He is warming up for his radio show, trying out new melodies. "I'll take you home again, Kathleen, to where your heart has always been," he sings, and I sing harmony with him, following the course of the melody, shadowing the song with another note that makes a chill of pleasure run up my spine.

"This tyke can harmonize with anything, even a car horn, a train whistle," he would say. He was always proud of the way I learned songs without struggling. I sang with the radio, I sang to put myself to sleep, I sang for anyone who would listen.

The Collins genes are strong. I have my father's melodic singing voice and his face; I learned his laugh and in photographs we look alike. I was like a film developing in the dark, a negative to his own positive and forceful imprint.

Daddy did not use a cane or have a Seeing Eye dog. He walked tall and straight, with his shoulders thrown back, his head held high. He called the sound of his shoes on the street his "radar"; the sound of his footsteps told him where he was going and gave him a powerful, greater-than-human presence. If you didn't know he was blind, you might not find out until he faltered in handling a fragile porcelain cup or stumbled into a table. It was not often that his radar system failed him, but when it did, he ran into things. His shins were covered with scars from encounters with wagons and bicycles left in the middle of sidewalks. He hit these at full tilt, walking his chin-up, face-front stride. He would come home wounded and cursing careless children, some of them his own.

"Which one of you kids left that wagon on the sidewalk? I'll thrash the living daylights out of whoever does that again!" A lot of his threats were for future reference, but sometimes he caught one of us, and a thrashing was what we got, as promised. We all tried to remember not to be the one who caused him to tumble on concrete.

Daddy had a secret language that none of us children ever learned. Braille is still a mystery to me, a sort of exterior landscape that must make people who read it feel they are living in a unique spatial dimension. If it had been a good day and he was in a good mood, he would read to me at bedtime.

"Will it be Jack London tonight, or will we go on with *The*

Wind in the Willows?'' When I was nestled under the covers, he would turn out the light and make his way to my bed. He'd open the Braille book on his knees and begin running his fingers over its pages in the dark.

I always tried to stay awake for as long as I could, so he would go on reading. Once I didn't answer when he asked me if I was asleep. I watched him tiptoe from the room and close the door. A blind person, I thought, cannot ever afford to think no one is looking.

My father was born in 1911, in Nez Perce, Idaho. He was the first son of Frank Collins and Ethel Booth. Frank was Irish and from a musical family; Ethel was Scandinavian and English. Her father, my Great-grandfather Booth, was a tall, thin, handsome man who kept a hundred silver dollars in a velvet pouch, which he would spill out onto the rug for me to play with on our visits to Idaho. He had a replica of an early slot machine with pictures of fruit—apples, oranges, and pears—that spun round and round when you turned the handle. Great-grandfather had been a banker in the eighteen hundreds, until his partner ran off with the bank holdings. Because banks had no insurance then, Great-grandfather paid back his customers with his own money. He wound up farming in Idaho. I remember the heavy, sweet smell of cream in the separating room and Great-grandmother Laurie Booth in the kitchen, bending over a platter of sugar cookies she had just taken out of the oven.

Frank Collins was wild and handsome and played the mouth harp, and Great-grandfather Booth practically disowned his daughter, Ethel, after she married him. They didn't settle their differences till long after Frank was dead and Ethel had remarried.

My father was born with musical talent. He was named Charles Thomas, after John Charles Thomas, the great baritone. Daddy was born sighted, but his vision was poor from some trauma before birth, and by the time he was four he was completely blind.

"Do you dream in black and white?" I would ask him, imprinting the family lore deeper with every telling.

"Not all the time. I can remember red, it was the color of the wagon. And green was the color of grass. I did all my chores on the farm after I went blind, same as when I could see; I hauled the wood and carried the water. They didn't give me any special privileges. I can remember the sky, so I remember blue. And I remember the Indians." Daddy would tap down the tobacco in his pipe carefully with his fingers, as though he were feeling the memories as he spoke. He'd strike a sulfur match against his thumbnail and light his pipe from the blue flame, continuing his story.

"Nez Perce was an Indian reservation. The Indians were peaceful, they made beaded leather purses and moccasins, and I remember their smell, pungent as wood smoke. But the farm was so far out in the sticks that when Aunt Violet came for a visit from Canada, in 1915, she slept with a butcher knife under her pillow to keep away the savages." Daddy would laugh, shaking his head at the memory.

One day when Daddy was five, he and Great-grandfather Booth were standing together in the farthest field. Daddy began clapping his hands, and when Great-grandfather Booth asked him what he was doing, he said he was seeing where the house was.

"What do you mean? You can't see it, you're blind, child."

"But I can hear it."

He had discovered his radar, the magic door that was to lead him away from the farm, into another world.

When he was seven, his parents sent him to a "special school" in Boise. It was an institution for children who were blind, deaf, or disturbed. The teaches assumed that the blind had only certain capabilities, so Daddy was taught basket weaving and piano tuning, but he refused to let his handicap define him. He asked his teachers to let him feel their faces when they were expressing different emotions so that he might be able to make the "right" face, and thus imitate their appearances. He went places on his own with no cane, learning to move everywhere as though he were sighted. The head of the deaf class once asked him to take the children skating, forgetting Charlie was blind. When the teacher came to his senses, Charlie had already come and gone, safely conducting the children to the lake and back without disasters.

Daddy learned sign language, and the deaf children held their fingers in the shapes of the signs while his hands encircled theirs, feeling the meaning. Once his mother sent him fried chicken in the mail, which sometimes took many days. As he sat eating his chicken under a tree in the orchard, a friend who could see but not hear tapped him on the shoulder.

"Charlie, what are you eating?" he signed.

"It's chicken my mother sent. You want some? It's delicious."

The child signed again, while Daddy's hand encircled his moving fingers.

"It may be good, but it's green."

While Daddy was away at school that first year, Daddy's brother Frank who was two years younger went blind as well, from glaucoma. A year later their father died, and Ethel moved back to the farm to live with her parents. Losing his father was a great blow to Charlie; he had loved him deeply. Soon his mother married Mac MacCready. Mac had a short temper and little patience for his wife and her two blind sons; Ethel soon became withdrawn. She had loved to sing, and now seldom did. She and Daddy didn't see much of each other, for Daddy stayed away at school. After they had been married for fifteen years, his mother and his stepfather had a child of their own. Billy MacCready was sighted.

Daddy and my Uncle Frank were very different, but they looked alike. When they were together, their double blindness made me nervous. Frank learned piano tuning as Daddy had, and he makes a good living in Idaho Falls. He is married to Mary, a blind woman, and they have four sighted children and what seems to be a calm, Christian life. Uncle Frank is a straight, tall, handsome man, like my father. He is accustomed to using a cane and does not refuse your arm if you offer him help. His life seems content, satisfied, and happy. He loves his work and feels comfortable with his blindness and with the world, which will always be dark for him.

I never felt this comfort or ease in my father. All his life he was fighting to become something different from what he was. He was both exciting and appalling to live with because he lived at such an energetic, fast-burning, passionate level.

Daddy graduated from the public high school in Boise in 1933, and with a scholarship went on to the University of Idaho in Moscow. He started a dance band and read everything he could find that was printed in Braille. There he met Holden Bowler, who became his lifelong friend and my godfather. Holden helped Daddy get into the Phi Gamma Delta fraternity, where his fraternity brothers delighted in Chuck Collins's being such a character. They thought it was great fun to put Daddy behind the wheel of Holden's Model T. One of the boys would put a hand on Daddy's knee to give him signals—start, stop, or go. Then they would drive through the campus, and every head would turn.

"Oh, there goes Charlie driving the car," they would say, and then, "But he can't be driving, he's blind!"

When Daddy graduated from college in 1937, he got a job singing at a club when he moved to Seattle, the city where he met my mother.

My mother, Marjorie, is a good-looking woman with big hazel eyes in which I always told her there were chunks of color that looked like fruitcake. She has wide cheekbones, a great smile, and is very strong and robust. I can never remember my mother being sick or staying in bed after seven in the morning. She was the middle child of nine and was born on January 23, 1916, in Nampa, Idaho, to Agnes Maye Cope and John Oscar Byrd. There are Quakers and missionaries on her mother's side, and one of her great-aunts was ordained as a Methodist minister before the turn of the century. Her father's relatives were members of the House of Burgesses and farmers in Virginia. Both families are English. Life wasn't always easy for my mother when she was growing up. My mother's brother Frank was killed in an elevator accident when he was eleven, and her brother Shannon disappeared when he was older and was never heard from again.

I often stayed with my mother's family in the Seattle house and I remember the way my Grandmother Byrd smelled after her bath, sweet like violets, and Grandfather Byrd carrying me around on his shoulders out under the pear and apple trees. He worked on the railroads, and it is said he once ran away to Chicago for a couple of years, leaving his family behind. I thought him a terribly romantic man, and I loved the feel of his beard on my cheek and the smell of tobacco from his old briar pipe.

In 1937, when Mother was living with her parents, she was on the bus on her way from the University of Washington when she first saw my father.

"I noticed a stocky, attractive man sitting opposite me, with his hands on the open pages of a book. He didn't look blind, but I realized he must be. I was surprised when he stood up to get off at my stop. I offered my arm to help him cross the street, and he declined with a brusque wave of his hand. Then he apologized and offered to buy me a Coke at the club where he was singing.'' Daddy told her he would be making his debut on the radio station KOMO the next day.

Next morning, my mother and her best friend, Eline, were glued to the radio. When Daddy came to the end of the old Buddy Green song "Once in a While," Mother burst into tears.

"I knew he was my fate, and there was nothing I could do about it," she told Eline. Four months later they were married.

My first memory of my mother is the feel of her fingers on my scalp, rubbing shampoo into mounds of white bubbles in my hair as I lay on my back on the steel kitchen counter, my head in the sink. She rinsed my long blond hair with water and then vinegar to make it squeak and shine, and when it was dry she braided it and tied ribbons to the ends.

"Now, out you go, and only play on the sidewalk," she would say. There were boundaries everywhere, and although I couldn't cross the street I dreamed of the time I could come and go as I pleased.

My parents were busy, active people who worked hard. Mommy was always cooking or driving Daddy somewhere or cleaning or sewing, and Daddy did his radio show. They loved to relax with their friends on the weekends. At those parties, drinking with their friends, my parents would sometimes get "a little tight," as they called it. Mother drank Presbyterians, 7-Up and bourbon, and Daddy drank plain bourbon. He would sing a little too loudly and be roughly affectionate with my mother, mussing her hair, and would hold me in a loving hug that took my breath away.

The house on Twenty-seventh Street was a place where I remember feeling mostly happy. My parents loved and appreciated me. I was the only child for the first four years of my life, ruling a private kingdom where everyone thought I was cute and adorable, even when I was behaving like a brat.

"Let me look at you, Brighteyes," Daddy would say, holding out his arms. He touched my clothes and my hair, and looked at my face with his fingers. I liked to play with the watch he carried in his pocket—its Braille numbers stood out in dots that told the time.

My godfather, Holden, was at our house a lot. He always told Daddy how amazing it was that my own eyes were so big and so blue.

"This tyke is the spitting image of you, Charlie, the poor little thing," he would say. He changed my diapers and baby-sat for me. Holden and my dad looked alike, both stocky Irishmen with wide cheekbones and beautiful tenor singing voices. Holden would sing John McCormack songs, Daddy playing the piano for him. They read books together, talked about authors, argued about politics, got drunk together, and hosed each other wet in their business suits, laughing until they fell down. My mother and Holden's wife, Ann, often looked on with disgust at their two grown adolescent husbands, but Daddy and Holden kept each other young.

Holden tried to teach me to swear as soon as I started to talk.

"She won't swear, Charlie, she takes after you in every other way. Don't know whatever's wrong with her."

Holden had met J. D. Salinger on shipboard during World War II. Later, Salinger wrote *The Catcher in the Rye*, naming the hero after Holden. Like the fictional Holden Caulfield, Holden was a breaker of molds, a rebel. He was often Daddy's eyes; they saw the world from the same inner point of view. And for nearly forty years, he was Daddy's closest friend.

"Let's hear Dreamboat sing just one song before Mommy puts her to bed."

Standing in my Dr. Denton's, beside the piano bench, I would sing while Daddy smiled and nodded, playing the piano for me. I experienced my first feelings of the joy and power and pleasure in singing during these nights when Holden and my mother and the rest of their pals—Dritch, Holden's brother, and Glee Melcher, and my aunts Jeannette and Louise, and their husbands, Uncle Al and Uncle Elmer—looked on. My parents were thrilled when I sang, and I wonder which came first, my own pleasure in singing or the knowledge of theirs.

"Charles," Mommy said after I had sung my song, "it's way past Judy's bedtime." I could usually convince my father to let me stay up later, and change his dark moods to sunshine when he felt a little sorry about life and scowled a little long. But my mother could not be swayed and would make sure I got to bed on time. But I knew she loved to hear me sing.

President Roosevelt sent Holden to Germany in 1942 to serve

in World War II, and that same year Daddy packed me and Mother into "Claudia," our slope-backed, shiny black Buick, and toured the West, performing concerts for a company called the National School Assemblies. I rode in the back of Claudia while my mother drove, and when it rained the windshield wipers whined and scraped across the glass, and I told my parents the song it sang was "Daddy works, Daddy works." He did, he worked like a dog.

My father, singing in his Irish-tenor voice, performed the songs of Rodgers and Hart, Irving Berlin, Cole Porter. His program was a mixture of humor and philosophy, which he called his "medicine show." That winter he did concerts in Billings and Helena, Butte and Salt Lake City, Carson City, Boise, Twin Falls, Gooding, Plentywood (called that because the settlers who first arrived there said there was "plenty wood for one fire"). Sometimes he did three shows a day, often in three different towns. I would stare from the wings of auditoriums, in my mother's arms or by her side, and sing along with the music. Then Daddy would call me out onto the stage, saying "Here's my little girl, Judy." I would rush into his arms. I loved the stage, the lights, the faces of the people in the audience and the thought that I was making them happy, just by being there. My father said I was a born ham.

That Christmas we were home in Seattle for the holidays. We found that my Uncle Elmer had been killed in Germany, leaving Jeannette a widow with two children, my cousins Pam and Tommy. Mother was four months pregnant with my brother Michael by January, so Daddy hired a driver, whose name was Glenn, to finish the spring tour.

As Mommy and I stayed in Seattle with Grandma Byrd, waiting for my brother to be born, Daddy's letters arrived, postmarked from Fargo and Butte, New Mexico and Colorado, Arizona and Kansas. They were written on a Remington portable typewriter while he rode in the passenger seat of Claudia and were addressed to Mother and me, telling about the West, about America, about how oil is made and mica is formed. He sent me miniature bars of soap from the motels in Montana and miniature milk bottles in their baskets; he wrote about getting caught in the snow and stuck in the mud, and ironing his own shirts, and about the guy in Grand Junction who gave him an extra gallon of gas with his gas-ration stamps. He wrote about hating Hitler and how, if he could, he would go to Germany to shoulder a gun alongside Holden. He found it humorous that a doctor had made a mistake somewhere in his college medical records so that he was classified 1-A, fit to fight. Daddy wrote about the kindness of people on the road and about the bastard who ran National School Assemblies, who wouldn't pay for the tires or cover the shows he had to miss because they couldn't make it over Whitebird Pass in a snowstorm. He was lonely, questioning everything in his life, or enjoying every minute of it, pleased as hell with himself. All through the spring the letters came from those long, winding roads.

> Spring, 1943
> Fargo, North Dakota

My dearest Judykins and Marjorie,

There is hope for the future, a quality of faith, a series of hunches, or luck happenstances that seem to guide us. I was thinking of a thing that happened in January in Colorado. We had run off a slick road into the ditch. We had pushed Claudia back onto the skating rink of a highway, and decided on chains. In trying to use the friction-type bumper jack I broke it, even before it had lifted Claudia clear of the ground. Glenn decided he would run Claudia up on the railroad tracks, a quick way of putting the chains on. This was a section of main line over which passed the heavy trains of the C.B. and Q. Glenn got in the car, stepped on the starter. For the first time, and the last, in my experience with Claudia, nothing happened. The engine spun, but would not catch. Five minutes later, as we were still trying to get her going, the Streamliner shot by like a streak of bright metal at near ninety, over the spot where we might have been if the engine had caught.

People say of me that I must be reconciled to my physical condition. That is, of course, ridiculous. To be reconciled is merely to sit passively on your jail bunk, weary of kicking at the interlaced ironwork in front of you. I am not reconciled to anything.

I do not know what the quality of faith is, or even that it is faith. Yet the long miles are well nigh over, and things have gone so smoothly you could hardly believe it. Why any beneficent power should watch over our destinies is more than I know. Even so, in common with witch doctors and fire walkers, priests and fanatics, it is somehow a good path to travel for me and mine.

> Your Loving,
> Charles

On May 25, 1943, my brother Michael was born. My parents named him after Michael Collins, the Irish patriot. Daddy despised the English for remaining in Ireland, often denied his own English blood, and said Churchill was the only Englishman who had any sense. Michael was a beautiful, strong baby boy, who ended my reign as an only child. Daddy came home at the end of May, and shortly after he took a job at NBC in Hollywood. We left the house on Twenty-seventh Street in Seattle and moved down to California and into a dark little house at 11572 Mississippi Avenue in West Los Angeles. My mother hated that house. Large trees with sticky brown pods shaded the front lawn, and crabgrass stitched its way among the lawn seed she planted every season. I missed the green of Seattle.

During the day, Daddy did his radio shows. At home, Michael, a little boy with big blue eyes, started walking. I was enrolled in Nora Sterry School on Sawtelle Boulevard. I walked there with my lunch, chocolate milk and a peanut butter sandwich, in a tin box. Mother put chopped carrots on the peanut butter because they gave you vitamins. I picked them off. After school I walked home past those Venus flowers that ate flies and past the Lark Ellen Home for Boys. The boys were often out in the field playing baseball in the afternoon. I would press my nose to the fence and watch, impressed that they looked normal in spite of their deprivation. Some of them went to Nora Sterry, and I was invited to their hayride at Halloween, where I bobbed for apples in the mountain lodge with a hundred children. On the ride back to Los Angeles one of the boys told me to close my eyes, and when I had, he put his lips on mine. I opened my eyes, and he looked at me.

"Do you know what that was?" he asked.

"No," I said, but I knew. It was the beginning of trouble.

My father always talked to me about grown-up things and assumed I could absorb ideas. He read poetry to me and encouraged me to write it; he talked to me about the state of the world and told me what he thought of it. When Roosevelt died my father was desolate; he took it personally. Daddy was a democratic liberal, convinced that the system worked, agreeing that anyone was innocent until proven guilty, but he felt that individual people are intrinsically different in both talent and temperament and not created equally. He thought men were mostly wrong and women usually right because women were emotionally more balanced than men and equal to any job a man could do. An admirer of Jefferson and the Founding Fathers, he thought this country was the most wonderful thing ever invented. At heart he was a believer in capitalism, where each could strive for worldly success, and a socialist, who believed we must care for our own. Loving his children, he wanted them to be the very best they could be, to do their utmost.

On V-E Day, May 8, 1945, my parents and our neighbors, the Pincocks, danced in the street on Mississippi Avenue. My father and mother cried, tears running down their faces, and laughed, as they hugged each other. My father was carrying Mike in his arms, and he put him down and picked me up, twirling me around and around until I was dizzy.

I have strong visual memories of my father: pushing a lawn-mower, his pants legs rolled up, a wide grin on his face, his feet bare, as he would say, "I don't know where I'm going, but I sure know where I've been"; looking sheepish when he had run the car through the back wall of the garage when he went out one winter morning to "warm it up" for Mother; playing Scrabble with pieces marked in letters and in Braille; and his holding a box of a dozen pairs of glass eyes that came in the mail from the Denver Optic Company. Mother would choose the one from the new batch that most exactly matched the color of the remaining unbroken eye. They were works of art, each and every one hand painted, and looked totally real. Though they cost twenty-five or thirty dollars a pair, he would say that his eyes were one of the best buys he ever made. When he took a job as the head of the State Agency for the blind in Colorado, I remember his outrage when the national director insisted he use a cane. "I've never used one and I don't intend to start now!" When the director insisted, his solution was a collapsible cane that he could keep in his desk drawer. When "important" sighted people came to meet with him, he would pull it out as a prop, and stand it by the desk, but he never walked with it.

On Saturdays Daddy and Mommy would sometimes take me and my brother into the NBC studios in Hollywood to watch the radio shows "The Cisco Kid" and "Let's Pretend." Michael was a gentle, sweet-natured child who had usurped my place, taken my crown, and I bullied him whenever Mommy and Daddy weren't looking. He was a tough, handsome, rugged little boy, and he could have clobbered me long before I stopped tormenting him, but my attitude only seemed to make his nature sweeter.

I wiggled my way between him and Daddy whenever possible and tried to get my mother's attention. On his fourth birthday Michael asked for a rosebush the color of peaches. My mother bought it for him and planted it out by the fence on Mississippi Avenue the night before his birthday. In the morning Michael walked to the bush, smiling with delight, utterly happy with his birthday roses. When we moved from Los Angeles to Denver, Mother uprooted that plant and took it with us. Sometimes, for old times' sake, I send Mike a dozen roses the color of peaches.

I started my first piano lessons when I was five. Three times a week, after school, I took the bus to my lesson, my music clutched under my arm. I learned to read music before I could read words, and from the beginning I could play a melody I'd heard only once, and make up pieces on the piano by just doodling. Sitting there, with my hands on the piano, thrilled me. Practicing Chopin and Debussy, I would often feel completely alone, totally happy and serene no matter what else went on around me.

When I was seven and Michael was four, our beautiful, tow-headed brother, David, was born. He looked like one of the angels hovering over a baptismal font at the Vatican, and had blue eyes like mine and Michael's.

Although Mother was always busy with us and my father, she made all my clothes for as long as I can remember. We pored over McCall's pattern book and shopped together for fabrics—blue corduroy for trousers, sparkling silver rickrack to trim my squaw dress for a Halloween costume, sensible stripped cotton for pants and shirts. Neither of us spoke as she took in the seams and measured hems with her mouth full of pins, but in those quiet moments I often felt a closeness and love for my mother that made me weak in the knees.

It sustained me even when she spanked me for chasing Marva Dawn Pincock down the street with a broom. (Marva Dawn was four years old, blond, and, as far as I was concerned, a pest.)

My best friend, Maria, was six and lived across the street. We shaved our legs and our arms, pretending to be grown-ups, and on our way to school in the morning we bought chewing gum and blew great bubbles that popped and landed in our hair and on our faces.

We sometimes prowled around the bushes outside the house on the corner. It was a spooky place with shuttered windows where a musty and reclusive old couple lived. The only time I saw their faces were when they came to the door to shoo me out of the avocado tree, where I liked to swing upside down with my knees over the lowest branch. I was afraid of this creaky pair and told Maria they had the bones of dead people in the attic. Once I fell from the avocado tree, landing on my back in the dirt. The fall knocked the wind out of me, and I ran all the way home without breathing. Unable to speak, I threw myself at my mother's feet and lay there, dreading what she would do to me if I were to die.

We lived in comfortable houses and wore good clothing, but we were a large family, and although Daddy's salary paid the bills, treats were rare. I liked treats and wanted to be able to afford them as often as I wanted them. My father and I both loved sugar, and sometimes I sneaked sweets from the drawer in my father's dresser where he kept candy hidden among his pairs of socks. The dark chocolate covered cherries were his favorites, and I often found his cache and depleted it. His socks always smelled of chocolate.

I often felt an awkward embarrassment about my father's blindness and a strange pride at his fame. People always knew who he was wherever we lived, because they heard him on the radio each day. But they knew only the public face of our lives. The private side was often chaotic. Sometimes my father drank, and when he did, his mood changes were extreme and confusing. I adored him and was dazzled by him, and he could be understanding, loving, tender, and kind. But he could also frighten me and send me howling to my room in anger and pain because I never knew when his usually sunny mood might turn black.

When my father drank, his whole personality changed. He would start the day with a smile when he was on the wagon, but when he wasn't he might come home late and curse the night and shout at the stars. My mother and father often argued at the dinner table while we children kept as quiet as possible. As Daddy's fist would pound the table, my heart would pound as well.

"Your father is such a marvelous man, Judy," people would say to me. "He gets around so, and he does so much good for other people." He was usually sociable; he liked people and they liked him. But his loud, full laugh could turn heads and

embarrass a child who was already aware her father was unusual. It was difficult to separate this mythical man, who was
loving and intelligent, from this "other" father. I thought one
of the reasons for his occasional dark moods was that he was
always under so much pressure to keep up his "normal" image.
Some nights my mother fed us and put us to bed before he came
home, and then waited up in the silence that roared through the
house. I would lie awake, waiting for the completion of the
evening—the arrival of Father and the fight or the reconciliation.
Until he came home, I rarely slept. Sometimes I lay awake and
trembled.

One night I awoke to screaming and the voice of my mother
threatening to leave. There was shouting, scuffling, the pounding sound of running feet. I ran out of my bedroom after my
mother as she tore out the front door with the car keys in her
hand, her nightgown flying. Daddy was out the door on her
heels. He grabbed her, tackled her as she reached the door of
the car, and hauled her back into the living room. We were all
crying. I was sobbing. As often happened after one of these
frightening evenings, the next morning everyone was quiet over
the scrambled eggs and buttered toast. Nothing was ever mentioned about the night before, and this burden of silence began
to dig a deep pit of fear in my heart.

Such extremes of behavior kept me off balance. I was always
waiting for the other shoe to drop. Daddy seemed to be as mys-
tified as everyone else in the family about why he drank and
about what happened to him when he did. But no one must know
this family secret; it must be kept behind the door, away from
the eyes of neighbors and friends.

I was sure my father's mood swings, and the resulting chaos
in the family, were my fault. Perhaps it was because of my being
mean to my brother Michael or not minding Mommy. Maybe if
I acted in certain ways, things would be different. Perhaps if I
just practiced hard enough at the piano, I could make Daddy
stop being the way he was. It was during this time that I remember first being aware of feeling different from other children.

"In the land of the blind, the man with two eyes is wise to
wear a blindfold." So, as I grew up I pretended not to see what
I couldn't bear to see. I learned that being invisible was a survival skill, like knowing how to breathe and read, like knowing
how to run.

* * *

Daddy asked me one day if I thought I would be married when I was his age.

"No, I want to be independent and make my own living," I told him. "I don't ever want to have to ask anyone for money." I was beginning to feel that it was better not to need anything from anybody. I decided I would learn to do everything in my life, in my family, without asking for help.

At nine I had pigtails and freckles and read a lot of books. I was outwardly self-contained, but inwardly insecure, and I wanted to tell someone what I was feeling. My friend Maria was Catholic, and I went to her church prepared to confess my sins, but was turned away because I was a Methodist.

The only times I felt pure pleasure were when I was practicing and singing in the choir at school and the choir at Wilshire Methodist Church in Beverly Hills, where my mother took us every Sunday. When I put on my choir robe and opened my mouth to sing, I was filled with a sense of peace. When I sang, my belief in God was strong, but I doubted if even He could quiet my inner, quaking fears.

After being in a dark mood for days, Daddy would wake up exuberant one morning and make a concoction of brewer's yeast, molasses, yogurt, bananas, and vitamin B_{12}. His conversion would be total and splendid and hopeful.

"Marjorie, this is the best thing in the world for you, you ought to have one yourself," he would say, handing my mother a glass of the foamy, foul-smelling mix he had whipped up in the blender. "Oh, Charles," she would say, praying that this would be the turning point, that after the last few nights, or weeks, we would have a little peace.

"This Gayelord Hauser knows what he's talking about. I feel as bright as a penny, I feel like a kid, I feel great. This is a brand-new day."

He would come home from work with jokes, smile with ease, and lose the few extra pounds he always hated and usually carried. He'd get a new tie, buy a new dress for Mother and new books for us—*Treasure Island* or *The Count of Monte Cristo*—and spend time talking to Michael and David about steam engines, maybe take us all to see a real one. With a chamois cloth he'd polish all his shoes to a bright, hard surface, and he'd tell Mother what a good cook she was and tell me I was doing great as he listened to me practice Chopin. Savoring the words, he'd read Dylan Thomas's poetry out loud to us and learn new songs for his radio show.

My father took a job in Colorado in 1949, when I was ten. Mother was pregnant when we moved into a duplex, in Denver on Willow Street, with a big lawn, neighbors everywhere, and no willow trees anywhere that I could see. I had my own bedroom, and a few weeks after we moved in, my youngest brother, Denver John, was born on the twenty-fifth of January. He was named after the city because my father loved it so much.

Daddy blossomed in Denver, with a new life, a new leaf. My mother had a new baby and smiled again, and she and my father seemed much happier together. I was enrolled at Ashley Elementary School and started music lessons with a new piano teacher, Mr. Rath. After riding to my lessons on the bus, I'd spend my change from the bus fare on those orange marshmallow peanut-shaped candies. I spent a lot of time in the dentist's chair getting my bad teeth drilled.

At Ashley Elementary I was put ahead a grade, and Mrs. Bush, my teacher, took an interest in my slight lisp, which I still have even now when I'm nervous or tired. She had red, wiry hair and was tiny—only four and a half feet tall.

"If you stay after school for an hour, we can work on your speech," she said to me.

She held a mirror to my mouth and I was as tall as she was.

"Say 'sorry,' " she commanded.

"Schorry," I said. We worked and worked on that *s* sound. During one of our sessions I told Mrs. Bush I'd been having pains in my leg. "That's growing pains, dear. Now, say 'seasons.' " The mirror was fogged over, and I couldn't see my lips or my tongue or my teeth. All I could think about was that my right hip ached.

I told my mother about the pain when I got home from school, and the next day the doctor came to the house. He took out a little hammer and hit me on both knees. My left knee flew up, kicking him in the chin, but my right knee just sat there. My mother went out of the room with the doctor, shutting the door. I could hear their voices talking, and then we all drove to the hospital, where I was examined on a stretcher. As they wheeled me out of the room, the look on my mother's face was tight and pained and she looked as though she was going to cry. I was put in a bed in a room of the isolation ward, alone. Though I didn't know it at the time, I wouldn't see my mother again for a month.

I asked the nurse what was wrong.

"Well, honey, you have polio, and it is contagious, so you have to stay here in this room. Your mommy can't come to see you, she might catch it, too."

That first night, I dreamed of a sheet on the ground held down at its corners by four stones. While my mother's voice floated in and out of the dream, I struggled under the sheet to free myself and begged her to set me loose.

The next day, a baby was brought to the room. When the nurses were gone, I went to the bed where he lay. I looked down at him and pinched him on the heel, but he didn't open his eyes or make a sound. The next day he was taken away, dead.

I took baths in the metal tub for physical therapy and the doctors gave me pills for the pain; I was frightened and didn't understand what was happening.

My flowers and my books were black from being put through the sterilizer. All my get-well cards looked withered, as though they were very old. I read and read, books by Jack London and Alexandre Dumas and Dostoevsky, and *The Secret Garden*. After I had been in isolation for a month, I was transferred to a different ward in the hospital for another month. There were other children, many of whom were walking on crutches. My mother and father came to visit me. We sat outside in the sun together and they were very nice to me. Though my parents must have felt enormous relief after the month of anxiety when they could not even see me, their faces still reflected their fears.

"Am I going to have this limp for a long time?" I asked my mother.

"No, dear, they say you will be just fine, you won't have any problems."

The night I went home from the hospital, I slept in my parents' bed. Trying to keep my breath even and my eyes still under my eyelids, I pretended that I was asleep when they came into the room to look at me. Through my eyelashes I watched my father's face. He sat with his turned toward me, a curiously tranquil look on his face. I felt a sense of peace from him there in the dimly lit room. Years later, when I wrote my song about him, "My Father," the look on his face that night came into my mind. In that look were all the hopes and promises he had for me, and for himself.

> *My father always promised us*
> *That we would live in France,*
> *We'd go boating on the Seine*
> *And I would learn to dance.*
>
>   . . .
>
> *I sail my memories of home*
> *Like boats across the Seine,*
> *And watch the Paris sun*
> *Set in my father's eyes again.*

He never heard this song. He died three weeks after I wrote it.

Golden Apples of the Sun

Wednesday, January 2, 1985 / En route, New York to the American Virgin Islands

Louis to my right in the next seat, our arms linked, we take off at ten this morning, flying over the island of Manhattan, the Statue of Liberty in her lace-like dress of scaffolding, and then over Long Island's cold stretches of beach. We are headed south, where we'll be in the sun for two weeks and I can recover from all the traveling I've done this year.

Indianapolis, Philadelphia, Minneapolis, Atlanta, Salem, Oklahoma City, Los Angeles, San Francisco, New Orleans, Valley Forge, Dallas, Quebec, Washington, D.C., Boston, Cincinnati. My schedule has been grueling. I have done about seventy concerts and shows—some with symphony orchestras—all over the country, concerts in Avery Fisher Hall in New York, Tanglewood in the Berkshires, the Greek Theatre in Los Angeles. I need to rest, away from airplanes, taxis, backstage doors, hotel rooms, promoters, problems, sound checks, waiting rooms, limousines, telephones.

The flight attendant cannot do enough. The coffee is not bad and we are almost giggling as we let the tension and the cold slide off our bodies. I feel I'm skipping school, playing hookey, leaving my assistant with bills and contracts, escaping off to the islands, leaving New York City for paradise, going to hell in a handbasket. I will burst if I don't get a break.

The resort where we will be staying is a group of tan stucco houses set on the beach around a point of land on a densely tropical island in a turquoise sea. We have come to this island in the southern Caribbean for many years. Still dressed in our woolen northern clothes, we finally arrive, weary from traveling nearly a full day on airplanes, taxis, and boats. The edges of my city nerves are still ragged, my inner clock still wound up on New York time.

"Welcome, Ms. Collins, Mr. Nelson. I'll be with you in a moment." The man at the desk looks comfortable and cool and turns back toward another guest. I'm irritated; I don't want to wait. I look out to the sea, where pelicans dive into the water in pairs and couples sit with pink icy drinks, their legs stretched out, their heads back. Louis's nose is covered with shiny sweat. He grins and puts an arm around me.

"Nobody is hurrying here," he says. In our room at last, with its white wicker furniture and windows that open out onto the sea, we pour club soda over ice into tall glasses, take off our heavy jackets, walk out onto the terrace. Across the sea, the island of Tortola is covered with twilight shadows, and a spit of land called Jost Van Dyke still holds pockets of sunlight in its valleys. I unpack two huge suitcases and, slowly, I unwind and begin to feel better. It's then, of course, that the thought comes: I don't deserve to be here when the rest of the world is dying, starving, wanting. Oh God, please let me get not what I deserve, but what you know I need. I need to rest, or there is no going on.

Evening on the island, and the sun sets like a golden ring over the blue-green water. The tanned faces of our friends the Perises, the Franks, and the Apfels, who have already been here for days, say good night to our white ones, and we walk back to our room through the moonlight. I'm so glad to be in Louis's arms with the sound of the sea in my ears and the feeling of peace descending over me.

Calling birds wake me from my deep sleep and I find coffee and breakfast laid out on the terrace, the sun already hot. Louis and I watch the yellow-breasted birds—bananaquits, they call them—and the brown, speckled nameless ones, whose calls are like the chattering of children. Louis's skin is already darker,

his teeth whiter. I don't really get tan, but Louis look
Indian already. His face is wreathed in a graying beard, his
is sunshine and light. He has blue blue eyes that look at yo
and you know he sees you. I am pale, with an Irish skin pebbled
by freckles. I always look like a wraith in photographs taken
here, my hair wild and reddish in the sunlight, but Louis is
photogenic. I am always cross-eyed or looking over my shoulder
at something or squinting, and he is . . . "that movie star, just
to her left—who is that good-looking man?"

The night I met Louis Nelson, on April 16, 1978, I thought
my life was over. Physically, I was ill from so many years of
unwitting self-destruction, and emotionally I was devastated by
the abrupt departure from my life of a man with whom I had
thought I had a good relationship. The blind date on which I
met Louis almost didn't happen, for I didn't want to go anywhere, or see anyone. My greatest pleasure would have been to
stay home, staring at what had become my familiar walls. But
my conscience provided the impetus for me to make an appearance at an event I had promised, months before, that I would
attend.

It was a fund raiser for the Equal Rights Amendment. The
dinner was held in New York at the Ginger Man, a restaurant
whose name was changed for the night to the Ginger Person. It
was the height of the eager, hopeful time when everybody was
sure we would soon have an amendment guaranteeing equal pay
for equal work for men and women. Bella Abzug, Stephen Sondheim, Barbara Barrie, Alan Alda, and Gloria Steinem were
going to be there to talk about the ERA and raise some money
and consciousnesses. I got myself together, looking better than
I felt. I had invited a lot of my friends, including my old friend
Jeanne Livingston. Jeanne was dating a man who was then
Louis's business partner, and she suggested he bring Louis.

"I want you to meet him. He's a Libra. I did both of your
charts, and he's perfect for you."

I had planned on getting politics out of the way and hurrying
home to my solitude. I certainly didn't want to meet anyone.

"It's very kind of you, Jeanne, but no thanks. Anyway, I don't
believe in all that astrology stuff."

Jeanne was undaunted. She brought Louis to the party anyway.

I liked him immediately, but I was sure he wasn't for me. He was kind and thoughtful that night, putting himself between me and a fan who kept poking a tape recorder in my face and telling me he had some songs to play for me. Louis graciously met all my friends and took me home in a cab, seeing me to my door. Lately, my lovers had been fast-lane drivers, men with little time for me. I thought Louis was someone I might get together with in another life.

Our meeting when we did was what people call a blessing. When Louise met me, I was at my worst, and while we spoke often on the phone after that night, it was more than two months before we had our second, real date, in July. By then, I had passed through deep emotional darkness. Meeting Louis coincided with the sunlight coming back into my life. We fell in love and have been together constantly ever since.

Louis is two years older than I am and is an industrial designer with his own business in New York. He designed the first brightly colored Fiberglas skis for Head, those purple, yellow, pink, and red beauties; his works include designing museum exhibits, album covers, and packaging; his designs are elegant and come from the imagination of an artist.

In the first years of our romance, there was an interlude when I didn't sing in concerts for about six months. So we had time to come to know each other, to meld our bodies and our hearts into a rhythm that continues even now when we are apart.

"I always wished I could be Jewish," he told me shortly after we met.

"Why on earth?" I asked him. It seemed a strange fantasy for a Norwegian from Queens.

"Because Jewish families always seem to talk around the dinner table, and we never did. It was as silent as a funeral."

A Norwegian, I have heard, doesn't say much until he gets started, and then you can't stop him.

One night, after we had exchanged keys and put our toothbrushes and a change of clothes in each other's apartments, Louis looked at me wistfully.

"I don't know if I can take another love affair of separation and tours and telephones," he said. His first wife was a biochemist who worked late nights and weekends, had to commute to the lab from home, and was sometimes away for days. His second wife was a ballet dancer, on the road frequently. When we met, he had been separated from her for two years and was dating a stable Norwegian woman who was a designer and, like him, always free on the weekends. A touring lover was the last thing he wanted. But love has no chronology, no logic.

Ever since I was a child, I have been trying to balance the demands of love and work. The competing passions of intimacy and music have always torn me.

After I recuperated from polio and came home from the hospital in 1950, I was put back the grade in school I had jumped ahead the previous January. Though I'd had a few piano lessons in Denver before I got polio, just before my eleventh birthday Daddy told me he had found me a new teacher.

Dr. Antonia Brico taught piano in Denver and conducted the Denver Businessmen's Symphony; she was famous for being tough and demanding, and took very few new students. Her studio was in an old stone building in downtown Denver. My mother and father took me to my first appointment with her: an interview with no guarantees. The door was opened by Dr. Brico's assistant, Mrs. Page. The studio was huge and the walls were covered with photographs of men and women, singers and conductors, scribbled signatures at the bottom: "To Antonia with love, Albert" Schweitzer, "Wonderful concert, love, Jean Sibelius," "To my beloved Antonia, Queen Juliana of the Netherlands." There were photos of people I had seen in *Time* and *Look* magazine—Toscanini, Casals, Rubinstein, musicians from all over the world, as well as royalty. The room had a polished wood floor covered by a carpet that stretched underneath two mammoth Steinway pianos. There were full-sized bronze busts of Sibelius and Beethoven, of Mozart. It was an awesome room, the habitat of someone important whose life possessed dimensions of which I could only dream. Dr. Brico's face matched the monumental look of the building she lived in and the room where she taught.

I scuffed into the room in my oxfords, gripping my grubby music in my hands. Dr. Brico had large features, and she looked to me like the busts of Schumann and Beethoven. I remember a scent of citrus in the room. She nodded at my parents, indicating the chairs where they could sit, and motioned me over to the piano bench, taking a seat beside me.

"All right, little Judy, what do you have to play for me?" I put my music on the piano rack and began a Debussy piece, "Snow Is Dancing" from *The Children's Corner*. I played very fast, stumbling over the eighty-eight keys. My fingers were jelly and I couldn't find the pedals under my feet. My father and mother sat a long way away, back at the other end of the room. They sat with their hands in their laps, and my father had a smile on his face. He always thought I was wonderful no matter what I did. My mother had a worried look on her face. She could see the room's heavy, imposing décor, whereas my father could only hear his little girl playing the piano, and he loved her and thought she was great, and he knew that this doctor woman would think she was great, too. His face said, She's my little girl, and isn't she wonderful? My mother wasn't so sure.

When I finished playing, Dr. Brisco sat still, looked at my hands, then turned to my parents.

"Little Judy has great hands, but her technique is not all that wonderful." A frown came over her face like clouds in an already dark sky. "This is going to be a lot of work," she said. She seemed enormous and angry, then her face was suddenly smiling and tender.

"I am going to take you as a student. We will have to work very hard, little Judy. The way the fingers scramble around, flying in the air, we will change all that. You have the feel, that is the most important thing, you understand the Debussy. Now we will teach you to express what you feel, and you have the hands! Your hands are of the best quality, good and strong across the back, with long fingers. I am going to show you how to make the Debussy speak! You could be a fine pianist, little Judy."

"Thank you, Dr. Grico."

"It's Dr. Brico," she said, rolling the *r* and searching my face. "Can you be your best for me, little Judy?" I was being asked to behave as though I were responsible and adult, and I felt about four years old. I looked down at my brown oxfords, wondering how the polish had rubbed off in so many spots. I suddenly wished I could hide them—maybe by sticking them under the x-ray machine they had at the shoestore to show whether new shoes were too long for your toes.

"Will you do your best for your Tante Antonia?"

I looked at Dr. Brico, and didn't know if I could live up to her expectations. But I sensed, as young as I was, that she would drive me until I longed to live up to my own. I didn't know how different from hers they were to be.

Dr. Brico had studied piano in music schools at Berkeley and in New York and Germany with some of the greatest teachers in the world, and she was an accomplished pianist as well as conductor. She taught a solid basis in technique using scales, exercises, Czerny, Hanon, and Chopin etudes; but her forte was the approach to the piano used by such masters as Horowitz and Rachmaninoff—that is, she thought of the piano as not a percussion but a stringed instrument. She taught the connected, lyrical line and what she held to be the greatest prize, a personal interpretation that stamped the performance indelibly as belonging to only one pianist. Technique was only the platform that allowed the personality of the individual musician to make itself known.

I raced through a Chopin etude at one of our early lessons, sight-reading from the page, hurrying to show her how fast and how well I could play, bundling dozen of notes up and flinging them into the room at rip speed. She stopped me before I could finish the piece, gently laying her hands across the keys so that I could not go on. She sighed.

"Anyone can play notes," she said. "I want you to sing, to lilt, on the piano."

I learned as much from her about singing as I learned about playing the piano. Melody must flow, the piano must sound like the line of a cello, the line of a voice. It was a pure magic she knew, and inspired.

"You will learn everything by analysis, and you will never play anything through without memorizing, except pieces for technique."

I shook my head, stared at the floor.

"When you begin a piece, take the first measure, and analyze it until you can play it without looking at the music. When you have it down, go on to the next, and then the next." Only when I had memorized the entire piece, at a slow, thinking tempo, would I know what the whole melody sounded like, and only later, after careful correction of my memorization, did she allow me to bring anything up to tempo. My early roughshod habit of speeding through pieces was over.

Dr. Brico always knew exactly what she wanted, as did some of the other strong, self-determined women I had known. Mrs.

Munson, my piano teacher in Los Angeles, had supported herself through her teaching. My choir teacher in school, Violet McCarthy, was a woman whose determination to teach music and be self-supporting was not thought of as unusual. Though they were self-supporting professionals, I wouldn't have known to call these women feminists.

From the scrapbooks she showed me, I knew Dr. Brico had studied with the best musicians in the world and conducted many orchestras. She was a woman, whereas everyone else in the pictures in her scrapbook and in her studio was a man, except the female singers she had conducted, her friend, Mrs. Page, and Juliana, the queen of the Netherlands. Sometimes a bitterness showed; she might speak of having had tough luck; she yearned for more contact with her friends, the people in the photographs. She went to Europe each summer on the *Queen Elizabeth* or the *France*, taking a piano student or two to listen to opera at Salzburg and Bayreuth; and though she went alone to see Albert Schweitzer in Lanbaréné, Africa, joining him at his little organ in the jungle to study Bach among the lepers, she always came home to Denver, home to me.

Something had happened to land her in Denver, like a big fish out of its depth. I had the feeling that someday I would know the real story of her life. Meanwhile, I saw her as the ultimate heroine, strapping her weapons to her back, the baton and the scores, roaming the forest like Diana the Huntress, the daughter of a god, the heiress to music and light.

For my twelfth birthday, in May, there was a surprise in the living room of our duplex house on Willow Street. The brown spinet both my father and I had played for years was gone, and in its place was a shining grand piano. Dr. Brico had told my parents I must have a fine instrument to practice on, and there it was. She was a wonder worker. I fell to it with a will, practicing with real pleasure.

But no matter how hard I did my exercises and learned pieces, according to Dr. Brico I never practiced enough. Our sessions together were soon tumultuous, filled with her praise, or tears, as she railed at me to practice more. She took me to rehearsals of her orchestra for inspiration so I could see what it meant to be committed. I sang in the choruses of her operatic productions: *Pagliacci* and *Eugene Onegin*, *The Marriage of Figaro* and *The Magic Flute*.

"Andiam, andiam!" I sang, dressed in a peasant costume for a performance at the Denver Auditorium. The clown in *Pagliacci* wept, the soprano laughed , and Dr. Brico's baton flashed. It was exciting and seductive. Sometimes I would sing so enthusiastically that my untrained voice would become hoarse.

Toscanini came to Denver to conduct the Denver Symphony and invited his old friend Antonia to join the rehearsals. He gave the board of directors hell for not letting her conduct the symphony as a guest, not letting her take over once in a while for the regular conductor, Saul Caston. She took me with her to the Toscanini rehearsals, and I followed her around, carrying her bags and her scores. We sat in the hall, listening to the rehearsal and watching the maestro, who was dressed in a black sweater and pants with his hair flying around his head, his baton flashing. He looked immense and conducted without a score, from memory. That impressed me terribly, and I wondered if he memorized by analysis.

After one rehearsal, Dr. Brico took me up to the podium and introduced me to the great man. He was hardly taller than I. His face beamed with a smile, his eyes lit up behind his glasses.

"I am pleased to meet you. Dr. Brico says you are a very gifted pianist," Toscanini said to me. "Take care of your hands, little one. They are very beautiful and will make beautiful music."

It was not that I doubted my own talent. I was at ease with music, and overcoming the difficulties of perfecting the technique was a matter of time, of practice, of minutes and hours behind the piano. But I doubted my ability to do enough, go far enough, be perfect enough. It was as if I had a shameful secret that prevented me from ever doing or being anything that anyone wanted me to be.

In Denver, my father's radio program was popular, and he made the transition into television. In 1951 he did a daily show and the city of Denver watched and listened to *Chuck Collins Calling* at ten-fifteen in the morning. He sang songs, read poetry, and philosophized for the audience. Everybody knew him and I loved being recognized as his daughter.

That year, Daddy first invited me to be on his radio show with him. Mother braided my long hair, and I played Mendelssohn's "Arabesque." There was a studio audience, and after I played the Mendelssohn, Daddy and I sang a duet together. The engineer adjusted the microphone for me.

"Just sing right into it, honey, don't be afraid of it," he said.

"This is Chuck Collins, your host, and that was my daughter, Judy." At the end of the show he always said, "Good-bye, good luck, and God bless you!"

In the format of my father's radio show, he addressed his audience about things that were on his mind. In between songs such as "Where or When" or "The Sunny Side of the Street," he would talk about his family and his philosophy of life. My father also talked openly about sensitive issues and was outspoken about politics on as well as off his show. He hated Senator Joseph McCarthy's parade of anti-Communist sentiment when the witch-hunts began and thought Truman a fool and the rest of the country likewise for listening to that "bull." He despised McCarthy for "ruining the lives of so many good, thinking people" and "making it criminal to think at all." He followed closely the progress of the United States in Vietnam's history. As soon as the United States signed a military assistance pact in 1950 with France to help support the French war in Indochina, my father predicted we would get involved, and from the beginning he was against it.

"We can't win there, those people in that part of the world are committed to a life we know nothing about, so what the hell does Truman think he is getting us into?" He would pound his chair, shouting so the neighbors could hear. He was never afraid to take an unpopular stand about something, and taught us that it was the American spirit to do so, that "Tom Paine had begun the fad, and you kids have a responsibility to continue it." We learned our politics at his feet, and we, too, were against intervention in Vietnam long before it officially became a war.

Our political education was woven into our lives with breakfast, over the news at night, reading out loud from *Time*, which Daddy said was too conservative for him, but at least he got news, and it had clever movie reviews. (Mother and Daddy like to go to the movies, where she would describe to him in whispers what was happening on the screen while they listened to the dialogue.)

Celebrities who traveled through Denver were often guests on my father's show, and during those years I met many of them, including Steve Allen, Eddie Albert, and the blind pianist George

Shearing. George often came to our house when he was in town, and one night after dinner he tried out the new grand piano.

"The Baldwin sounds great, Charlie," he said to my father. His guide dog lay at his feet, the harness loose around his mouth, his chin on his paws, watching George's every move.

"Judy, your Chopin will sound swell on this piano." My parakeet, Chris, flew around the room, distracting George's dog and Koko, our cocker spaniel. Koko would have loved to eat the powder blue parakeet, but instead he submitted to having the bird ride around perched on his head. A crown of feathers. Now, Chris landed on George's shoulder, ruffling and fluffing himself into a puffed ball.

"Birds can't talk," the parakeet said. George turned his mouth to the bird's and made a kissing sound. Chris nudged him with his beak and said, "Pretty bird." I had taught him to speak well.

Then George played his arrangement of "Laura." I had never heard the song before. Hearing it made me weak in the knees, the harmonic changes in the song were so beautiful.

"Please, George, teach me to play that song," I pleaded.

"Oh, I wouldn't want to spoil you for your classical studies!" He was smiling, but very serious. George read Braille music and played concertos with orchestras, as well as doing his jazz, yet he wanted me to continue with my classical studies. My father, who made his living in pop music, also wanted me to be a classical pianist. It seemed strange that both of them wanted me to have what they had left behind.

I begged, and he declined again, but he finally gave in, and I studied his fingers as they formed around the chords to "Laura." I learned it note by note. I memorized it by analysis! Dr. Brico found out about it, of course.

"Little Judy, you'll ruin yourself with all that jazz!" she said to me.

My Debussy and Chopin scores had bite marks on all the corners, where my parakeet, who kept me company as I practiced, had taken little chunks out of them with his beak. Practicing scales was pure drudgery, and it always seemed to me that everyone in my family was having a good time while I plodded through my exercises. My only consolation was that sometimes I could prop up a favorite novel in front of my score and read while I practiced. So there were parakeet bites in *The Count of Monte Cristo* and *Madame Bovary* as well.

During this time I took baby-sitting jobs and helped Mother clean the house, do the dishes, and wash the clothes. My brother Denver John was still a little boy, a year old. David was four, and Mike already had a paper route at eight. My Saturday afternoon chores were always accompanied by my favorite radio shows, and I can trace my lifetime habit of trying to do more than one thing at a time to the day when I got my arm caught in the wringer while I was listening to "The Shadow." I howled. Mother came down, got me untangled, told me to watch what I was doing—and I never missed a beat of the plot. "The Shadow knows!"

We moved from Willow to Oneida Street, into a white house with stucco arches and a sweet-smelling Russian olive tree in the backyard. I was working hard at the piano, trying to be as good as Dr. Brico said I could be. One day after a lesson, she said she had a surprise for me.

"You have been making good progress, little Judy, and I want you and Danno Guerrero to play the Mozart Concerto for two pianos in E-flat in February next year, with my orchestra." I was overjoyed. Danno was a sixteen-year-old student of Dr. Brico's whom I had only seen at master classes. He was a very advanced pianist.

"Mozart composed this concerto for his sister and himself when he was twenty-three, to perform together at court in Austria. Since you'll be thirteen next year, you will be mature enough to play it." Over the spring and summer, I had memorized the entire concerto, and during the winter of 1952 Danno and I chose the pianos we would be playing in the concert; mine was a shiny black Steinway with a rich sound and an easy action. It sparkled in the treble and roared in the bass; it was a piano you could really get your hands around, responding to every breath, every gesture. Our rehearsals with Dr. Brico were exciting, both of us sitting behind the Steinways at the studio, Danno's face shining at mine as we nodded to each other for entrances and endings and burst into smiles at the end of our rehearsals.

Danno and I appeared with Dr. Brico's orchestra in February 1953. The largest snowfall in five decades had hit Denver the night before the concert. The cars crawled through a dense white-out and the city was practically at a standstill. Though Mother always made my clothes, for this occasion she bought me a dress for the first time, white organdy with a big red bow. Mommy curled my hair, let me wear lipstick and my first high-heeled shoes, and I put on a huge woolen coat and went to Phipps Auditorium in City Park with my mother and father and my brothers, and joined those brave souls who had made it through the storm to see us.

Danno and I had gone over this concerto so many times that it was in my fingers, I owned it. But nothing had prepared me for the feelings I experienced as I walked out onto the stage. I was taken over by an energy that was never present even when I practiced with the orchestra in the weeks preceding the concert. My lungs seemed filled with something light and apart, helium perhaps. My head spun and my stomach found its way into my throat. I could barely keep my breath coming evenly, and I was afraid that I might not make it to the piano. I seemed to float as I walked.

There are two kinds of energy one brings to the stage. One is total fear, a paralyzing, life-threatening feeling that sinks into the pit of the stomach and makes the breath come fast and the heart beat wildly, and happens if I am not totally prepared; it is a horrible thing and comes to me at times in dreams when I am playing a concerto I do not know, with an orchestra I haven't even heard of, and must somehow go on.

The other kind of energy is what I experienced that night in Denver. I was as well prepared as I would ever be for anything. I reveled in the music; in the big, resonating hall. I loved the people in the audience, who had come in their boots and heavy coats and hats, plodding through the snow to hear Danno and me play Mozart. The feeling of joy at playing the music was sweet, exhilarating, and was over before it had begun. I knew Danno and I had been good.

My parents came backstage, along with a handful of enthusiastic members of the audience. Everyone was smiling.

"You were wonderful," said my mother, "and you looked so beautiful!" My father bundled me into his arms, squeezing tight, grinning from ear to ear.

"Dreamboat," he said, "you did us proud!"

Dr. Brico came through the door, looked from Danno to me,

and put her hands on her hips. She frowned. I had a moment of horrible doubt against my inner feelings of triumph.

"You were brilliant," she said, breaking into a huge smile. I could not have asked for more.

After the Mozart concert, I fell into a kind of slump. The letdown was enormous after the year of pressure. I turned fourteen in May, and felt unhappy and depressed. I had started memorizing a Lizst transcription of a violin piece of Paganini's. It was complex, with technical demands that were within my grasp, but they were taking a long time to get. I was slowly, diligently practicing to bring the whole thing up to tempo. Lizst had captured the flash of the violin's dancing melody so that the piece sparkled and clamored for attention even at a slow speed. My father listened, inspired by the music and crazy with his inner vision.

"You must play that on the program I am doing for the automobile show next month," he said. I said I couldn't possibly, it was much too hard, it was more difficult than anything I had played before. He insisted.

I told him I couldn't do it.

"You can if you want to," he said.

I became more and more despairing as the day drew nearer and I knew it was not possible.

I thought for a week about how outrageous my father was being, and one day while I was alone in the house ironing shirts in the utility room, the thought crossed my mind that there was only one solution. I went to the medicine cabinet, pulled out a bottle of a hundred aspirins, and began taking handfuls of them with glasses of water. They were the strongest medication that my family took, and I was sure they would kill me. I finished off the bottle while I finished ironing a shirt collar. I thought about how simple it would be to be dead. I thought about my mother and how she would have to make do without me and about how angry my father would be. My thoughts became hazy, and as I started feel sick I became frightened. The sickness turned into raging nausea. I was no longer depressed, only desperate. I might in fact die.

Panicked, I went to the phone to call my close friend Marcia Pinto, whose father was a doctor. When her mother answered, I told her what I had done. She talked to me in a calm tone.

"Judy, go to the bathroom, put your finger down your throat and throw up, and Sherman will be there as soon as possible."

By this time my brothers were coming home from school. I was lying on my bed, cold sweat standing on my face. The boys peeked into my room, shifting from one foot to the other, and when Dr. Pinto arrived they let him in the front door. He wiped my head with a cold towel and said reassuring things to me until my mother arrived. They stood together, looking down at me.

"She'll be all right," Dr. Pinto said. "Sometimes children are given as many as twenty aspirins a day if they have scarlet fever. She took about a hundred, but I think she got most of that out of her system. Just let her rest, and she'll be like new in the morning."

After he had gone, my mother shook her head. "Why did you do that? What is the matter with you?"

"I'm afraid of failing Daddy, he expects so much."

Mother sat down on the bed and put her arms around me. "You know he thinks you can do anything, Judy, because he thinks he can."

Daddy was so upset that he couldn't talk to me; instead he wrote me a letter of apology the next day in which he spoke of how frail and human adults can be, and how wrong. He wrote that he had pushed me too far. The remorse in his letter expressed his disappointment in himself; for the first time in my memory he spoke of his own limitations.

His attitude toward me softened a little; after that, there were fewer fights about the piano. But he was still demanding, and just as determined as ever that I fulfill his idea of what I could become. He and Dr. Brico wanted me to be a perfect pianist, I thought my mother wanted me to be the perfect daughter, but I was beginning to understand that I would probably grow up to be myself.

My sister, Holly Ann, was born on the twenty-third of December in 1954. The afternoon my mother went into the hospital, I was reading Dylan Thomas's *Under Milk Wood* out loud to my father in the uneasy truce that had settled in since our autumn confrontation over the Lizst. I remember hearing "Hernando's Hideaway," "Three Coins in the Fountain," and "Hey There, You with the Stars in Your Eyes" on the radio. Because it was almost Christmas, my parents had already decided that if the child was a girl they would name her Holly for the holly berries. Mother called from the hospital and told me I would have to play Santa Claus that year, so I went around to the closets and pulled out hidden bikes and books and meerschaum pipes, and took care of Daddy and the boys. I did the cooking, and when Mother came home with Holly, Daddy had white spots on the inside of his mouth. The doctor said they were from vitamin C deficiency.

Holly was a beautiful baby with big brown eyes and blond hair, and even as an infant she had a glint in her eyes, an indication that she knew of things mystical and magical. From the moment she was born she was my best friend.

At East High School, I had a teacher named Jack Shearn, who taught me writing and lived in a house over our back fence with his wife and seven children. I thought Jack Shearn's veins ran with poet's tears and James Joyce's blood. Teachers had always encouraged me in writing, but during my junior year a new English teacher came to East High. For our first paper she asked us to write on anything we wanted so that she could see what we were doing. I wrote about *The Cocktail Party* by T. S. Eliot, a play that had had a powerful effect on me. One of the characters, an elegant, intellectual English lady, winds up going out to Africa as a volunteer nurse. In the jungle, while doing service for a native tribe, she is eaten alive by giant ants. The play's central theme of obsession stimulated my imagination, and I was so excited by the paper I had written that I could barely sleep the night before turning it in.

When the papers were returned in a few days, I waited for the A I knew I would get. All the papers were handed out but mine. I thought, She is going to read my paper in front of everyone. When the bell rang, the teacher asked to see me. "Miss Collins," she said, "I don't believe you wrote this. I'd like to know where you found it." My cheeks burned. I felt humiliation and rage. It was unjust, but because of the accusation, I felt guilty.

Mr. Shearn came to plead my case, bringing with him other papers I had written. My other teachers assured her that this was the kind of work I could do, and had done. The look on her face said whatever they showed her would not change her mind.

I stayed in her class, hangdog, for the rest of the year, barely passing. It was years before I wrote again with any joy.

* * *

Apart from practicing the piano, when I was fourteen I began to have more of a social life outside of school. Sometimes I even went to the school dances on Friday nights with my friends. My first crush was on a boy named Wally, and when we went to the movies together, we would neck like mad in the back row between mouthfuls of popcorn.

Throughout these years I did a lot of singing in the choir at school and at church. Never having studied singing formally, I had a "natural" voice. I picked up the songs my father sang at the piano, and sometimes, as we had done when I was a little girl, he would play while I sang. When Jack Blue, a friend of Daddy's, came for dinner one night, he heard me sing some popular songs and asked if I would like a job singing with a local pop band that did shows on the weekends. I said I would love it.

Wearing the white organdy dress from my Mozart concert, I stood in front of a sign that said JACK BLUE'S DANCE BAND and sang "My Funny Valentine" and "Long Ago and Far Away." I was terrified Dr. Brico would find out because she would see it as a perversion of my talent. We went out to Lowry Air Force Base and did shows at the officers' club, where they didn't seem to mind that I was under age. But when Jack tried to book us into a club in town, the owner objected because I was only fifteen. That ended my brief career, but Jack told me I had the "stuff" and could become a pop singer if I wanted to. Though these were nice songs, I was relieved that now Dr. Brico would have no reason to be angry at me.

I had another brief job, singing for a man named Leigh Baron who had a supper club out on the highway going north. I sat on a little stage set in the wall above the tables like a window frame while he played the piano for me. I was fifteen and sang "When I Was Seventeen," but that lasted only a couple of nights. These two experiences told me that singing purely popular songs was not for me. Though I enjoyed them, I sometimes found the lyrics to be lacking something. I was still practicing the piano two hours a day after school, and had begun to learn the Rachmaninoff Piano Concerto no. 2. Dr. Brico expected me to perform the concerto with her orchestra when I was ready, but I no longer pretended that classical music was the only music that interested me. And by this time I had met the three people who were to become my closest teenage friends.

Marcia Pinto was tall, dark-haired, and she studied classical ballet. Carol Shank was blond, and studied modern dance. We wore felt skirts with poodles and chains on them, and I remember soaking my crinoline petticoats in the bathtub with sugared water, then hanging them to dry overnight; the sugar made the petticoats stand out under the felt skirts. John Gilbert was my best friend among the boys. I adored him, but we did not date; ours was a platonic relationship. He wanted to be an actor, and he and I were in the same Shakespeare class together, where we both memorized Hamlet's "To be or not to be" soliloquy. Marcia, Carol, John, and I went to lectures about the Committee for a Sane Nuclear Policy, saw avant-garde movies, and talked about what was happening in Algeria. We saved our money and went to see *Cyrano de Bergerac* and the New York City Ballet when they came through Denver. We had potluck dinners and talked about our visions of our lives beyond the present. We were considered "oddballs" by our schoolmates.

Often we met at my house. My parents liked my friends. One night when Marcia was over after dinner, Daddy asked if she would dance around the living room so that he could feel the movement in the room. At fourteen, Marcia was already a prima ballerina, a star in her class, and when she was dancing "The Blue Danube" with the Denver Symphony in an evening of Viennese waltzes, Daddy told her, "I'm coming to see you dance."

Marcia and I talked about putting together an "act" and taking it to Las Vegas. One night, after a Friday potluck dinner at Carol's, I sat down at the piano and played some Debussy. Finishing, I continued to experiment at the keyboard.

"Are you just making up those melodies as you go?" asked Marcia. She was twirling around the room in time to the music.

"Sure. It's easy," I replied.

"Why don't you make up theme music for a story we can dance to?" she said. We settled on "Little Red Riding Hood." I made up some themes for the characters, and that night, over vanilla frozen ice and tollhouse cookies, our new ensemble, which we called the Little Reds, was born. We performed "Little Red Riding Hood" that year at the East High talent show.

While looking for the Little Reds' next story I heard my first folk song, a version of "Barbara Allen" sung on the radio by Jo Stafford.

> " *'Twas in the merry month of May,*
> *When green buds they were swelling,*
> *A young man on his death bed lay*
> *For the love of Barbara Allen.* "

The song took my breath away. The melody was minor, with a mournful tune. It was nothing like the lyrics of the Broadway songs my father sang, and nothing like classical music. With the emotional excess of adolescence, I was sure by now that I would end up dying for either love or passion—as happens to the hero in "Barbara Allen." I had to sing "Barbara Allen"; I felt it belonged to me. With no idea that the song was originally sung with just a guitar, I got the record and learned it, accompanying myself on the piano. I kept the song to myself; it was too personal for the Little Reds.

I was listening more to the radio station where I had first heard "Barbara Allen." There must have been a disc jockey out there who had no way of knowing he was changing an innocent girl's life, for I heard my second folk song on his station as well. The next song to win my heart was "The Gypsy Rover." I called the station immediately to find out the name of the song, went to Wells Music to buy the record, and learned the words. I told Marcia and Carol the plot—a young girl leaves her castle, her husband, her baby, and her wealth to follow a gypsy into the woods. It would be a perfect piece for the Little Reds.

> "*The gypsy rover came over the hill,*
> *Down through the valley so shady,*
> *He whistled and sang till the green woods rang,*
> *And he won the heart of a lady.* "

That spring, the Little Reds performed again at the school talent show. I sang "The Gypsy Rover" with a flute, piano, and guitar trio; Marcia, wearing tights and heavy makeup, danced the Gypsy, and Carol, in a pale blue tutu, was the princess.

Singing for people was a very different experience from playing the piano. Standing up in front of the audience, looking out at them instead of just sitting behind the piano and playing, I had the sense of eyes, faces, hopes, turned toward me, embracing me in a way that they could not have when half my body was facing away from them as I played the piano. Despite how much I loved them, Mozart and Chopin paled in comparison.

People wanted to hear "The Gypsy Rover," and clubs all over Denver asked us to perform it. Over the next three months the Little Reds performed for the PTA, women's groups, and luncheons, with Marcia and Carol dancing and me singing about this girl who traipses off into the woods with the gypsy. Folk music, this new combination of melody and story, was to change my life. As much as classical music nurtured me, I was discovering that playing the piano fulfilled only half of my musical needs; here was the other half, the story. My life as a folk singer had begun.

Soon after, I talked my father into renting me an old National guitar with a twangy sound and ancient strings. It came with seven free jazz lessons. I skipped the lessons and taught myself.

I was still working on the Rachmaninoff concerto, trying to get it ready for the concert with Dr. Brico's orchestra, but I had fallen in love with folk music. I was terrified to tell Dr. Brico that I didn't want to study the Rachmaninoff anymore. But I knew I had to.

On the day I finally summoned up the courage to tell her, I walked to the door of her studio like someone condemned, imagining the worst; and it was worse than I could have imagined. We had a terrible scene: she cried, she begged; I cried, I begged her to understand. Finally, she became furious.

"Can't you see you are throwing your career away?" I bowed my head. "Do you know how many pianists would give up everything just to be able to play as you can? You are ungrateful, you cannot see the thing that is right in front of your nose. I can't believe you are able to be this callous to what God has given you. You have the hands, you could go right to the top."

She didn't know I had a guitar, and when I told her it was the last straw. I was ruined, Dr. Brico said.

I walked out of her studio and onto the sidewalk without looking back. In my heart, I would look back for years, and perhaps even today a part of me still looks back. The call of folk music was stronger than even this strong and powerful woman. The wonderful Rachmaninoff Piano Concerto no. 2, which I had memorized, would go unplayed with her orchestra. She had said I was making a mistake and I had to struggle not to believe her. I didn't know then what the Buddhists say, that all decisions are right.

* * *

Though disappointed that I wanted to give up the piano, my father ultimately respected my decision, which is why he agreed to rent that beat-up National guitar for me. I fingered the strings until I found the right chords to go with the melody—something that would have driven Dr. Brico wild. I became a hunter of songs, searching for folk music records and getting my father to sing me old Irish melodies, songs I hadn't realized were also folk songs; songs that McCormack and John Charles Thomas had sung. I discovered many folk songs hidden among my father's repertoire.

At the beginning of 1956, when I was sixteen, I met Lingo the Drifter. He had a radio show that played nothing but folk music, which Daddy and I used to listen to together on Saturday afternoons. We both loved these songs of Woody Guthrie and Pete Seeger, people whom we had never heard before, and one Saturday after the show, Daddy called Lingo and asked him to dinner.

Lingo arrived at the house with his guitar around his neck on a leather strap. He was wearing buckskin pants and a hat with a pine bough sticking out through the top. We discovered that he lived in a log cabin up on Lookout Mountain, a stone's throw from Buffalo Bill Cody's grave, in a place he called his homestead. Later I learned from my friend Studs Terkel, the writer and journalist, that Lingo had lived in Chicago for years and that his wife and child had been killed in an automobile accident. He left, never to return to the Windy City. He never talked about his family or his old life. He wanted people to think he had dropped out of a cloud onto the mountains, materializing fully dressed, singing and playing the guitar; but Lingo was also articulate, cunning, and sophisticated under the buckskin and pine boughs. My dad said Lingo was about as much a hillbilly as Adlai Stevenson.

From Lingo I heard more songs that had "political" themes. I heard union songs, the songs of Woody Guthrie and Cisco Houston and the Weavers, songs of the newly fired movement for integration in the South. After the bus boycott in Montgomery, Martin Luther King, Jr., emerged as the leader in the struggle for desegregation; the United States was getting involved in Vietnam as more advisers were sent each year; and these things found their way into many of the songs I was hearing. Folk music was a means to stir people about matters of the heart and matters of politics. It was not only a reaction to the moon-June-spoon lyrics of current pop music, but also a vehicle for expressing a depth of feeling about things political as well as personal.

"Why don't you and Judy and Marge come up to the homestead this weekend, bring your guitar, and I'll show you some real live folk music. There'll be home-brew, and lots of homemade borscht and a whole mess of guitars and banjos." We were all excited by Lingo's invitation.

"What'll we wear? I've never been invited to anything like this," I said.

"It's not as though he's a heathen. We'll just wear clothes, for God's sake," said my father.

I wore my oldest Levi's and a checkered shirt and my rough-out boots, of which I was terribly proud. I looked Denver to the toes. There were a lot of people there with guitars and banjos. As soon as one person finished a song, another would say, "Here's a song that reminds me of," or "This is another version of that one," or "Here's that one with another melody." If a lot of them knew the same song they might sing on the chorus, but for the most part they let the singer sing. When my turn came, I was shy for a moment, feeling the outsider. I was the new girl singer in the group, an unknown quantity.

"I learned this from John Jacob Niles's recording," I said.

> *"Black, black, black is the color of my true love's hair;*
> *His face is something wondrous fair,*
> *The purest eyes, and the finest hands,*
> *I love the ground where-on he stands."*

The crowd around the room was silent while I sang, and when I was finished, Lingo put his arm around me.

"She's really good, isn't she?" Everyone nodded and smiled, and I had made it into the group with Lingo's seal of approval. They asked me to sing again, high praise. I knew I belonged.

I met two singers that night who were to have a strong influence on my music and my appreciation of the interpretive nature of the folk singer. Dick Barker, a rancher's son who would later run float trips down the Colorado River, sang with a sweet and haunting voice:

"Spanish is the loving tongue,
Bright as music, soft as spray
'Twas a girl I learned it from,
Living down Sonora way.
I don't look much like a lover,
But I say her love words over,
Often when I'm all alone;
Mi amor, mi corozon,"

After Dick had sung this song, a gangly young man named Mart Hoffman sang, with an equally haunting voice, the song that would become the anthem of the sixties, the theme song of a generation of dreamers.

"This land is your land,
This land is my land,
From California to the New York island
From the redwood forest
To the Gulf Stream waters,
This land was made for you and me."

Years later Mart, who had become a friend and confidant, died in Arizona, a suicide. In my mind, Mart's voice is the one I will always hear singing Woody's great song.

Lingo brought out wooden bowls and served his homemade borscht, which was steaming hot and very good. The whole night was unforgettable. Denver stretched below us like a jewel box, shining and twinkling. Toward the end of the evening as we all stood outside in the light of the stars, I said to Lingo, "I think I know what I want to do, Lingo, I want to be a folk singer."

"Well," he said, "I've done it, and I know two things for sure. You'll never starve, and you'll never be lonely."

Late afternoon, the Virgin Islands

Last night I dreamed about Freddy DeMann, my manager. In the dream he is in an argument, shot in the head, and can't see out of one eye. Wounded. Imperfect.

After managing myself for eleven years, I started working with Freddy DeMann two years ago. He and I had first met when he was a record promotion man with Elektra. He worked on the promotion of "Send In the Clowns." I have sold millions of records, but in the changing music business, I felt I needed help. I've been told for years that I should have a manager. But Freddy's attempts to get my new record played and exposed to the world don't seem to be working. Have I given things enough time? Is two years enough time? Maybe I've been on my own too long. If I had the courage to break off with Freddy, I feel my wings would be let loose to fly.

I lie awake tonight, listening to the sea, my eyes open in the dark, thinking about "my brilliant career."

A few months after I met Lingo, I met Peter Taylor, my husband-to-be. Before I stopped studying with Dr. Brico, I taught piano under her supervision, and I still had a few students, one of whom was Peter's sister, Hadley Taylor. During my teaching sessions with Hadley, we giggled about her two older brothers, thinking it would be great if I could meet them. The Taylor kids worked summers at Sportsland Valley Guest Ranch, a dude ranch in the mountains above Berthoud Pass with horses, a fishing lake, pack trips, and a dozen young high school students who did all the work for practically nothing plus room and board. The summer after my sophomore year in high school one of the girls left early, and Hadley suggested me as her replacement. Her cousin, Patti Gwen Huffsmith, was going up to the ranch the same weekend, so Hadley was able to arrange for her brother Peter to drive us both.

"Hi, I'm Judy, and you must be Peter." He was tall and handsome and wore a Stetson, faded blue jeans, a soft cotton shirt, and a pair of roughouts. Pete Taylor looked like what the designer Ralph Lauren later tried to imitate.

"Hi," he said, and opened the door for me. I stood on the curb in front of our house on Emerson Street. Behind me on the lawn I remember my sister, Holly, who was one and a half and dressed in her pinafore, waving good-bye, and Denver John standing by the screen door. Peter and I loaded my suitcases and guitar into the trunk; I squeezed into the back seat, with Patti Gwen in front with Peter. It turned out she was going up to be with her beau, Ray Fox, who was the son of a mountain rancher near Granby. Peter was "free." So was I. But by the time we arrived at the lodge, neither of us was.

After we had unloaded the gear and had dinner that first night, Peter and I walked down the highway in the moonlight to Wally's Bar, the local mountain watering hole in Hidden Valley, the nearest town. We danced to the music on the jukebox—"Earth Angel" and "Rock Around the Clock"—and we told each other all about our lives.

Peter was two years older than I and was about to start his second year at the University of Colorado. We had both read Camus and Sartre and Evelyn Waugh; we forgave Graham Greene for writing thrillers because in spite of his being a converted Catholic, he was still a brilliant thinker; we talked about James Agee's tragic life and how neither of us would consider reading an Agatha Christie novel; we both listened to Beethoven, Smetana, and Charlie "Bird" Parker. Peter identified with my troubles with Dr. Brico. He, too, felt he had let someone down by the choices he was making. Though he wanted to be a scholar, a writer, he planned to enlist to fly for the Naval Air Cadets the following year so that he wouldn't be drafted.

We walked back down the dark highway to the lodge. It was very late. We stood out by the Sportsland Valley gas pump, next to the pickup truck, and under the stars we talked about our dreams.

I stayed at Sportsland Valley for a month. Though Peter went back to Denver, where he was working for the summer, he came up to visit me on weekends. The Beavers, who owned the ranch, were Christian Scientists, with bright, cheery smiles and handsome faces, but I soon learned they were tough as nails to work for. After I had poured coffee into a guest's lap at breakfast, I was told I would have to get my act together. The other girls told me that the Beavers warned you once, they warned you twice, and then you were out, back to Kansas or Ohio or Denver. It was rumored that Hortense Beaver had a round bed covered in a red quilted silk, but I never found out for sure.

Although I was not a very good dishwasher, cabin cleaner, and table setter, I played the piano and sang songs around the campfire after dinner. We'd take my guitar on a packhorse so I could play "Cool Clear Water," and everyone would sing while they cooked S'mores over the campfire. Or I'd sit at the piano in the lodge and sing "Barbara Allen" while people gazed into the flames in the stone fireplace. I taught everyone rounds and sang the hours away while all of us washed hundreds of dishes after dinner.

In the afternoons, when the rooms in the lodge were cleaned, the cabins done, the lunch served, and the dishes washed, I would go up to the dormitory under the pine eves of the lodge, lie on my bunk, and dream the hours away. I read Peter's letters and wrote back to him, sitting on the back steps of the lodge after dinner, smoking Kool cigarettes with the cook and his wife, watching the sunset.

That fall I entered my Junior year in high school. On weekends, Peter would come to the house in Denver and he, my dad, and I would discuss books and politics and history. The three of us smoked pipes. I was allowed to smoke only pipes or cigars in the house because although Daddy loved cigarettes, he referred to them as coffin nails and would smoke yours, but never buy his own. The scent of Briggs and Seventy-Nine mix floated through the house, and as the Saturday afternoon wore on, Daddy would break out the sherry or the rum. I remember the taste of pecans and apples and good dry sherry, mingled with sounds of my father's and Peter's voices reading lines from T. S. Eliot or Walt Whitman.

That year, 1956, Mother went to work at Neusteter's, a fancy women's shop in Denver, and she began to be more her own woman and less our mother and my father's wife. Holly grew into a little girl from a baby; Michael began junior high; Denver and David were in grammar school. "Blue Suede Shoes" was playing on the radio, and Elvis was rolling his hips on television, but I was much more interested in art movies, folk music, and going with Peter, when he was in town, to see *The Seventh Seal* or Cocteau's *Orpheus* at the Esquire Theater. We would hold hands while straining to read the subtitles.

I learned that my friends and I were not "odd," but that we were members of the "beat generation;" my friend John Gilbert carried a battered copy of *On the Road* to class. When we went out to the movies, John wore a black leather jacket, and we were all learning to smoke French cigarettes, coughing and choking—but determined. We talked about having "substance" in our lives, and "meaning," and we didn't like the "moon-June-spoon" lyrics of popular songs because they were vapid and hollow.

After the second summer at Sportsland Valley, I started my

senior year in high school and Peter joined the Naval Air Cadets. A friend entered me in the four-state Kiwanis "Stars of Tomorrow" contest, which I won by playing the guitar and singing "Pretty Saro." The father of one of the other contestants, a very fine classical violinist, complained that his daughter had been "beat out by a hillbilly." I went to Atlantic City for a weekend to sing at the International Kiwanis Club convention, where ten thousand Kiwanians nodded in their red hats and clapped enthusiastically when I sang "Pretty Saro":

> *"Down in some lone valley,*
> *In some lonesome place*
> *Where the wild birds all whistle*
> *And their notes do increase.*
> *Farewell, pretty Saro, I bid you adieu,*
> *But I'll dream of pretty Saro*
> *Wherever I go."*

I always loved the saddest songs, and as young as I was, I already had a sense of loss in my life. I couldn't have told you what I had lost, but I knew that whatever it was, it was irreplaceable.

My friend Marcia Pinto had gone to England for our junior year at East High School, studying with the Royal Ballet in London. She came home for our senior year with stardust still on her feet, and told us of the magical world she had visited. I had no thoughts about what to do myself when I graduated and was depressed that Peter was away in Pensacola, Florida, learning to be a pilot and that I had had such a rift with Dr. Brico. I still sang in the choir at Park Hill Methodist Church, but my faith was flimsy, and my heart wasn't in it. I felt at loose ends.

That same year Toscanini died. I found the experience of previous knowledge of the deceased, no matter how slight, unnerving. I was beginning to understand that life does not last forever.

When I graduated from East High School, Peter was flying airplanes for the navy in Pensacola and his letters arrived every few days. I got a summer job working at Lemon Lodge on Grand Lake. It was a small, charming place at the mouth of the Little Colorado River as it ran into Grand Lake, at the foot of the mountains that rose up toward the continental divide. Jenny

Lemon was a fair boss, and I liked her. Every day we cleaned the dozen cabins that were scattered about the property. In the evening I would pull out the guitar and sing. Sometimes I went dancing at night in the local bars or jingling-riding up into the mountains with the wranglers from the local stable to bring two dozen horses down from the meadows where they had spent the night. One of the cowboys would bring a saddled horse and wake me at six in the morning with a whistle at my window, and we would ride to the mountain meadows. We hunted the horses among the pine trees and the low bushes, bending our heads to avoid the boughs, and calling, "Come, come, here Paint, here Buffalo Bill, come this way, Honey Bun," wrangling our quarter horses in among the flowers.

One afternoon, during a summer shower that fell loudly among the pines, I was ironing when there was a knock at the door. One of the guests, whom I'll call Mr. Golden, stood outside in the rain, wearing a hat whose rim was dripping water. His boots were soaked, his clothes hanging, and in his hand was a fishing rod, the tackle kit slung over his shoulder. The kit was drenched, water falling out through its threaded reed sides. I could smell gutted fish, a clean raw scent. His face was wet and tight under his hat.

"I can't wake her, you better come, and get the doctor."

How do you know someone is dead, without knowing? I said, "Just a minute," and went to the phone and dialed Dr. Frazer. He cared for all the broken arms and pregnancy scares in town, as well as tick bites and infected burns.

The nurse answered, and I said, "Bring a stomach pump," as though I knew what I was doing. I tramped behind Mr. Golden through the wet pine needles on the ground, a slicker over my jeans, my moccasins soaking through with every step. The cabin was one of the two that had a second floor, the stairway doubling upon itself, twisting up to the second-story bedroom. I followed his back climbing the narrow passage and stood looking down at a body.

The dead woman was sprawled across the bed and looked like a doll thrown against the wall, dropped into a bundle of arms and legs and bones, her pelvis and pubic hair showing. She wore a silk nightgown that was shoved up along her hip and was rumpled and torn at the shoulder. Her brunette and blond-streaked hair spread out from her worried face. She was very stiff, very still, and very dead.

Probably too many pills and a great deal of booze, I thought, an accidental suicide. I grinned, a wide, violent, tight-lipped, automatic grin that would not come off my face. I smiled, looking around for a suicide note. Murder, maybe.

Mr. Golden stood looking down at his wife. Rain still dripped from the brim of his hat. He stopped over her and took her hand in his, twisting and pulling at the enormous jeweled ring that was on her index finger.

"They would steal it at the morgue," he said. Rain dripped from his nose onto his wife's nightgown.

I asked him if there had been a note. I have always believed that there was a note, that he arrived first, cleaned up the pills, the evidence, and took the note with him, crumpling it into his wet pocket, or maybe thrusting it down among the dead fish in the basket. It must have recked, full of oil and scales, when he pulled it out later.

"No note, no, nothing," he said fumbling with the ring, finally getting it off her finger and slipping it into his pocket. I couldn't stop grinning.

"She is dead," said the nurse, who had come in a station wagon rigged up as an ambulance.

We wrapped what had been Mrs. Golden in an army blanket and tried to bend her arms and legs. They were stiff from rigor mortis. As we forced the joints to give way they made a soggy, scraping noise. We angled the body down the narrow staircase, pressing each limb around the corners. I couldn't believe how her fragile body could be so ungiving in the army blanket. My face was contorted in laughter; it was all I could do not to howl.

Later, I became hysterical. I called my parents on the phone.

"Mom, can you come up to see me? I feel awful."

"Honey, its all right. Of course you're upset." Mother put my father on the phone.

"Relax, Dreamboat," he said, "you just saw your first corpse. It's natural, the first time you see a dead person the mind doesn't know how to react, it is stunned. You'll get over it, but we'll be right up this weekend. Friday, as early afternoon as possible." My parents' voices sounded so comforting. I'd thought I was glad to be away from home for the summer, but I couldn't wait to see my family.

"They drank a lot, the couple in Seven-D," said Jenny, when she returned from her twice-a-month trip down to Denver. Her eyes took in the afternoon's tale, unspoken looks saying: It wouldn't have happened if I had been here, if you had gotten there sooner, if you had ignored the DO NOT DISTURB sign on the door and gone in to clean when you are supposed to clean, in the morning, at nine. I tried to tell her about the rigor mortis. The woman had been dead for hours.

That afternoon there were rainbows over Grand Lake and drops of water hung like veils in the dusk under the big pine trees. I got terribly drunk that night. I couldn't get the dead woman out of my mind.

At the end of that summer Mother and I packed up my suitcases, and she and Daddy drove me out to Illinois, to continue my education at MacMurray, a four-year college for women in the middle of the wheat belt of the Midwest. Though I'd never heard of the school, I chose to attend MacMurray because I'd been given a working scholarship. I paid the rest of my way by shelving books in the library. The year I spent there seemed like two.

I was utterly homesick and missed Peter, my mother's cooking, my father's pressured enthusiasm, and my brothers and sister. I went home for Christmas to see Peter, and in March we went on a skiing trip to Colorado. Between my visits home, I spent most of my time thinking, What am I doing here? I hated the landscape, the brutally cold, bitter winter, and got through it by playing the guitar, singing "This Land Is Your Land" and "Black Is the Color of My True Love's Hair." I smoked cigarettes, and in the melancholy, long winter I started practicing the piano again: scales and exercises and the Rachmaninoff concerto and all the Chopin and Ravel I had spent so many years learning. Practicing soothed what was saddest, as it always had. I knew that I wasn't "playing seriously," which would have meant that I must give up everything else in my life, but it gave me comfort.

In 1958, I went home to Denver and married Peter Taylor.

Late afternoon

Rough and cold all day, but when the sun came out to warm the wind I snorkled out to the reef by myself. I am a strong swimmer today, although it took me many years to feel comfortable in the water. I was looking for French angelfish, but they seem to have left or were hiding from the heavy surf. The reef isn't far from any beach but the surf was very strong. Before I knew it I was a long way out, with the tide bearing me farther. My breathing was shallow. I began to hyperventilate as the adrenaline flooded me. When I reached the calmer water my heart was pounding. In those moments of lucidity as I swam back to shore I realized that fear of the water was still with me, and fear of the future.

Last night the clouds parted, the sky cleared, the stars came out, and I looked into the endless black and silver above me and wished upon a star as it flew over the Pleiades, Give me the faith to just let go

I have my tours, I have Louis, what more do I want?

In My Life

Wednesday, January 9, 1985 / the Virgin Islands

The sea is a thousand shades of blue this morning. Not a cloud anywhere. The sound of the surf reaches me on the terrace, and the warbling conversation of a bird hidden in the leaves of a cypress tree. Tranquil. Quiet. The day is holding its breath with me, waiting for a sign.

Yesterday we took a snorkel trip to a romantic, remote beach. I saw a queen triggerfish and dove to retrieve two yellow-orange, double sunrise shells, the first I've seen this trip. We saw shoals of purple tang and a million sparkling fish turning in an instant together, moving the water in a wave of silver.

We went out to dinner in Blues Bay last night, and on the way back from town in the Jeep we stopped to let a huge crab walk his slow crawl across the road, toward the mountain.

"He is going the wrong way, the water is in the other direction," I say.

"It's in that direction, too, as well you know; this is an island. No matter which road you choose to travel, you face the same lessons and get to the same place," Louis says.

Louis is reading *The Name of the Rose*, and I, for a change, am reading nothing. I am letting my thoughts wander over the years when I was a girl, before the circus began, before the tours

54

began, before the recordings began, to the time I was innocent, or at least invincible.

Peter had been my sweetheart for three years and he and my family were very close. I was eighteen when we were married and Peter had already finished his tour of duty in the navy and was planning to go back to school in the fall to finish the two years necessary for his undergraduate degree in English literature. It was the beginning of the summer, so we agreed that we would work in the mountains for three months, then move to Boulder. In June 1958, we headed for the town of Estes Park to look for a job. We stayed in godfather Holden's cabin in Rocky Mountain National Park, a preserve of mountains and rushing streams, raw wilderness and beauty. Peter went to town the first day, and came home to our cabin very excited.

"There's a job for us running Fern Lake Lodge. It's owned by Jim Bishop, who owns the big lodge at Bear Lake. It's a nine-mile round-trip hike to get to Fern; the lodge has no electricity, and our food will be brought in by packhorse once a week; the water has to be pumped from the mountain springs, and I will chop wood for the fires, and you will—here's the catch—bake bread and pies on the wood stove!"

"Of course I will!" I already knew I was pregnant with Clark and I felt vibrant and healthy, capable of anything. Euphoric.

We first moved into Bear Lake Lodge, where Jim Bishop made us comfortable. The cook taught me to bake bread, and we waited for the snow to melt enough so we could start for Fern Lake. Jim told us how for years his mother had run Fern Lake Lodge year in and year out, accommodating two dozen guests at a time. Burros were sent in loaded with steamer trunks, and she kept three wood stoves burning all year. People would walk the nine-mile round-trip on snowshoes and go ice fishing on the lake in the winter. The lodge had been closed for a few years, but Jim wanted to open it up again because it had been so special in his mother's time and it was his favorite lodge in the national park.

Finally, when the snow was melted enough to get over the high trail, Peter and I each assembled a fifty-pound pack of clothes and food for a week and started out for our new home. It was a brilliantly sunny morning the day we began our trek.

The wild mountain flowers were in bloom, the snowmelt roared down in streams and waterfalls. There were a million purple, white, and yellow columbines blooming, and I saw an orange hummingbird, a little bigger than my thumb. I have never seen one that color since, and I have been told that this species lives only in the Andes at very high altitudes. I have always thought of those red-orange wings as a special sign.

We arrived after four and a half hours and put our packs down. The lodge sat on the banks of Fern Lake, nestled beside the crystal water, its windows boarded up. We began opening doors with the big loop of keys Jim had given us, and as the slats came off, the daylight flooded the puncheon-floored main room. On the walls were enormous old photographs of people in furs with long wooden skis, snowshoes stacked against the lodge. There was a blackened stove in the huge kitchen, and behind the main lodge were eleven cabins scattered throughout the pines. Each cabin had beds and a potbellied Franklin wood-burning stove in perfect condition. A storage cabin was filled with quilts, ancient canned goods, parts for lanterns, pillows for thirty. We made up a bed in the cabin closest to the lake, and Peter went out to chop kindling. I lit the Coleman lamps in the kitchen and got the stove going. We were home.

That first night Peter and I fell asleep exhausted. Next day, he got the spring water running through the pipes; I got the bread baking. Soon mountain hikers were stopping in at the lodge for lunch.

A few days later our packhorse arrived with my old National guitar, a quart of Jack Daniel's, and food for a week. Occasionally friends would hike in to spend a few days, bringing avocados, Mexican beer, and fresh tomatoes, but mostly we relied on the arrival each week of the packhorse loaded with fresh meat and vegetables, letters from home, and sometimes a newspaper. Peter fished trout out of the lake, and in the woods under the pine trees was our "Girl Scout refrigerator," a cooler made by dripping water from one of the spring pipes over a tin box covered with cheesecloth. Primitive, but it worked just fine.

In the mornings, after the fires were started, the bread baked, the chores done, the wood chopped, and the spring pipes checked, Peter and I would sit out on the porch of the lodge and play chess as we looked across the clear surface of Fern Lake, awaiting our hikers. We would hear their voices first, coming down from Emerald Lake, above us at thirteen thousand feet. I would go into the kitchen and make the final preparations for the pies and slice the bread for sandwiches.

"It's amazing to find you here in the middle of "nowhere," they would often say. Peter would settle them around the wood tables, get them mugs of coffee, and then I would serve the hot apple and cherry pies and sandwiches while they oohed and ahhed.

After lunch I would bring out the guitar and sing "Spanish Is the Loving Tongue" and "Barbara Allen." People leaned their faces back in the sun, their eyes closed, sometimes singing along on the choruses. With their legs stretched out, hiking boots crossed, they often had a look of reverie that told of their innermost dreams. Fern answered a need I had not known I had—during the day we had the company of friends and strangers, but at night, as the light of the sun left the lake, there was solitude. The only sounds were the owls calling and the stream talking to itself as it ran out from the lake down the mountain. I was happy with only my husband and the moon for company. Fern Lake was a dream in the wilderness, something we knew was rare, like the hummingbird of a color not seen everywhere.

At the end of the summer, Pete and I moved into Boulder, where he enrolled at the University of Colorado to study English literature. I got a job filing papers in the administration office, and we paid Peter's tuition with most of the three hundred dollars we had made during the summer. We lived in a two-room basement apartment; after paying for rent and food, the rest didn't go very far. Peter got a job delivering newspapers at four in the morning and I took a typing class. I had a healthy pregnancy with no morning sickness, so as I grew bigger and bigger with the baby I felt very comfortable about having a child and Peter seemed at ease with his future fatherhood.

On January 8, 1959, Clark was born at the Seventh-Day Adventist Hospital in Boulder, Colorado, while the snow fell outside onto the mountains. I had wanted a "natural" childbirth, but after fifteen hours of labor they gave me saddle block anesthesia, which didn't help the pain but seemed to make Dr. Lockwood, my gynecologist, and the nurses feel better. After I had been in labor for twenty-six hours, Dr. Lockwood drew a long, red line across my belly and said, "I'm going to call in another doctor and your husband will have to sign a release for a Caesarian if it's necessary.'' Peter huffed and hemmed and said he didn't know if he would sign anything.

When they wheeled me into the delivery room my mother was there. She and Peter both watched me curse and scream my way through the birth. ''Push, Judy, push.'' Clark was big, nine pounds and two ounces. I was nineteen years old, and finally I was swearing. Godfather Holden would be proud.

Clark was a good-natured baby who slept through the night after only a few weeks. One cold February night, when he was just a month old, Peter and I were sitting in the living room, the snow falling outside.

''I hate to bring up an unpleasant subject, Judy, but we don't have any money left.'' I wasn't working, and we had borrowed some money from his parents to pay my dentist's bills when I was pregnant. We discussed borrowing money from them again or from the university. The thought of borrowing went against every fiber in my body.

''Why don't you get a job doing something you know how to do?''

''You mean singing?''

''Sure. There's that club in town, Michael's Pub. Why don't you see if you can get an audition? Everybody loves it when you sing for free.''

Michael's Pub was a hangout, a beer-guzzling joint where all the college students went to eat pizza and drink gallons of ''horse-piss,'' which is what we called the 3.2 percent beer you had to drink in Colorado if you were under twenty-one. It would get you drunk, but you had to nearly drown first. At Michael's you could sometimes hear a barbershop quartet or one of the pop acts from Denver, but never a folk singer.

I called Al Fike, a friend of my family's who knew the owner, Mike Besessi, and asked him if he would arrange an audition. Then I went to see Mike.

''Come in one evening, sing a few songs, we'll see how it goes,'' he told me.

One the night of March 2, 1959, I walked into Michael's Pub with my guitar case, my hair cut short in a pixie. The room was filled with a noisy crowd of college students, half of them a little drunk, all of them intent on their beer and their pizza. The microphone sputtered and coughed, gave a high-pitched squeal, and finally his voice came through.

"Ladies and gentlemen, I have a special guest for you tonight. Let's give a warm welcome to Miss Judy Collins."

I climbed up onto the partially raised platform that served as a stage. There was some sparse clapping. I sat down on a chair, my guitar in my lap, and waited. The smoke rose from the dark, the lights were dim. Slowly people put down their beer glasses and looked at me. I looked out at them. It was a mutual dare: they dared me to show them what I could do and I dared them to give me a chance.

I sang "Black Is the Color" and "Barbara Allen," "This Land Is Your Land" and "Pretty Saro." I sang everything I knew.

When I finished singing, they started clapping and calling for more as soon as I stood up. Mike came and put his arm around me.

"You have to go back, they want more."

I had sung for school shows, for my father's radio show, on the stage for the Kiwanians; I had played the piano with an orchestra, in front of an audience. But when I went on stage at Michael's Pub I felt as exposed and vulnerable as I'd ever felt before. Singing in front of those college students was somehow primal, a primitive ritual that would take me from childhood to adulthood. Like sex, like motherhood, this was a visceral experience, after which I would never be the same.

For an encore I sang an unaccompanied version of "The Dowie Dens of Yarrow." It is a very fine song about a maiden whose seven brothers murder her lover, and the melody is heartbreaking. It was very still in the room, and when the song was over the clapping started again. Mike came up to the stage, through the standing students, and led me to the back of the pub, where waiters stood in mid-act, balancing trays of pizzas and pitchers of beer.

"I want you to know I hate folk music. It is the only form of music for which I have exactly no tolerance." Mike said, smiling a huge smile. He was a slim Italian with a bony, attractive face. He wore glasses and looked intelligent and ageless, although I think he was then about forty.

"But as much as I hate folk music, the audience loves you. They went crazy, did you hear them? You've got a job here. I'll pay you a hundred dollars a week, plus all the beer you can drink and all the pizza you can eat. You start Tuesday night. Don't be late.''

Poor Mike. After I started working at Michael's, it became known as a folk music club forever. A barbershop quartet never darkened its door again. And I never again had to work in the administration office at the university. My life was changed forever.

A hundred dollars a week was a fortune. Pete quit his job delivering papers and settled down to go to school full-time. We moved out of the little basement apartment and into a log house by a rushing river. Shoes for baby, school for Peter. And for me? A career?

While I sang at Michael's five nights a week, Peter took care of Clark. I baked bread and made dinners that I put in the freezer for Peter when I wasn't home. During the day, while Peter was at school, I took Clark with me everywhere I went—to the laundromat, to the grocery store—in a baby pack on my back.

I worked at Michael's Pub all of March, April, and May. I tried to make the performance a good one, working on sets, learning new lyrics. The urgency that I had felt when I heard my first folk song was a constant hum in my blood. Through folk music I could express anything people felt. There were songs about having babies and falling in love, songs about jealousy, anger, joy, and fear. I discovered I was a pacifist and sang songs against war, and I sang songs about the union movement, about building railroads, about the feelings of a woman who had sold her body to a judge who lusted after her in exchange for the release of her condemned brother, and her curse on the judge, who deflowered her and hung her brother anyway.

I searched for songs everywhere. I listened to records, haunted the tiny record store in Boulder where you could buy Richard Dyer-Bennet and Woody Guthrie, and went to Denver to the Folk Center, where Harry Tuft had started a store with a wealth of records, songbooks, volumes of Child Ballads, and hundreds of Alan Lomax field recordings from The Library of Congress. I finally bought a really good Martin guitar from Harry and got rid of my old National. I worked to learn ''Scruggs picking'' and longed to have a twelve-string like the one on which Bob Gibson played ''Sailin' Down the River on the Ohio.''

I practiced my songs during the day by singing to Clark as I did the housework, playing him to sleep, trying out "So Early in the Spring" and "The Prickilie Bush" and a mystical song about a seal who is actually a human being, called "The Great Silkie of Sule Skerry," which was to serve as my audition for the Gate of Horn in Chicago. The lifelong habit of listening for the right melody, hunting the song, had begun.

I didn't think about the future, I lived in the present. But I began to fill in the shadowy outline I had had of myself as a child with something that felt more like me. I had a growing sense of who I was, and an urge to communicate with my singing. At Michael's Pub I met most of the local singers, who would come by for a beer at night to listen to a set. Michael's was becoming a mecca for folk music lovers, and its reputation traveled beyond Colorado, as Mike hired singers from out of state. By the summer of 1959, the pub had become famous, and I think Michael was even starting to appreciate folk music.

In June, when Clark was five months old, I had an offer to sing in Central City at a funky club called the Gilded Garter, on the same bill with a rock-and-roll band. Peter and I decided that another summer in the mountains would be great, so I took the job.

Central City was rough in spirit but had a lot of class, for a broken-down mining town. The cultural vultures from Denver were already restoring buildings and renovating hotels when Peter and Clark and I moved there. At the Central City Opera House you could hear really good singers in concert, as well as opera. I opened at the Gilded Garter six nights a week and sang "The Prickilie Bush," "The Gypsy Rover," and "Greenland Fisheries." The rock-and-roll group sang "Till There Was You" and "Rock Around the Clock." It was a strange combination, but people seemed to like it.

That summer I met Nancy and Terry Williams, who came to see me sing at the Gilded Garter and became lifelong friends. Terry taught English literature at the Colorado School of Mines. We gave parties on my nights off at the apartment we rented across from the hand-painted Bull Durham sign down in Blackhawk, a stone's throw from Central City. We entertained a peculiar assortment of people—drummers, jewelers, rock-and-rollers, bartenders, countertenors and sopranos from the opera, and a stripper who worked for Warren St. John, the owner of the Gilded Garter.

Bob Dylan was singing at one of the clubs in nearby Cripple Creek that summer, and one night he came to the Gilded Garter to hear me and the rock-and-roll band. Whenever we meet now, he says, "Remember the night I sat at your feet?"

After that summer, we moved back to Boulder. Peter was in his last undergraduate year at the university, and I sang at Michael's again. That winter I was offered a job for a hundred and fifty dollars a week at a new club in Denver called the Exodus, which had become another good club for folk music. I commuted back and forth each night, driving the forty-mile round-trip on the turnpike between Denver and Boulder.

At the Exodus, in 1959 and 1960, I met the Tarriers, a group from New York with Eric Weissberg, Clarence Cooper, and Marshall Brickman. Marshall later became a writer for Woody Allen and a producer and writer of his own movies, and Eric Weissberg went on to become one of the top studio players in the recording industry. Bob Gibson was a singer I worked with many times at the Exodus. Also, I worked with and got to know Josh White.

Josh was one of the most unselfish and generous people I have ever met, in or out of show business. He must have been in his late fifties when I was working with him, and his son Donny was an infant. Josh is dead now, for many years. But he was a friend of mine. There was not an ounce of competitiveness in him. Anything he knew about the music business, he would share. He would listen to my show and come backstage to talk to me about how I could improve it.

"Those sad songs are beautiful," he would say, "but you got to break them up. Don't sing only sad songs all in a row." He made me laugh, he loosened me up. I was so intense and took everything too seriously. "See, you got to have things to say. Develop a patter, so when you get stuck, tuning or something, you don't have to stand there with your mouth hanging open, boring them till they wish they'd gone to the drive-in." Josh's routine, when he got "stuck," as he called it, or broke a string, was to put the guitar behind his back and sing "Summertime" while he replaced the string. "Contrast, that's the thing." He had a fungus that took the nails right off his fingers and caused him a lot of pain, but he didn't complain about it. "You don't complain. You just say how it is." Josh taught me a lot about how it is.

In January I sang at the Limelight, in Aspen, with the Smothers

Brothers and the Limeliters. I lived for two weeks in a room at a dingy boarding house and I roamed around Aspen, practiced the guitar, and worked at night. For the first time since I had started working I was away from home. I felt lonely, and there were nights I drank too much and did things I remembered only vaguely. I had my first taste of the price of the road, a bitter flavor at the back of my throat.

Back home with our friends in the university community in Boulder, I slipped into my role of mother and housewife, cooking, cleaning, going to parties on the weekends with Peter and our friends. John Clark, our friend who was a national park ranger, and his new wife, Judy Holland, were at our house a lot. The Soviet Army Chorus record came out that year, and we listened to the Communists sing "It's a Long Way to Tipperary" and their folk songs and national songs, and decided that we ought to be friends with people who could sing like that. We ate huge batches of spaghetti and drank gallons of red wine. I always played the guitar and sang at those parties; there was much talk of the problems in Vietnam and of the CIA's secret dealings and illegal surveillance of civilians. We commiserated over the death of Camus that year, and read Sartre and Simone de Beauvoir. We went to see Melina Mercouri dance in *Never on Sunday* and demonstrated against the death penalty when Caryl Chessman was executed.

When I was growing up, my father had always behaved as though I was his confidante. My mother often must have felt excluded from our closeness, as I realized when Clark was about a year old and I received this letter from her:

> Dear Judy,
>
> I have been thinking for a long time that we have become very far apart. It is upsetting to me, as I think it has not so much to do with you and me as it has to do with me and your father. He is always insinuating to me that you are his child, he is the one that gets along with you, and that I am the outsider.
>
> I love you. I would like us to sit down and talk about this, please. It is very painful to me.
>
> Love, Mother

So we made a date for lunch. I got a baby sitter for Clark, drove to Denver, and met Mother in a fancy restaurant at Writers' Manor. We ordered the most expensive entrées on the menu, got very drunk together, and bared our souls. We had the first heart-to-heart of our lives.

"It was hard to reach you when I was growing up," I told her. "I felt you didn't listen to me, and Daddy did. I thought you were too busy."

"After the clothes were clean and the meals cooked and the dishes washed and I drove all of you children to school, or lessons, or basketball practice, or the dentist, I guess I was worn out. There wasn't much left, and I gave what my mother gave me, probably. A lean mixture, with a lot of grit in it."

I had known my mother had done the best she could do. After those long days, did she dream sweet dreams, a dream lover? That day an understanding began between my mother and me. She taught me how to survive.

"I came to have lunch with my mother," I said to her after we had paid the check, "and found a friend."

Peter was due to graduate in June, and in April of 1960 he found out he would have a Guggenheim teaching fellowship at the University of Connecticut in the fall, so we would be moving. By that time we had lived in Boulder for a year and a half. I was slowly becoming known. At about the same time I was offered a job at the Gate of Horn in Chicago for the coming summer. Alan Ribback, the owner of the Gate, had heard a tape Bob Gibson had given him of my version of "The Great Silkie" and wanted me to sing at his club. We also had an offer to live as fire lookouts that summer, at Twin Sisters, in the mountains. We had hoped to spend our last summer in Colorado before moving east and were torn about what to do. Alan wanted an answer, and so did the park rangers at Twin Sisters.

I have a vivid memory of sitting in the sunshine beside a mountain road on a Sunday afternoon with Peter and Clark. We were at a picnic table with our lunch of cheese and wine and apples set out on paper napkins. Pete had his Swiss army knife out and was cutting wedges, just so, and handing them to me and to Clark, who was running around at our feet. It was one of those moments in which you see the course of your life change, alter, move inexorably from one stage to the next. It was very simple. There was nothing dramatic about it except that it was the moment of decision.

"Well?" Pete smiled over at me, squinting in the sun.

"Let's go to Chicago"—we both said it at the same moment.

It was settled, and although we didn't know it, it meant our idylls in the mountains were over. I wonder if, had we stayed in Colorado that summer, our lives might have been different.

That May, I turned twenty-one. Soon after we'd decided to spend the summer in Chicago, I was driving in Denver with Margaret, Peter's mother. I was sitting in the passenger seat, with Clark in the baby seat in the back.

"It's great that you have this job in Chicago." She looked in the rearview mirror at her grandson, the recipient of good fortune and glad tidings. He had a working mother and a glowing grandmother—two glowing grandmothers. My own mother, so comfortable with her five children, was also thrilled by her first grandchild.

Margaret checked the oncoming traffic. She spoke without turning her head.

"It will be fine for the summer. But now that Peter has his fellowship, you will be able to quit working when you settle in Connecticut. You don't have to go on with the singing." It was a statement. She put the car in first gear and pulled away from the curb.

I looked at the dashboard. It was a new car, her car, an expensive car, very comfortable.

"I don't want to stop singing." I said. "I want to be a singer. I want a career as a singer."

It was the first time I had said it. I think it was the first time I had thought about it at a conscious level. Margaret said nothing, just kept driving with her eyes straight ahead, but her mouth was tight. We didn't talk of it again. I had crossed an invisible line.

School was finished in June, and we packed everything we owned from the house in Boulder and drove east in the Chevy to Chicago. Alan Ribback had arranged a sublet for us for the summer, and Clark, Peter, and I walked into our apartment on the South Side and nearly fell over. It was so big, so beautiful, so "elegant," like nothing we had ever seen.

July 6, 1960

Dearest Mom and Dad,

The bedroom is large, with a KING-SIZED bed. The baby's room is carpeted wall to wall, as are all rooms except the bathrooms, four of them. Everything is here, dishes, pots and pans, linens, records, silverware, handsoap, Clorox, and spices and EVERYTHING . . . all that is needed is us, and here we are . . . I spent a day yesterday straightening out my dues at the Chicago Musicians Union . . . DID YOU KNOW!!! The Chicago Union is still separate for blacks and whites, in 1960, the enlightened era! . . . Our neighbor is Bill Berry, head of the Chicago Urban League, they are fighting hard to change that. . . .

The opening night at the Gate, my show was a hit with the press, who said I sang well and thought it was very funny that I was wearing a cast (I had broken my leg skiing in March) since I was from Colorado. Alan was not amused at first, but he was a good sport and finally laughed at the situation.

"I guess it doesn't make you sing any better or any worse," he said, "and as long as you sing "The Great Silkie of Sule Skerry" every night, I don't care how you look."

The Gate of Horn was on the corner of Rush and Division streets. Alan's partner in the club was Albert Grossman, who later managed Bob Dylan and Peter, Paul and Mary. The Gate was at that time one of only a few folk-music clubs in the country. I was on the bill with Will Holt and Dolly Jonah, who sang songs of Kurt Weill and Bertolt Brecht as well as their own. I was the opening act.

"I want a forty-minute set, no shorter and no longer," said Alan, rocking in his chair in the back room of the club. I sang my forty minutes, and then would sit with a drink through Will and Dolly's show, soaking up everything I could. That first night, Will sang a song based on a Yeats poem, "The Song of Wandering Aengus," or, as Will had named it, "The Golden Apples of the Sun." As I listened to the song, I felt the familiar thud of recognition in my stomach, the aching feeling that it belonged to me, a feeling like seeing a lover you have lost. I had to sing the song; I was not myself without it. Dolly Jonah sang a version of a Brecht-Weill song, "Surrabaya, Johnny," that left no dry eyes in the audience. From Will and Dolly I began to learn that the term "folk music" is a misleading one: it could mean Big Bill Broonzy singing the Delta blues; it could mean Dolly Jonah singing a song written by a German anti-Fascist; it could mean me singing "When Johnny Comes Marching Home Again," an antiwar song from the American Civil War. Folk music was diverse, rich stuff, and there was endless choice.

The second two weeks I opened for Bob Gibson and Bob Camp, and then was held over for an additional two weeks, when I was the opener for the Tarriers, as I had been at the Exodus. After the six weeks in Chicago, with good reviews and a lot of exposure, my "career" was on its way.

In the fall of 1960, we drove east to Storrs, Connecticut. We rented a two-bedroom house with a study on a farm, a comfortable place with new red paint, cows in the pastures, a pond in the back of the house, rolling hills of green and brown lightning bugs in the summer evenings. It was an expensive house, a lot more than university housing, where the other students with fellowships had to stay. We were getting spoiled.

September 10, 1960

Dear Mom and Dad,

Day dawned early here at the big red house on Bent Hill, and there to greet it were Peter and I, being solicited at that early hour by a visit from our friendly Watchtower representative. . . . We've been here a few weeks, and though in the Chevy our luggage and furniture were an immense cargo, straining the windows, piled high to the roof, in this big house it has dwindled to a few things, and we bounce around like loose peas in a pod . . . in Willimantic, an old mill town nearby, while looking for beds, I found a miniature captain's chair for two and a half dollars, just right for Clark. I feel we are really settled, the little chair makes it feel like home . . . Rock walls wander for miles, the pond in back is surrounded with oaks, maples, and tangled berry bushes. With the gray sky this morning, all the greens seem even more lush. There is a huge turtle that lives in our pond, and I can see him sometimes from the kitchen window, lolling in the water. . . . Peter and I are glad that I have arranged to spend all of September and part of October at home, here in Storrs. (Six weeks off!!!) I feel like a happy housewife, cleaning, waxing my floors, putting in tomato plants, feeding Ishmael, the German shepherd puppy, his three pounds of food a day— he is growing spatulas for feet. . . .

Clark sends his love to all, and a special kiss to Holly Ann. He decided tonight that he was a cow, but reneged when we told him he would have to sleep in the pasture. . . . We went to pick up Daddy after school, and at the library Clark heard the big bell in the tower ring six o'clock, and he got very excited about churches that have bells on them and when he came home he went upstairs and built a church out of blocks, complete with a steeple. He is a constant delight.

Motherhood and living in the country were good. Our landlord was Vic Scottron, who taught chemical engineering at the university. His wife, Jan, hooked rugs, made jam and New England clam chowder, hunted through the foliage in the fall looking for dried cones and flowers to make into wreaths, and also taught me all these country skills. But the road beckoned, there was work to be done, a living to be made.

That winter I was hired at Gerdes, on West Fourth Street in New York. In 1960 you needed a cabaret license to sing in a club in the city, so I had to go to the police department, in the bowels of Manhattan, to be fingerprinted and have my picture taken. If you had a history of drug arrests or other offenses, it could mean not getting a license and therefore not getting a job. Billie Holiday, Lenny Bruce, Lord Buckley, and a lot of other performers were constantly being hassled by the cops and had to work under scale, illegally. This practice of having to register with the police was outlawed in the late sixties, but meanwhile a lot of us are there, prints and pictures and all. That was the start of my police record.

I stayed at the Broadway Central Hotel for four dollars a night, a week at at time, driving home to Storrs for my days off. Nights at the Broadway Central and other hotels on the road could be lonely and depressing, but every now and then I'd find a friendly face. One night I met up with Bob Dylan again. Dressed in his sloppy clothes, with the funny railroad hat and a drink in front of him, grinning at me in the mirror across the bar at Gerdes, hunched over like a bum off the street, slouching up to the stage, he looked like a lost soul. We talked about Colorado and Minnesota. We were both a long way from home.

"What are you doing now?" I asked him.

"I'm going to sing here next week, you can hear what I'm writing then." As it turned out, I heard his songs on a tape that Al Grossman played for me. He was thinking of managing Bobby and wanted to know what I thought of his voice.

"The record companies tell me he can't sing," he said.

I listened to the tape and was bowled over. I could barely speak. Never before had I heard such songs, such ideas in lyrics. I thought Dylan was brilliant, a genius.

"It's not his singing, it's what he's saying," I told Albert. "But I love his voice, too. It's rugged and sweet." I wrote Bob my first fan letter when "Blowin' in the Wind" was printed in *Sing Out!*

Peter Yarrow and Albert Grossman founded Peter, Paul and Mary that year. I always liked Albert; we had spent a few nights getting drunk together in Chicago when I worked at the Gate, wandering the streets of the Windy City's Old Town at three in the morning singing sea chanties. In 1961 Albert suggested putting me in a female trio.

"I'll tell you the first thing I want you to do, Judy, we're going to get you some brown contact lenses." Albert always did have a strange sense of humor.

Albert had Jo Mapes and another female singer interested in the trio as well, and we were all quite serious until I told him I preferred to continue on my own.

"You're the boss. But it's nearly impossible for a single to make it now, unless you're a man, or crazy."

"I would rather be crazy," I said.

Bob Shelton, who wrote for the *New York Times*, was often in Gerdes, and when I was singing he would listen to my sets and talk to me about songwriters. Tom Paxton would come in with a new song, sit down in the corner, and sing it to me, and along the bar that was lined with mirrors I watched other performers do their sets. I first heard John Hammond, Jr., sing at Gerdes. John Phillips, Scott McKenzie, and Dick Weissman were in a group called the Journeymen. Scott once took me on the subway to look at Tiffany's, all the way to Fifty-seventh and Fifth. I hadn't known there was more to New York than Greenwich Village.

In the daytime, I would hang out at the Folk Center on MacDougal Street. It was owned and run by Israel Young, Izzy, as we all called him. There I bought guitar strings and copies of *Sing Out!* and heard the latest gossip of who was in town and what was going on. Izzy was a walking encyclopedia of the political and social history of folk music, plus he knew where everybody in the country was singing. It was a folk music clearinghouse.

The man who owned Gerdes was an Italian named Mike Porco. In 1958, Izzy Young had suggested to Mike that he turn the small back room of Gerdes, which was then Mike's Italian Restaurant, into a folk music club. Izzy would book the talent, take a door fee, and Mike would make his profit from the drinks.

The back room at Gerdes was a great success, and soon Mike turned the whole restaurant into a folk music club. Mike Porco booked not only Peter Yarrow, Bob Dylan, Carolyn Hester, and myself, but also many old blues singers, including Lightnin' Hopkins, Son House, and John Lee Hooker. It was very gutsy for a guy who started out wanting to run a pasta parlor.

"You wanna pizza, Judy, you wanna nice piece-a veal parmigiana?" I would accept gratefully, often having driven down from Storrs just in time for my first show.

"You're good-a, you deserve-a the best," he would say, and set a plate of veal and spaghetti in front of me. I would eat my supper at the table in front of the mirror downstairs. Then I would unpack my guitar, tune up, and put on my makeup in the dressing room, which smelled of cat piss, the calicos and tabbies begging and meowing around my feet. I would straighten my homemade skirt and my peasant blouse and go on at nine for my first set.

At Gerdes there was usually somebody to have a few drinks with around one in the morning, after I had done my three sets, then I would walk the couple of blocks to my hotel feeling no pain. I would work Sunday nights, sleep at the hotel, and then drive back to Connecticut for my days off, Monday and Tuesday. Sometimes I scraped the guardrails on the Merritt Parkway in my haste to get to the farm, to Peter, to my son. Back from the wicked city, I would swing into the drive and up the hill to Brown's Hill Road.

"I'm home," I would holler, coming up from the big garage, slamming the kitchen door, greeting Peter with a hug and a check.

January 1962 [Part of a letter to my parents, written from Storrs]
. . . Someone at a movie asked me the other night if Clark recognized me when I got home. I replied that, yes, Clark had recognized me, and, more amazing, I had actually remembered Peter . . . .

Peter's brother, Gary had been away at Amherst College in Massachusetts and in 1958, at Christmas, he came home with his fiancée, Minky Goodman. They had met at a Smith prom. Minky was from Rye, New York, the daughter of the founder of Bergdorf Goodman. My first memory of Minky was how "eastern'' she was—very sophisticated for Denver, which was still a mountain town, wide open and western.

Gary and Minky were married in 1960 and moved to the suburbs of New York. While I was home from touring, we went to visit them. We talked about Gary's work at Bergdorf's and about Minky's life. Minky had been a straight A student at school, and I had always found her easy to talk to, but now I felt uncomfortable and out of place when we were together. I saw a tight look in both Gary's and her faces when we talked about the way Peter and I lived.

''So, is Clark in school when you travel?'' Minky asked. I said we had found a nursery school for him during the day. ''How does Peter manage, without you there?'' Very nicely, I wanted to answer. We had a housekeeper by now, and a baby sitter in the evenings when Peter wanted to go out.

Our life seemed perfectly normal to us, but when we talked to them, it seemed odd. Peter was what feminists would later call a liberated man, and I was an independent woman. We were doing what had to be done.

''I love the singing and I hate the traveling,'' I would explain. It's the same thing I say today.

That winter I took Clark with me to the Gate of Horn in Chicago for my two-week gig. I couldn't bear to be away from him any longer. I stayed with Carol Margolis, who had three children of her own. Having Clark along made working easier, but it wasn't great for him. I came home to Connecticut for the holidays knowing I must change things.

''Peter,'' I said to him, ''what would you think if I didn't take any more work for a while? I don't see enough of you and Clark, and I'm exhausted from the traveling.''

''Well, the only problem is that we might have to move to faculty housing. I can't pay the rent here on just my teaching salary.'' We talked about it for a couple of days. I felt rested, and we agreed that we didn't want to move. So we decided to leave things the way they were.

That year, I had jobs lined up in Denver, New York, Washington, Boston, Tucson, and Philadelphia. I knew that Margaret, my mother-in-law, would not approve. Clark was growing from a baby into a little boy and it was not easy, living as we did. I knew my career was going well, but I felt that my marriage was slipping from me. I brought home the checks, Peter made progress in his field, and by now he had a master's degree in English literature. But we were away from each other so often that we were no longer able to meet each other's needs. I began to hunt for love in other places.

It all flooded back to me so clearly when I was on the phone with Clark yesterday, which was his twenty-sixth birthday. I called to sing him "Happy Birthday."

"I've been up since before dawn to celebrate the hour of my birth," he said. "Thanks for the William James and the other goodies. I love you, Mom."

"I love you, too, Clark, I'm proud of you."

I hung up the phone and thought to myself that it is a miracle that we both made it thus far. Our lives had been entangled in more difficulties that took years to unravel. He's a man now, and I feel sadness for the part of his babyhood I missed. But through the tough and tender times, the love between us has grown, as we have grown up together.

Last week, before we came on vacation, I had a letter from Clark.

Dear Mom,
   When you become a Minnesotan one of the first things that you are expected to learn is that talking about the weather is not superficial, it is rather one of the highest and most meaningful forms of communication possible. . . . The summer brings that kind of beautiful storm that we both love . . . big, dark, heavy sky, flash and crash. God's fireworks . . . I took to calling on the great spirit and watching the sky in hopeful anticipation of rain when I really should have been painting. I love being able to share with you the weather report of the soul. I have some of those dark clouds gathering but I believe the storm coming is meant to clean up the dirty winter snow and bring forth green shoots. . . . I'm very grateful that you're my oldest friend. . . .

Love,
Clark

Reflections

Saturday, January 19, 1985 / New York

We must return from paradise, and Thursday morning I took one last, long snorkel while the sun danced down into the water, pebbling the depths in shadowed light. I saw no angelfish, but a barracuda hung like a piñata just below the surface, very near me, black spots on his silver tail, his bright eye watching me swim away from him, toward air, my element, and toward home.

When Louis and I arrive back in New York it is very cold, and snowstorms have left six inches on the ground. In my travel bag, swimsuits are exchanged for silver heels, cotton shirts for silk robes. I'll pack my bags with the threads and props of my trade and go off tomorrow as the wandering minstrel again. I'm on my way to Scotland in the morning.

Monday, January 21, 1985 / Glasgow, Scotland

It is raining and we are in a tiny, depressing hotel, exhausted after the flight from London. Maria Pizzuro, who is a makeup artist and my traveling assistant, and Shelton Becton, my pianist, and I came over on the the morning flight from New York, stayed over at Heathrow, and flew up here today. Small room, small view. Unlovely wallpaper. This is the glamour of show business, I keep telling myself, trying to take comfort in remembering that I live better, even in this peculiar, depressing room, with its ugly, brownish-orange white-and-black-spotted bedspreads and curtains and its dull brown rug, than Mary, Queen of Scots, or Elizabeth I, or any king before the invention of hot running water, electric teapots, instant coffee, and indoor plumbing.

The show I'm doing here is called "Corry and Friends." I had to agree not to sing "Send In the Clowns"; they said they wanted folk music. I suggested "Both Sides Now," and that made everybody happy. "Both Sides" has magically turned itself into a folk song by being called one.

The Corry Brothers are a pair of gifted men who sing songs of the British Isles. When we arrived this afternoon for the rehearsal, I had the familiar feeling that I did not fit amid the guitars and banjos, alongside the traditional singers. The setting for the show is a bar with an invited audience, who are smoking, drinking pints of bitter, and singing along on the choruses. I sang "Grandaddy," my ode to the old country and my Grandfather Byrd, and Amanda McBroom's "From Where I Stand" and "Amazing Grace," and remember again that folk music is an elusive creature. It is full of contrasts, and that is what drew me to it in the first place. In many places people still think of me as a folk singer. Stephen Holden in the *New York Times* has called me an "art singer." I don't know if either one is right. The feeling that I don't belong is strong—I am different; I have always been different.

As did most of the women who sang folk music in the early sixties, I grew my hair long and wore clothes in baggy shapes. When the music became popular, that type of clothing became fashionable and I was one of the people who helped make it fashionable. I always envied Joan Baez's sleek figure and her long hair. She could put on a silk blouse with a black skirt and look avant-garde even in the early sixties. I was wrapped in layers, hiding in my *shmatte*, then in vogue.

I walk into the rehearsal area and open my mouth and begin to sing. I am comfortable, it is suddenly good to be here. I am dressed in black pants, a black turtleneck sweater, and a black Borsalino hat—very au courant. Joanie would be proud. When the lights go down and the filming of the show begins tonight,

I know that life is what happens next. And I know that I do belong.

I went to the theater last night to see Maggie Smith in *The Way of the World*, and she was brilliant. Everyone else got better alongside her; she shines on the stage.

Afterward, dinner at the White Elephant with Barbara Howell and Alan Woltz. Barbara is a fine writer, with a number of books published in England and the United States. I don't see her as often as I would like. Her husband, Alan, is the head of a British company that is based in London. Over a festive dinner with them and some of their friends, I hear the following story:

A scientist was watching a monarch butterfly emerge from its cocoon. It was such a long struggle, the creature fought on and on with the rough material of the cocoon—tearing, pulling, and struggling, fighting to get out.

"If I only snip this little bit at the top, I could help this creature," he said to himself. And he reached in with his scissors and cut away the last piece of the cocoon.

The monarch went on for a few moments, but seemed to grow weaker, and finally, his wings still partly folded, he fell back onto the table, dead.

The scientist realized he had killed the butterfly by trying to make things easier. Each push by the struggling insect forces lifeblood into those glorious wings, and their beauty in flight comes only after the fight to emerge from the cocoon is entirely finished.

In 1961, while my marriage continued to stall and my career continued to improve, I met Jac Holzman for the first time. He came to see the television show I was taping at the Village Gate, in Greenwich Village, with the Clancy Brothers and Tommy Makem. My eyes were shut, my head was thrown back, I was singing a whaling song under the lights of the television cameras. I always liked songs about driving trucks, hunting whales, herding cattle, riding the range, and punching cows in the lonely

West. Working songs suited my nature, in combination with songs about "maids of constant sorrow."

When the song was over, Jac came up to me as I was leaving the stage and held out his hand.

"I'm Jac Holzman, the president of Elektra Records," he said. He led me to a table and slid in beside me. We watched the rest of the show, listening to the Clancys weave their Irish magic in the smoky room. It was dark except for the television lights that shone on the Clancys' white cable-knit sweaters. During the break, Jac turned to me and got straight to the point.

"You are ready to make a record, Judy, and I want it to be on Elektra."

"No, I'm not," I said. I had never given a thought to making a record because I didn't think of myself as a singer. My voice was a deep and husky contralto, and I thought of it solely as an instrument with which to tell stories.

"I want you on Elektra. What is your schedule? When shall I book the studio?" That was that. That was how it was with Jac.

Jac is tall and thin, with an intelligent, handsome face. His energy is always at a high level; he speaks quickly and directly. He knows what he wants and with whom he wants to work. He had started Elektra when he was a student at St. John's University. The first Elektra album was by Georgia Bannister, singing the songs of John Gruen. Jac made it just because he wanted a good recording of the songs. By the time we met, the tiny company had become established as one of the foremost folk music recording companies. Josh White, Oscar Brand, Cynthia Gooding, Jean Reid, and Ed McCurdy were recording with Elektra. He knew how to market records and his artists were reaching a widening audience. Jac was ambitious, smart, and very good at what he did. He had great taste, and he wanted me on his label. After the shock wore off, I was flattered.

"What will I put on the record?" I asked him.

"All the songs you are doing in concert, the ones I have heard you perform at Gerdes." He had sat in the club, night after night, listening to me sing, before he decided he wanted to record me. "You should include 'The Wars of Germany,' 'The Great Silkie,' and 'The Prickilie Bush.' " So he *had* been listening, following me, and already knew he wanted a certain repertoire.

I went home to the country full of excitement. Peter was enthusiastic and told me he thought it was wonderful. We hoped that with a record out, perhaps I wouldn't have to be on the road so much. That August, I recorded the album in only four days. I left Peter and Clark one morning, drove in from Connecticut, parked the Chevy, and carried my guitar to the Great Northern Hotel, on Fifty-seventh Street, to record in a studio called Fine Sound. Freddy Hellerman, of the Weavers, played second guitar, and Eric Darling played banjo. Jac gave me a thousand-dollar advance.

In September, I ran down to the mailbox on Brown's Hill Road every day, waiting for the record to arrive. I had done the cover in New York with a photographer named Lida Moser. It was a dusky blue cover, and my face and hair were silhouetted. I had bleached my pixie-style hair blond, and refrained from hating it long enough to have the cover picture taken before I dyed it black. *A Maid of Constant Sorrow* was released in October of 1961. When my copy arrived in the mail, I raced up the hill shouting to Peter that I was on wax at last, that my record career had begun.

Jac believed in me, and gave me all the loving support and confidence I needed. From the beginning I listened closely to what he said. "Sing what you love." It was the same thing my father had said to me. It was the only way.

Jac is a complicated man, but we have always gotten along. I got a fair deal from him, and he is often surprisingly generous in a manner that can take your breath away. He is essentially a very private man who is at ease with the music business, and he knows how to make the people with whom he works feel comfortable. Jac can laugh easily, even on a tough day. Though we have had our scraps and tough moments, our friendship has lasted longer than most of our friends' marriages, and Jac is my oldest friend in this business.

Elektra had its office down on Sixteenth Street when I began the first of my twenty-four years with the company. It was a small label with a small staff, and we were all close. Vera Hertenstein was the executive secretary, Bill Harvey did the covers. I was always involved in the entire process, from beginning to end. Every part of it was important: the material, the musicians, the mixes, final vocals, sequences—what time and heartache I have put in trying to decide the sequence of an album! "God is in the details," Jac would say. "The secret, after the right songs, is getting the sequence exactly right, so that it flows and attains a magic of its own." I learned that I could never leave any of it to others, so I chose photos for the covers, talked to art directors about layouts, proofed credits, and checked color corrections. Every breath. Every note. Do it right. We will have to live with it.

These were the halcyon, bright days of folk music. All around me, interesting, creative music was being made, and I was in the middle of it, recording the songs of writers who were legends even then. At Gerdes, after my shows, Robert Shelton, Tom Paxton, Jac Holzman, I, and many of the others spent time talking about what was going on in the country. And living as I did near the campus of a state university, I was unusually aware of the protest movement in the country against the U.S. involvement in Vietnam. Folk music seemed to galvanize these sentiments. I hoped that when I sang "The Wars of Germany," the lament of a woman whose husband goes to war and never comes back, the song would make a difference, make people think. I imagined that if people thought about it, they would see how mad war was, how useless the loss of life.

The country's political mood in 1961 was one of great contrasts. John F. Kennedy had been inaugurated in January, and there was a feeling of hope and challenge in the air. At the campus in Connecticut, our friends talked about Kennedy's defeat of Nixon and were cheered to think that the country wanted the man with the dream. Kennedy started the Peace Corps that year. The United Nations condemned apartheid, and Freedom Riders in the South were making headlines, for both their bravery and courage in trying to secure the vote for blacks; they were often hassled, sometimes injured. But despite these provocations, the dream of real international brotherhood was on the move.

By the end of the year, the United States was sending helicopter pilots stationed in Germany to Southeast Asia, where their average life expectancy, when flying missions over Vietnam, was twenty minutes. The military advisers in Vietnam, a small force begun with the Truman Administration, was becoming larger every day; even the president with the bright dream was in trouble in Vietnam and would lead us deeper into Southeast Asia as the years went on. In 1961, there was still hope that

Jack Kennedy would wake up, and wake us up with him. We thought we were in Camelot; I and people I knew believed we would change the world, and the music I was hearing and singing convinced me we could not be wrong.

My personal destiny was to be part of the protest and the history of the times, social as well as political.

Jac and Nina Holzman and their son, Adam, who was two, were then living in Greenwich Village. Often I would go to dinner at their apartment, listen to music, and talk into the night. Nina was pregnant with their second child, Jaclyn, by the time my second album came out. As the years passed, Nina would give parties to celebrate the release of my albums as well as my yearly concerts at Carnegie Hall. After she and Jac had moved out to Los Angeles, she started a catering company called Pure Pleasure. The Yellow Pages refused to list it because they said it sounded like an X-rated business. Nina did have exotic tastes, and I often look to her for the sign that we were on the right track with an album. She had a way of seeing its pattern as a whole, and her input was invaluable.

Jac and I discussed music and went to see singers. He was always looking out for good songwriters and for material that was right for me. We went to Dylan concerts and folk festivals together and plowed through demo tapes till our ears were worn out. I remember sitting next to Jac one night at a Dylan concert, elbowing each other at every new song, and once in a while his whispering in my ear, "That's perfect for you, dear. Let me see if I can get him to send you a tape of it. . . . You ought to consider recording 'Masters of War,' 'Tom Thumb's Blues,' and 'The Lonesome Death of Hattie Carroll.' "

Jac gave me a long tether and a hard argument. There is no doubt that our tastes were very similar. I didn't always agree with him—but our differences gave the collaboration snap and vitality.

The hunting of the song is mystical, mysterious. It begins somewhere down near the solar plexus and moves through the whole body until it reaches the ears. I can tell when I love a song because I am not aware of even listening to it. Rather, I am absorbing it, like a bird who is changing its body color to match the color of a tree or a flower. I become the song physically.

This has happened to me from early childhood. My "ear"

for melody was strong. When I listened to the stories in the first folk songs I learned, it was their nature that drew me to them, as though they were not songs but personalities whom I either liked or cared nothing for or became passionate about and had to live with.

A singer can record many, many songs, but of those there will be only a few that remain in the heart of your conscience, in the hearts of your audience. They are wheat sifted from chaff; they take a long time to collect. Like good friends, they don't come along every day. When they do, you have to fight for them, hold on to them. In the lyric is the magic, the "secret" of a song. So the lyric must fit the personality of the singer so closely that the union is seamless. The relationship is intimate and vital and subtle.

"Maid of Constant Sorrow" was taught to me by Judith Weston in St. Louis. I learned "Mr. Tambourine Man" from Bob Dylan when he sang it in the middle of the night at Albert Grossman's farm in the Catskills. I was asleep upstairs, and the rough, sweet voice, weaving through the dark house, found me in my bed and drew me down, as if the song were a line and he were a fisherman, luring me to the surface. "Golden Apples" was the song Will Holt sang so beautifully those first nights I worked at the Gate of Horn in Chicago. These songs were not luxuries; they were necessities, they nourished me. I had to have them, as I had to breathe.

They are rare, like pearls.

The first two albums on Elektra were primarily traditional folk music, although the lead song on the second album was the wonderful poem by Yeats "The Song of Wandering Aengus," or "Golden Apples of the Sun." In 1963 I moved to songs that were being written by the city singers I had come to know in Greenwich Village and Boston—the songs of Pete Seeger, Bob Dylan, Mike Settle, Shel Silverstein, Jim Friedman, John Phillips. My third album contained "Turn! Turn! Turn!," Pete Seeger's song about the seasons of life, "Mr. Tambourine Man," and "Hey, Nelly, Nelly," a song written by Shel Silverstein and Jim Friedman about the integration movement. Jac supported this shift from purely folk music to nontraditional music. He was a purist in the best sense in that he loved what is good.

Izzy Young had led me to Billy Edd Wheeler's writing, and on the fourth album I had a group of Billy Edd's songs. I found

Richard Fariña's work in 1964, then the songs of Malvina Reynolds. Malvina and her husband, Bud, became close friends; she was a white-haired, sixty-year-old matron whose fame had spread with Pete Seeger's recording of her song about the ticky-tacky houses in San Francisco, her hometown. "Little Boxes" made her famous. "It Isn't Nice" was a protest anthem by Malvina and Barbara Dane. The country was beginning to wake up to the terrible war in Vietnam.

> *It isn't nice to block the doorway,*
> *It isn't nice to go to jail,*
> *There are nicer ways to do it,*
> *But the nice ways always fail,*
> *It isn't nice, it isn't nice,*
> *You told us once, you told us twice . . .*
> *But if that's Freedom's price, we don't mind.*

Malvina and Barbara's song embodied the movement of folk protest; I sang it at rallies in Mississippi when I worked for voter registration, at concerts and protests against war in Vietnam.

Although I was always involved with political protest, I could never choose a song simply because it was a protest song. In looking for material, there was a level of "timelessness" that had to be there; the song had to transcend a particular situation and apply to all situations. Dylan's material always did that, from songs such as "The Lonesome Death of Hattie Carroll," about the brutal murder of a black woman in a Baltimore social setting, which I recorded on the live concert album in 1965, to "The Hostage," Tom Paxton's great eulogy to the guards and the guarded at Attica. The interesting thing about both Paxton and Dylan was their ability to write fine love songs as well as scalpel-sharp social commentary. "Masters of War" transcends all wars, and "Lay Lady Lay" does the same thing for love. "That Was the Last Thing on My Mind," Tom's love song, is balanced by his broadside about the fallacies in the press, "I Read It in the Daily News."

I believe all the best writers of that time were able to do this. Jacques Brel wrote "La Colombe" ("The Dove"), an antiwar song, but he also wrote "Chanson des Vieux Amants" ("Song of the Old Lovers"), a heartbreaking song about the inevitability of imperfect love. Woody Guthrie's "This Land Is Your Land" is an anthem to America, but he could also write "I Woke Up in a Dry Bed,'' about childhood's triumphs. Pete Seeger could write ''Turn! Turn! Turn!'' and then sing a love song to humanity, ''Golden Thread.'' Craftspeople, all of them. I was honored to be the instrument of their powerful songs.

By the time I started recording *In My Life*, all the rules and musical boundaries were dissolving. My musical background was surfacing. I could not continue to record only folk music. The years spent learning Bach and Debussy and Ravel, singing in opera choruses, singing with dance bands, creating my own ''operas'' with my high school friends Marcia and Carol, were all affecting my musical choices in a powerful way. I wanted to venture as far afield as I could go. I wanted to stretch and to reach.

I recorded ''Pirate Jenny'' from *The Threepenny Opera* by Kurt Weill and Bertolt Brecht and ''In My Life'' by the Beatles. In 1963, I first heard Jacques Brel's early record, with ''Marieke'' and ''Amsterdam'' on it, and I later recorded ''La Colombe'' in French. Mark Abramson, a sensitive man and a musical adventurer, was my producer on my first eleven albums, and we decided to ask Josh Rifkin to write orchestral arrangements for *In My Life*. Thus began a collaboration that continued on two other albums, *Wildflowers* and *Whales and Nightingales*. Next, we found a fourteenth-century piece of music by Landini, ''Ecco la Primavera,'' and recorded it with sackbuts, harmoniums, and gambas.

Dylan went electric and was bitterly condemned by *Sing Out!* in an editorial written by the publisher, Irwin Silber. The Beatles used a string quartet when recording ''Eleanor Rigby.'' The tide was moving. Popular music was becoming something entirely new. Juilliard students, who were graduating with degrees in composition and with great technical ability, were arranging for groups such as the Blues Project and flooding the folk music revival with great diversity. Classical music had used folk music themes for centuries. The marriage of diverse musical forms was inevitable. It was a vital, exciting, daring time. There was no turning back.

Jac sold Elektra to the Kinney Corporation in the late sixties, but he stayed on as president and was as much involved as ever. In 1972, Kinney sold Elektra to Warner Brothers Records. By then, I had been with Elektra for eleven years. I had recorded ''Both Sides Now'' and ''Amazing Grace.'' My albums frequently went gold—a million dollars in sales or more. The artistic combination with Holzman was working well, as it always had. In March of that year, I got a call from Jac the night before the public announcement was made that he would be leaving Elektra.

"I'm sorry to upset you, dear, but you will be fine at Elektra. David Geffen is going to be the new president of the company, and he loves your work." I was furious. I didn't go to the farewell party Jac was given. I felt betrayed.

It was months before we spoke again. Jac would have given me the shirt off his back, but he couldn't stay at Elektra. He had to move on, but I stayed. Jac went to Hawaii, where he did freelance technical consulting for Warner's cable company, then in its infancy. Eventually, at the end of that year, I went out to visit him, to forgive, to try to forget.

Meanwhile, David Geffen had taken over Elektra, making it a joint venture with his own company, Asylum Records. This new company Elektra/Asylum, was now my company.

Disco was becoming the hot thing, and the kind of records I was making were being heard on the radio less and less. I was upset and nervous about the music business and my place in it. I went to see David Geffen and I bared my soul to him, shared my fears. He is a sensitive and caring man, and he understood that I would naturally miss the man with whom I had made records for so many years. He proved himself to be someone I could trust.

"Whatever is happening in music today should not deter you from your path. Do what you love, do what you are good at."

I was not going to Broadway shows in 1973, but my friends were, and they told me I must listen to a song from *A Little Night Music*. Patricia Elliot, a woman who was to become one of my best friends, was playing in the show at that time. I had the album sent, found the cut, put the needle down on "Send In the Clowns," and began to weep. I had to sing this song.

I called Hal Prince, who had produced *A Little Night Music*, and said "Mr. Prince, I think you have a great song in this show of yours." He was kind.

"Have you seen the show?" he asked.

"No," I told him.

He laughed and then said the show had been running for two

years and people agreed with me, there was a great song in it. I asked him who had recorded the song.

"Everyone, including Sinatra."

I said I didn't care, I had to sing it. I asked him who he would suggest for the orchestration, and he said Jonathan Tunick, the man who had done it on the album and for the show and who does all of Sondheim. When I called Jonathan, he said he would love to arrange the song for me. And so began a great relationship, which continues till this day, and the song became a lifelong companion. Every time I sing "Send In the Clowns," it reveals some other aspect of itself and of me, something I had never thought of, never even suspected. "Send In the Clowns" became a major hit in 1975.

David Geffen arranged for me to work with Arif Mardin, who was a staff producer for Atlantic Records. Elektra/Asylum and Atlantic are both with Warner Brothers, and David was on the board of directors, so I was able to work with Arif on three albums, *Judith* and *Bread and Roses*, for which Phil Ramone was the engineer, and *Times of Our Lives*, which I produced with Lew Hahn, with Arif as executive director.

David Geffen was with Elektra for three years before he left in 1976 and Joe Smith became president. "Send In the Clowns" had another big surge in 1977, going onto the pop charts again.

What the record companies want is hits, but creating hits is a self-fulfilling prophecy. If a company puts money into promotion, a song can become a hit, and if they don't, it may not have a chance. *Hard Times for Lovers* was released in 1979. Joe Smith put money into it for promotion, and it did very well, with the lead song, "Hard Times for Lovers," going onto the charts. But since then I've released three albums—*Running for My Life, Times of Our Lives*, and *Home Again*—which Elektra has not supported. The struggle has been difficult, but I stayed, believing in promises, knowing the tide must turn at last.

Monday, February 4, 1985 / New York

There are ice floes on the river and the sky is filled with clouds and the clouds are filled with light. Home again in this glorious apartment. Nine rooms that I share with my beloved Louis. I am amused that it was I who could not bear living with anyone,

I who insisted I must be free. I could not imagine the barriers to intimacy breaking down as they have.

Dinner last night with Jac Holzman and David Braun, at the Four Seasons, I still have jet lag, and over dinner felt a little strange. Partly it was seeing Jac, whose presence brought back the early years when I was still married, a country girl with a career in the city, the circus just starting up.

Jac has been telling me for a long time that I should leave Elektra.

"You always had peculiar hits. Anomalies. Songs that with any other artist would never have worked," says Jac. " 'Amazing Grace' was especially strange. Who would think a song sung a cappella about a spiritual experience could become a hit? Your successful songs were out of the mainstream of what is usually considered pop music."

"Well," I said, "I'm free from Elektra at last."

"I'm so glad." Jac gave me his most reassuring smile. "You'll find the right company, don't worry about it. As for hits, 'The Life You Dream,' the song you wrote about meditation, may be your next single. You never know."

Last night, over second cups of coffee as the restaurant was emptying, Jac, David, Louis, and I still sat, contemplating our cups and one another's faces.

"You were spoiled, Judy. People today are backing the things they believe in. They just believe in different things than you and I did. I think it's the same as it always was," Jac says.

"They say I need a hit. What is a hit?" I ask.

"You have to do what you love," he says.

"That's the only way I know how to make records," I say. "I don't know why I stayed for all those years, but there must be a reason."

On the way home with Louis, I am depressed. I know I am better off, but I feel rudderless.

Wildflowers

Friday, February 15, 1985 / Connecticut

I woke this morning in a kind of anxious frenzy. I had not felt that kind of panic for a long time. No money coming in, in this feast-or-famine business. I lay in bed, listening to the sound of the water pump, the scratching of a squirrel on the roof, the wind chimes in the trees.

Louis and I drove up to the lake Friday night from the city. This is Louis's house, but I feel at home in it. The house is an open space; floor-to-ceiling windows look out on a spring-fed lake that is inhabited by some geese, a few swans, and three or four ducks, even in the bitter winter. When you look out the windows, it is as though you were at the prow of a boat, you see only water, and trees, and birds.

If we are in the city and I don't have to go out on tour, we come up on Friday nights. We have dinner at a rustic, charming inn. At the house we unpack, open the shades, turn on the heat, settle down for a peaceful couple of days. But now the house is in chaos; Louis decided this year to build a room for me where I can put my piano, to build a hot tub out on the deck, to finish the basement, and to install skylights. There is dust everywhere, piles of wood on the lawn, covers on the furniture. A new spiral staircase plummets down into the cold, as-yet-unfinished basement. The new windows have been put in downstairs, and wood shavings surround the lower entrance.

I feel this house is a metaphor for my life; I am under major renovation, in chaos, under reconstruction. So while this whole process is making Louis crazy, as he fights with his contractor and the work drags on through the year, I am philosophical about it. As I look out through the raw, new skylight, I feel I am looking into a mirror that reflects my own overhauling.

When I awoke this morning and could not go back to sleep, I watched the birds, the titmice and downy woodpeckers and a brilliantly red cardinal. Red against the wood, red against the snow, red against the evergreen, as if saying, "How do I look here? How about over here?" I love these mornings in the country. From the double bed I can look up at the clouds through the new skylight or out the window where each day, each season, each year, the view is different.

I think of how, in the sixteenth century, Brother Lawrence, in a monastery in France, looked at a bare tree in winter and realized that the branches would be full of green leaves, singing birds, and summer light dappling the ground where the flowers bloomed; this experience led to his religious conversion. His book, called *The Practice of the Presence of God*, talks about looking at everything as the chance to see the Maker behind the world.

Usually I make breakfast when we are in the city, bringing Louis coffee and fruit. When we are here, I get breakfast in bed, hot coffee served on a tray, the luxury of waking up to Louis's face. This morning I got out of bed and went downstairs, where I lay on the floor and did my stomach exercises, then made the coffee and eggs. In the open space the sound of the coffee grinder will wake him, but he will be so happy I am making the breakfast today he won't mind. I put on my running gear and go out for a jog around the lake, two miles in the wind. The lake is wrapped in ermine, white on white in the flying snow.

In a few days the feast will begin, for I will be working. This tranquil moment today will be broken into many days in many different places. I have concerts in Seattle, Los Angeles, San Francisco, then Salt Lake City and Denver before I come home again.

Monday, February 18, 1985 / New York

From May Sarton's journal *At Seventy*: "The discipline this time must be . . . to make every effort to live in eternity's light, not in time. . . . To live in eternity means to live in the moment."

A rainy day in New York. New spring tulips, white and yellow, are in vases in the front hall and the studio; the blossoms lean over, their slender stalks bending gracefully. Spring dancers.

Last week I went to Susie Crile's opening at the Graham Gallery. Susie is one of my closest friends and a fine painter. Last summer at her farm in Cambridge, New York, many of these paintings were just beginning. I was staying at the farm for a few days after I did a benefit for Yaddo, the arts colony near Saratoga Springs, and Susie and I stood together and looked at her new work, as we have done for years. The grass waved outside in the August breeze and the bees bounced against the screen doors of the barn she has turned into a studio. When we met in 1970 she was doing work that was partly representational, big canvases of overlapping Chinese rugs and still lifes of fruit on patterns; over the years the subject of her work has moved from rugs to landscapes, to geometrically rhythmic paintings in which the overlapping layers of color still seem to sing with the basic theme of dense color patterns that has always underlain her work. When she moved from painting rugs and still lifes to working on geographical views of the earth, she went on barge trips on the Mississippi and airplane rides from Martha's Vineyard to New York to look at the earth from different points of view. I feel close to her work in a physical way. It is part of me, as her friendship is part of me. I own many of these big, extraordinary works. They hang on the walls of my apartment, reminders of my own outer victories and inner struggles.

"How I wish our 'group' was still meeting, I could use the support!" Susie says to me tonight.

In 1972, Susie Crile, the poet Cynthia Macdonald, the painter John Grieffin, another poet, Al Levine, the novelist Richard Elman, and I formed a work group. We met each week at one another's homes and studios to discuss work in progress. Over the next two years, we drew on our friendship and critical responses and discussed the interrelationships between the different forms in which we were working. We were all trying to find the courage to make changes; me in my songwriting, the others in their own efforts to break through into new frontiers in their own mediums.

"I can't think of anyone anymore who has the time to get together as we did, or the inclination. Everybody is much too competitive, with the exception of you and me, of course!" We laugh, but our smiles are only partly from amusement.

"Did you see Cindy Child's new piece at the Brooklyn Academy, with Philip Glass? It is very good." Cindy is a strong choreographer, very innovative. For a while she, too, came to the group when she was doing no dancing and was rethinking her entire approach to her work.

"But," Susie says, "the time is not always right for such a group. Artists are so seldom synchronous in their timing about anything, it's difficult enough to get a date with you to go to dinner!" For two years, it was the right time for our gang of six, or seven, or eight. It was one of the most exciting creative situations of which I have been a part.

Susie and I talk of everything: the men in our lives (she is married to Joe Murphy, the chancellor of the City University of New York), and our health, and our work, and our dreams. I liked the shoes she was wearing last night, and like the good sister that she is, she assured me I could borrow them. (Most of the clothes we buy we can both wear, and we go through each other's closets from time to time.) She looked happy last night, as she should. This is fine work, a beautiful show.

Andrée Hayum, my friend who is an art historian, is also here tonight. She is tall, with hair that is almost black and a Mondrian face. We share a reservoir of mutual friendships.

"I can't see the paintings for the people," she says, angling for a better view.

I keep my eyes open for friends—Esther Kartiganer, a producer of *Sixty Minutes*, and Susan Lyne, George Crile's wife, who is expecting her first child. George is Susie's brother and a producer for CBS. Carol Hall, who wrote *The Best Little Whorehouse in Texas*, should be here as well as Muriel Levitt. Seeking a quiet talk amid the noisy exuberance of the opening, I look for Doris Dallow and Jane Cecil and find Judith Goldman, the writer and art critic, who looks wonderful tonight.

"I've quit smoking and finished my book," she says, putting her arms around Esteban Vicente and his wife, Harriet.

"Judith's new book is brilliant," Esteban says, smiling his wonderful, crooked smile. He is tall and slender and eighty-four and one of the finest painters in the world.

Louis and I stay at the opening for most of the evening. Afterward we go across the street to Leo's Delicatessen for a quick bite of dinner. Gene Hackman comes in, sits down by himself at a table, orders a steak and a baked potato. Stardom, fame, fortune. Dinner at Leo's, alone.

Tuesday, February 19, 1985 / Los Angeles

In the rain I left the L.A. airport and drove to Holly Ann's in Santa Monica. As soon as I walked into the house, I knew why I had come to Los Angeles to sing on *Solid Gold*. It was not to push the album, it was because I needed to see my sister. After talking to her for no more than a few minutes, I feel unburdened. She makes me laugh at myself and sees the humor in every situation.

Holly is thirty. She and I are the bookends, with Michael, David, and Denver John between us. Perhaps that is why we have always been close. My sister and I look alike. At my best moments I see her face looking back at me from the mirror. I am slender as a stick at my lowest weight; she is voluptuous and sensual at hers. (She must have inherited her figure from Grandma Byrd.) She has big, brown eyes that seem to look right into you rather than at you. Her face is heart-shaped and her skin fair, her hands are strong and beautiful. Though she is shorter than I am, she looks taller. She laughs easily, and has a serious, passionate side to her nature. Her work is rich with color, and she is a fine and productive artist whether she is weaving on her looms or doing oil paintings or watercolors or making the jewelry she creates out of found pieces of pottery and glass from the sea.

Holly's house is filled with light and sun, with an oval skylight in the living room ceiling that illuminates hundreds of rolls of wool in shelves on the wall and two enormous looms. In every room of the house today is a clear glass vase filled with ranunculus of orange and red and flame and peach. There is even a glass of roses next to the gerbil cage in her son Kalen's room.

Holly and I both have the same voice shouting at us all the

time, no matter how we are doing: "You are not doing enough, and anyway, you should be doing it differently!" The internalized, hammering voice of the Nazi. Why is it so hard for each of us to accept our own pace, our own way of growing?

Holly and her husband, Jim Keach, have been separated for a year. Jim's brother, Stacy, is a man with whom I had a long relationship. Stacy is Kalen's uncle, and I am Kalen's aunt, and it will be ever so.

"Jim and I must find another way to relate to each other now that we're no longer together," says Holly. "He's not my lover anymore, but he is still the father of my child."

"I hope you can sort it out in a friendly way, Holly, without a court battle."

I was in a long and bitter struggle for custody of Clark during and after my divorce from Peter. It was in February 1962 that things started to fall apart in what had already become a difficult marriage.

Some people need an analyst, some need a rabbit. I had been given a psychedelic mushroom. On that February evening I made tea, dissolved the mushroom in it, and drank it. It was a rainy night, and we went to see *Breakfast at Tiffany's* at a drive-in movie in the Chevy carryall. The mushroom was my first psychedelic, and I was not prepared for the tumult that came with it. The rain on the windshield turned into the Nile River. Holly Golightly was Everywoman, her effort to be free the effort of each woman. I laughed and cried, convinced the movie was changing my life. Peter drove on the way home, and I was very stoned. The fireflies lit up in the dark trees along the road. I had come to know fireflies very well those summers in the country. When I was home between tours, Clark and I watched them fly under the big elm trees on summer evenings, lighting up like lanterns between the pond and the road, in among the dense foliage.

"Why do they light up, Mommy?" Clark would ask.

"No one knows, honey," I told him. "They say it's a chemical reaction, like love." Was I still in love? I put the flying lights in a bottle for Clark, toddling beneath the arms of the elm tree. Gazing up at the fireflies, he said, "Oh, ah," trying to say firefly. I let them out of the bottle and the next day they fell dead, their lights out, their bodies very rigid.

What is love, then? I thought; I wanted to be free to light up among the trees, mysteriously. I did not plan my escape, but I became more frightened of staying than of leaving.

I was traveling a lot, I had a record out, and things were starting to go well in my career. At home Peter and I saw less of each other and were drifting apart. I didn't know how to tell Peter I was dissastified, and my silence built a wall.

As we sped home that night, we came around a curve, and a rabbit streaked in front of the truck; Peter braked too late. The rabbit's body slamming against the truck cracked through my fog and suddenly I could not go on with my denial.

When we got home we were both dazed. While Peter took the baby sitter home, I sat alone in the living room, rehearsing what I would say. When he came up the steps from the garage and had closed the door behind the cold wind coming up from the basement, the mushroom and the rabbit had finally given me the nerve to speak. I blurted out what I had been holding in for months.

"Peter, I want a divorce." What simple words, only five of them. Irrevocable. The damage had begun and the silence was ended.

"You can't be serious, Judy. This is sudden; I don't know how you can be saying that." We were standing in the kitchen. Peter had his hand on the refrigerator for support.

"But I mean it." I went into the living room and sat down on the pullout couch.

"I haven't been happy for a long time. It's painful to tell you this, because I do love you, contrary to what this may sound like."

"How can you say you love me and still be telling me you want a divorce?" Peter had begun his voyage as a scholar; he was a stickler for logic and correct thinking. To me, it was logical.

"I wish we could keep what is good about our marriage," I said. I was too young to know you can't have everything, ever.

"I was going to get a beer," he said, "but I think I'll make myself a real drink. It isn't every night that your wife tells you she is leaving. It calls for a celebration, don't you agree?" He raised his eyebrows. "Would you care to join me?"

We were both deadly serious. So this was what it was like, not what I had imagined. This was the real thing.

We had one drink and then a few more, talking long into the night. We sat on opposite sides of the room. He kept saying, "Let's try to work this out." I kept saying, "I want to leave." Toward three in the morning, he leaned his elbows against the table near where I was sitting and brought his face close to mine.

"Where do you want to be in five years?" he said.

"I would like to have five more children and be happy with you, but I don't believe that is possible." It would have been much easier, but I knew everything had changed and would never be the same.

The next day we were both extremely civil, and although we stayed together through the summer and into the fall, our marriage never recovered. We said it was for Clark's sake; perhaps time would heal things. I was terrified that the longer I stayed, the more difficult it would be, finally, to leave. But by then I knew no matter how hard it was, I would.

My career went along as if on a schedule of its own. I worked in many clubs around the country during the spring and summer, and in the fall, after my second album had come out, Theodore Bikel invited me to be his guest at his Carnegie Hall concert in October.

The beginning of October found Peter and me no closer to separating, but no closer to reconciliation. The night of my concert with Theo, my mother and father came from Denver to be with us; I had told Mother nothing of our troubles. Peter's sister, Hadley, and brother, Gary, and his wife, Minky, were there as well, and afterward Minky invited the whole family up to the Bergdorf Goodman penthouse on Fifty-eighth Street. Central Park spread out beneath us, the streetlamps etching the park drives, the lighted apartment houses lining Fifth Avenue. Horse-drawn carriages made their way around the circle in front of the Plaza Hotel as the water fountain played in the air. A romantic, exotic place for a family fight.

Peter and I celebrated so much that we said what was really on our minds. Before the evening was over, Peter had discussed the situation with Gary, who caught me in one of the hallways, between an early American landscape and the molding of a bedroom door.

Gary let me know that the family would fight for custody of

Clark. I wasn't worried because I was sure I would never lose custody, no matter what happened. But the battle lines were drawn. Gary backed down the hall to the living room, where his sister was standing with my mother and father, looking out at New York's radiant lights. The city was shining for us.

"Oh, look," Hadley said, "the fountains are silver." She knew nothing yet of the dramas in the other rooms, and later, when she did, she refused to take sides and remained my friend through everything. It was courageous and I never forgot it.

My success at Carnegie Hall was over in a few moments and my marriage was finally finished. Back in our hotel room I couldn't sleep, tossing in bed till dawn.

In the morning Peter, Mother, Daddy, and I drove to Connecticut. My parents were going to look after Clark for a couple of weeks while I went to Arizona to work. On the three-hour drive to Storrs, I remember "Blowin' in the Wind" playing on the car radio and our talking of everything except what was really happening. Maybe if we didn't speak to it, the elephant in the living room would just go away.

I left the next day for Tucson and went to work that night at a folk music club. After the first show I was so ill, I could barely perform.

"What in the world is the matter with you? You look awful!" said Bill Taxerman, one of the owners of the club. "You ought to see a doctor tomorrow."

"I'll be all right. I've been under some emotional strain." I felt weak as a kitten. For months, I had had a gurgling in my lungs that I assumed was a symptom of a ruptured marriage.

"You've got a fever," Bill said, putting his wrist to my forehead. "It just so happens that you are in the right place. We all"—he nodded at the other two owners, Irene and Phil Janicek—"work as biochemists during the day for a doctor at Tucson General Hospital. In the morning we'll get you in to see the best internist in Tucson."

They were as good as their word. They came to get me at eight o'clock, and we drove in the morning light to the office of their employer, Dr. Schneider. He thumped my chest, looked into my mouth and ears, checked my pulse, took my temperature, and told me to get dressed.

"I'll meet you in my office in exactly five minutes. Be there." He smiled, his face wrinkling up in a handsome way, putting dents in his suntan and lines around his eyes. Fully clothed, I sat in his office, waiting for him. On the table were framed pictures of two little children with black hair and blue eyes, a boy and a girl, and a woman who had her arms around them. They all laughed out into the room at me.

"You have tuberculosis," Dr. Schneider said as he walked into the room and shut the door behind him. "I am going to admit you to Tucson General. Your lungs are full of liquid; they have to be drained, but we can't do that until the fever comes down a little." He sat in his chair, next to the pictures, and looked at me.

I think I was relieved. At least there was a name for what was wrong with me.

"I've asked Bill and the others to drive you over to the hospital, and they will get you admitted. I will be by after lunch to give the instructions for your medication. In the meantime, they are going to want to do all the standard blood tests and so on. I hope you feel up to it. You look beat." He got up and walked me out of the room. As I left, I looked back at the photographs. Maybe marriages had a better chance in the West, all that clean air and sunshine.

I was put in a secluded ward at the end of a ground floor, far away from the other patients, because the hospital was wary of tuberculosis.

I was isolated, apart from the others, just as I had been when I had polio. After my lungs were drained and I was put on the beginning of two years of medication, I collapsed. I slept, mentally and physical exhausted, for days.

When I was rested enough to think about what had happened in New York, I wrote letters to a lawyer requesting forms to file for divorce, and custody, and started writing in my journal: "Painful, too much memory, ghostly realization of the permanency of this separation with Peter . . . but there is some order coming into my life at last." I had been stopped in my tracks, and now I lay for hours, just thinking and planning, staring out at the naked Arizona desert beyond my hospital room. I was, as I had wanted to be that previous year, off the road.

"You are going to need months of hospitalization, Judy," said Dr. Schneider. "Do you have any insurance?" I liked this man very much. He had been kind, brought me books, taken time to visit me here in Tucson, where I knew no one.

"I don't have a sou, no insurance."

"I'll tell you what the treatment is for this kind of TB. Months of rest, antibiotics, plus two other drugs, INH and PAS. You're lucky you have TB now, if luck is a word I may use." We both laughed. He had brought books by Gide and Camus, and said he wouldn't give me Thomas Mann's *Magic Mountain*, about a long recovery from tuberculosis, because it might depress me.

"Until a few years ago, doctors were insisting on at least a year to recover from what you have. There is one place that takes care of entertainers. It's at Saranac Lake. Why don't you look into that in a few days when you're feeling better? You will have to have, oh, my assessment would be for now, about five months. Rest first, and then I'll try to help you find out about the Will Rogers Sanatorium and Saranac."

As it turned out, I got help from Jac Holzman and Theo Bikel, who were able to arrange for my admission to the National Jewish Hospital in Denver. It was closer than Saranac Lake.

"Besides being closer, National Jewish happens to be the best research hospital in the country for tuberculosis and other lung diseases. They only take charity cases, so it's a good thing you ain't rich!" said Dr. Schneider. He laughed again. I always felt better when he came to see me, whether he was draining my lungs or bringing me books. He was a good guy.

"Charity begins at home," I said. "My mother will be glad to see me."

After I had been in Tucson for a month, I went home to Denver.

Peter brought Clark out to stay with my mother, so I could be with him every day. I was able to leave the hospital and go to Mother's house in the afternoons and return to the hospital in the early evenings. We got Clark into a nursery school, and Mom took care of him at night. Peter's parents also saw a lot of him during the next three months.

I put my typewriter on my hospital bed and wrote letters to my lawyers and my husband. My roommate was a Vietnamese girl name Pho Tuit Lan, which means Snowflower, and she was very beautiful. She had spots on her lungs, and she and I would smoke cigarettes while she told me about her life. She was in favor of the American advisers in Vietnam because her father was part of the South Vietnamese government. By then it was the end of 1962, and Buddhists were setting fire to themselves in the streets of Saigon, her home. As we watched the news together at night on the television set in the lounge, she would point out the places she thought looked like her neighborhood and wonder out loud whether her relatives' homes had been bombed.

Nearly all of us smoked—standing in line to get our shots of penicillin, sitting in the auditorium listening to lectures on TB, in our rooms, and at our meals in the cafeteria. At that time most medical researchers had not yet linked cigarette smoking to lung disease. There were people there who, like Pho, had been x-rayed at school or at work and sent to Denver to get well or who had been diagnosed at the medical screenings at immigration centers. In the TB ward I had my first facial, from a Rumanian woman who had not even set foot on United States soil; when they found spots on her lungs, she had been sent directly to Denver as she got off the boat in the harbor at New York. We were a strange community, bonded by a virus, thrown together willy-nilly from all over the country and the world.

These three months were a strangely tranquil time for me. At Christmas Peter came to Denver and we talked about reconciliation. I wanted the marriage to be over, and the holiday, the gaiety, the tequila, the hope in the season, nothing changed that. By the time Peter left to go back to Connecticut, we both knew divorce was next.

Letters continued to flow between the hospital and my lawyers in the East. I had to find a place for me and Clark in New York, where I had friends and a support system. During this time I had kept in touch with Walter Raim, a friend in New York, and he helped me find an apartment in Greenwich Village. In January I worked hard to plan for the move east. I would be getting out of the hospital at the end of March, and by then I hoped to have everything ready.

When I called Mom on Sunday, February 24, to find out if Peter's parents had brought Clark back after a weekend visit, her voice was strained.

"No," she said, "he's not back yet." I called Peter's mother, Margaret, to find out where Clark was. She told me he had gone to the dump with his grandfather. I didn't worry.

At the hospital later that night, I was called to the phone. It was Peter.

"Judy, I have Clark with me. We are in Chicago. We're on

our way back to Connecticut, and there is nothing you can do, so don't try to stop me." I was frantic. I called the police.

"Are you a state resident, Mrs. Taylor?"

"No, I live in Connecticut. I'm temporarily visiting in Colorado." I was tempted to say, I'm temporarily insane.

"Do you have a court order that gives you custody of your son?"

God, I hadn't thought he would do this, this was a nightmare, it couldn't possibly be happening. Of course I didn't have a court order. I hung up the phone. Because it was Sunday night I couldn't reach the district attorney till morning. By then I was almost sick from worry when I dialed his office number.

"He has every right to take your son," he said. "He is the father, he is returning with his son to your legal residence, and you have no court order. There is nothing I can do for you."

My world shattered. I made calls and found a lawyer in Hartford, where any suit for custody would have to be filed. I sent them a small retainer and let them know my fears in a long letter. Their return letter should have been reassuring. The lawyer who would be handling my case was quite clear that "all things being equal, the mother is generally awarded custody of children." I had no reason to doubt that all things would be equal, but now, away from my son as well as my husband, I was sick with worry and anxiety.

There was nothing to do but wait it out. I wouldn't get out of the hospital for another month. I kept forging ahead, making plans for what I would do when I was released. It was now more important than ever that I continue to work. In late February, I got an invitation to sing at a salute to President Kennedy in Washington, D.C., and the hospital let me fly there for the weekend. "Dinner with the President" featured Odetta, Josh White, the Clancy Brothers, Will Holt, Lynn Gold, and myself. I met John F. Kennedy, and he was even more vibrant in person than he was on the radio and television; his charisma was breathtaking. After the weekend, I flew back to Denver, finished my treatment of drugs and rest, and continued to talk to my lawyers about the divorce procedures. I was becoming more agitated about the custody issue in spite of the reassurances.

In early March, I was released from National Jewish and given an eighteen-month supply of pills. Going to New York, I took the apartment in Greenwich Village and visited Clark as often as I could. Peter had moved from the farmhouse on Brown's Hill Road to university housing. He sent me my skis, my clothes, and a couple of silver platters, gifts from our wedding, but I didn't want things, I wanted my son. We began to struggle for custody.

As I waited for the divorce and custody settlement to be over, I continued with my career. It had come to an abrupt halt, and now I put one foot in front of the other to make a living.

Soon I was invited to go to Brown University to tape a concert for a show called *Hootenanny*, which was scheduled for broadcast in the fall by ABC. On the show with me were the Clancy Brothers, John Phillips of the Journeymen, and Theodore Bikel. Harold Leventhal was managing Theo, and during the coming year was to become my manager as well. Shortly after the taping, ABC refused to hire Pete Seeger and the Weavers to perform on *Hootenanny*. Although ABC claimed it was for "professional" reasons, I assumed, as most people did, that it was political. (Pete and the Weavers had been blacklisted during the McCarthy era in the fifties.) In response, I helped found a committee protesting ABC's position. The protesters included Erik Darling, Leon Bibb, Tommy Makem, and Izzy Young. We met at the Village Gate, gathering place for so many social and political causes, and drafted a letter to the press, the attorney general, and the FCC, asking them to outlaw hiring decisions made on political grounds.

In the summer, Harold Leventhal called a meeting with Pete Seeger, Theo, and me to discuss the situation at ABC. I was surprised at Pete's response. He said that *Hootenanny* would help to make folk music popular, which was something he had fought for all his life, and urged Theo and me to accept invitations to go on the show again.

With Pete's words in mind, I did two more concerts in the *Hootenanny* series, but in addition to the mixed feelings I had about doing them, I found the show's artistic direction to be slick and commercial. The production staff changed lyrics and insisted on cuts in material that made no sense. After those performances, I told ABC I would not do the show again.

Pete Seeger and I have worked together often in the years since then, and recently I told him I was sorry I had taken his advice about doing the ABC show.

"I've always said you can't tell about a boycott," Pete said.

"You must be cautious, and I feel they seldom do what they are supposed to do. That was the reason I felt people should do the show." It wouldn't be like Pete to say something he didn't believe. Yet, doing *Hootenanny* is one of the few things in my life I would have done differently.

I would often drive to Connecticut, to pick up Clark for our visits. My friend Linda Leibman, whom I had met in Chicago years before and who was like an aunt to Clark, suggested I not return him after our visit.

"Why don't you just not take him back to Storrs?" she asked me. "Two can play the same game. What have you got to lose?"

There was no court order yet, and I had registered to vote in New York. Clark was my son.

"I just can't do it. I would never be able to look my son in the face again. I'm going to get custody, my lawyers tell me it is just a matter of time."

Perhaps I should have taken Linda's advice after all. The divorce suit dragged on through the summer, as did my suit for custody, which, my lawyers advised me, must be handled as separate issues.

I did benefits that year at the Village Peace Center Theater and worked with Oscar Brand at Grossinger's; I performed concerts for the Southern Christian Leadership Conference, led by Martin Luther King, Jr. I recorded radio jingles and did whatever New York studio singing work I could get to make a living. Walter Raim was a musician who arranged and produced a lot of radio jingles, and he hired me as often as he could. I sang back up for ads about soap products and hair sprays. Advertising Cover Girl makeup, I sang, to the tune of an old sea chanty, about loving a man who went to sea. Between clubs and the occasional concert, in 1963, singing jingles paid the rent.

Walter had played guitar on my second album and introduced me to some unusual songs. We were close, and I learned from his mother in Brooklyn how to make kreplach, the Jewish ravioli, from scratch. I learned what *kvell* and *kvetch* meant. Perhaps because of his Jewish heritage, Walter carried the guilt of the ages on his sympathetic face and was often depressed.

I rented a grand piano and started playing again. The practicing made me feel better, as it always has. I got to know Paul Krasner, who was a publisher and writer, and I helped raise money for his pet school, Summerlane. And I continued talking to my lawyers about the progress of my divorce and custody suits, the lawyers continually assuring me that there was no way I could lose custody.

In looking back, the national violence that occurred during 1963 seems forever entangled with my personal pain at not being with Clark. A public tragedy appeared to confirm my private turmoil. On the afternoon of November 22, 1963, I was taking the bus to La Guardia Airport, planning to catch a plane for Washington, D.C., where I was doing a concert that night. As I stepped onto the bus, the driver looked through me as I handed him my fare.

"Kennedy's been shot," he said to the air.

He closed the door behind me, and we drove in silence to the airport, the other passengers as quiet as the driver. I prayed he would live. When we arrived at the shuttle terminal and the door opened, a woman stuck her head into the bus.

"He's dead," she said. I remember my first thought after her words: Please let the murderer be caught, and please let him be white.

I continued on to Washington, knowing there would be no concert, but wanting to be as near the nation's capital as possible when the next day came. I went directly to Beverly and Lee Silberstein's house, friends who lived in Georgetown. We watched the alleged murderer, Lee Harvey Oswald, being murdered on television by Jack Ruby, and then, in the next awesome days, followed the entire funeral, the sad and mournful ending of the dream.

In 1964 I finished my third studio album, a group of songs by "city singers." *Judy Collins #3* was recorded at Plaza Sound in New York. In the spring, I did Steve Allen's show and worked again at Newport, with John Hammond, Jr., on a workshop, after which the *New York Times* said I was in the "front rank of American balladeers." I went to Mississippi in July to work with voter registration, and when I got home after two weeks, went to see my lawyers, who filled me in on the progress of my custody suit. I learned the stipulations of visitation preliminary to a final decision, I had been granted "liberal visiting privileges." I would be allowed to see my son every other weekend and for six weeks in the summer. The custody suit itself was yet to be settled.

The Connecticut social worker who had been assigned my case came to visit me. I doubt she had been to New York before, let alone broached Greenwich Village. I was dressed like a matron from Westchester, hoping to look the part of a correctly attired mother, and she and I were both extremely uncomfortable.

"How can your son adapt to living here, Miss Collins? His friends, his school, all his activities are in Storrs."

On West Tenth and Hudson streets, below my windows, the Village hummed with eccentrics, musicians and artists, blacks and whites. On the corner down the street was the White Horse Tavern, where Dylan Thomas used to drink and where I now went drinking with Pete Hamill and Dave Van Ronk.

"But I am his mother, and I am here . . ."

I was afraid her disapproval of the Village would prejudice my case, so I took a large apartment uptown, in a more acceptable neighborhood. There was plenty of space for Clark and me to have our home together. In late December there was another custody hearing, with no final conclusion, but the divorce was granted separately from the custody suit and went through by Christmas. Peter remarried immediately, on December 27. Sue, Clark's stepmother, was a Quaker from Boston, and though she seemed nice enough, I felt an almost mythical antipathy toward her from the first. She had come between my son and me. She was a primeval rival.

"Mommy, why can't I live with you part of the time and with Daddy and Sue the other?" I had no answer, and I knew it. His life was settled at the house in Storrs in a way it couldn't be in New York. If I didn't have him with me for a long time, then I couldn't get him into a school or a play group or a niche that he could call his own.

"I can't get custody until I have custody!" I said to Linda Leibman.

"What do your lawyers say? Are they still telling you there will be no problem?

"I'm beginning to doubt these experts, Linda. The men with the answers don't seem to have any."

Linda went with me to the final custody hearing on April 1, 1965. The courtroom in Connecticut was full of Peter's family. My lawyer was there, as well as Ralph Klein, the therapist I had been seeing since I had moved to New York. Harold Leventhal, my manager, came to testify in my behalf. Everyone said what they had to say, and we were told the decision of the judge would be handed down the next day. I drove back to New York to wait. In the morning, the voice of my astonished lawyer informed me on the phone that the court had found against me.

"They always find for the mother," he said. "This is appalling. It is a stunning decision. I cannot believe it has happened."

Nor could I.

Later, my lawyer told me, "They are very prejudiced against therapy in Connecticut. They didn't want to give you custody if you were not 'all right'; they think anyone seeing a shrink must be crazy."

Linda tried to console me, and I sat with her, letting out all my rage against the situation. I told her I hated Peter's family, the judge, anyone associated with the decision against me.

"I know how you feel," Linda said. "You must feel ganged up on as well as disappointed. But let go of it and get on with your life, because you know they say you belong to whomever you hate."

I still feel that bitter pain. It was devastating to lose custody of my son. I had been able to wrest a sort of "permission" from somewhere to choose the path of an artist. The cost was travel and fragmentation, time away from home, isolation, and the risk of having an "unusual" lifestyle, an unusual relationship with my husband. I had accepted that it probably had cost me my marriage, but to have it cost me my son was unbearable. How could I justify my work if it resulted in my no longer being able to mother my son in the real sense, the one we are taught counts?

"Most women are given custody of their child as a matter of course," my lawyer had said to me. I was the exception; I must be a monster. My revulsion at myself was complete.

A few days after losing custody, I had an offer to perform concerts in the Soviet Union and Poland. Harold said he thought it would be a good idea to accept. I called my mother.

"I won't go unless I can take Holly with me, I will not be able to survive." Holly Ann was ten.

God bless my mother, for she never rebuked me for the loss of my child. I felt I had been given the responsibility to go out and try to be an adult and had failed miserably. She never suggested that I was anything less than a loving, perfectly adequate parent. I felt she understood and sympathized. She helped make it possible for me to live with that loss. When she said that Holly could come with me, she gave me a priceless gift. It was as though she had said, "You are a nurturing and a good parent, and I will prove it to you by giving you your younger sister to shepherd to a strange and unfamiliar place; I trust you to do the right thing."

And now, twenty-two years later, I am here in Los Angeles, troubled about my life, feeling anger and frustration about my career, aware of how human and how flawed I am. But after an hour with my sister, I feel absolution and clarity. My sister inspired this song, which I wrote when she was living in northern California.

> She is a weaver,
> Through her hands the bright thread travels,
> Blue green water, willows weeping, silver stars.
> She sings and sighs as the shuttle flies
> Through the yarn like a Kerry dancer,
> Pink and purple velvet red for a lover's bed.
> Living north of San Francisco
> With a man who built his house alone,
> Living peaceful in the country,
> The lights of the Golden Gate will lead her home.
>
> . . .
> She is a spinner,
> In her hands the wooden wheel turns the wool around,
> Then around again.
> The gypsy from Bolinas sits and plays the mandolin,
> Faces smile in the firelight of a foggy night.
> Living north of San Francisco,
> Sometimes it's nice to be alone.
> She says it's peaceful where she is living,
> The lights of the Golden Gate will lead her home.
>
> . . .
> You can see the bridges of the city
> Hanging in the air by steel and stone.
> She says it's peaceful where she's living,
> The lights of the Golden Gate will lead her home.
>
> . . .
> She is a weaver,
> Through her hand the bright thread travels,
> Blue green water, willows weeping, silver stars.

She is my sister, the baby born when I was older,
Her hands are light, her hair is bright as the summer sun.
Living north of San Francisco,
Sometimes it's nice to be alone.
She says it's peaceful in the country,
The lights of the Golden Gate will lead her home.
The lights of the Golden Gate will lead her home.

I put my things in the tote bag and head off to do *Solid Gold*. I feel lighter. She is an angel near me, on my side.

When I return from the hours at the studio, Holly has made roast chicken. "How did it go?" she says.

"Fine. I can't figure out why they asked me to be on this show singing 'Only You.' But I had a great time."

"I guess someone out there was supposed to see you smile," says Holly.

That night, sitting in the living room among the looms and the flowers after Kalen is asleep, we talk more about the trip we took to Poland and the Soviet Union.

Early in June 1965, we took off for Europe. There were six of us, Holly, Arlene Cunningham, my manager's assistant, the Tarriers, and me. En route to Warsaw, we stopped over in Paris for a night, where Holly and I took a tiny hotel room together. It was just a simple pension, but to us it was magical and charmed. A balcony opened out above the street, and we stood looking over the houses, the rooftops, and up into the Parisian sky. We were in a fairyland. That night we had dinner with Harold Leventhal, who had come with us on the first leg of the trip, and "Big Joan" Baez, Joan's mother, and her husband, who were living in Paris. Al Baez, a scientist, was working in France. I had known the Baez family for a few years already, having met Joanie and Mimi at festivals and concerts in the States, and had come to love Big Joan. Her "fan letters" to me, on blue paper, in her tiny neat handwriting, are scattered throughout the years of my correspondence. The next day Big Joan came to the airport to see us off, her arms full of flowers, her black hair shining, her face a warm, smiling presence. I thought, All the mothers are coming through for me. Those hours in Paris will stay with me forever. The pain in my heart moved over to make room for the loveliness of Paris, and some sense of hope began to return.

Clark was still my son, after all; I would always be his mother. That thought gave me a night of sleep before the numbness returned the next day.

We spent three weeks touring the cities and the countryside of Poland, and I wished my son could have seen these places. We passed farmyards and stared with wonder and delight at chickens and bright red dogs standing on the sloping grass roofs of the farmhouses. With flowers poking up between their paws, their feet in straw, the dogs barked at us as we rolled by in our minibuses. We slept in beds with strange silk coverlets. We stayed over an extra day in the town of Jedrzejow, because the coal mine needed the electricity the night we were scheduled to do our concert. We walked around town with our traveling companions, the Tarriers—Clarence Cooper, Eric Weissberg, and Al Gargoni, the group's members at that time. Clarence, a black man, was followed everywhere by a string of blond children, their eyes wide with amazement. They were all under five and had never seen anyone with skin the color of coal. We had a Polish translator named Edwina whose estranged husband followed us for three hundred miles, wooing his unsympathetic wife. Edwina offered us only three choices in every restaurant, and we learned later that she hadn't wanted to translate more than chicken, veal, and beef, because she was distracted by the pursuit of her enamored husband.

While on a road near Warsaw, we saw a sign for Auschwitz and asked the driver to take us there, although he didn't want to. We went in through the wire fences and walked around the desolate ruins. The smell of the Holocaust was there. In that horror of eyeglasses piled high and hollow iron ovens, Holly found the children's museum, and the watercolors of butterflies and rainbows. As we walked away from the main gate, blowing the stench from our nostrils, she pointed to the sky where a sparrow was singing and flying. There were hawkers in front of the gate, selling Auschwitz memorabilia, flags and buttons with a picture of a wire fence. We were all speechless. We couldn't believe they would commercialize the Holocaust.

The ads in Poland had announced our tour as "Judy Collins and Her All Negro Band." In Odessa, someone threw an apple at me, mad because the ads in the Soviet Union read, "American Rock-and-Roll Band." Our Russian translator, Ilyana, had borrowed a corset from the Bolshoi, and Holly and I strapped her into it every night, one of us putting a foot in the middle of her back, all of us howling as Ilyana got her figure together. She spoke good English and we invited her to come to a party given for us at the American Embassy in Moscow. She refused, saying that the authorities would find out and accuse her of spying. As I looked out the second-story window of the embassy, I watched her leave alone, driving off into the Moscow night.

The American ambassador, Foy Kohler, and his wife gave us a very nice party, but we were disappointed that Ilyana wasn't there. The Cold War was hot again; North Vietnamese MiGs had shot down United States jets in Vietnam, and the U.S.S.R. had admitted they were supplying arms to Hanoi. While students demonstrated in the United States to get us out of Vietnam, the Soviets demonstrated for the same thing.

After leaving Moscow, Holly and I watched Russian boys play chess and volleyball on the beach at Yalta; on the radio, a pirated record of the Beatles singing "Help!" wafted across the black sand from a portable radio.

In Lublin, Poland, we met a magician who performed tricks for us and gave me a ring made of green nephrite, a stone that is a type of jade. It was too big and kept falling off my finger. Three times Holly found it again, once on the high road to Odessa, where it had fallen off my finger out the window. The bus stopped and she searched the shoulders of the road, and found it in a ditch on the downhill side. Once it was lost at dusk on a beach at Yalta, and she reached into the sand and brought it out. Another time it rolled under a piece of furniture in the Tzar's Hotel in Krasnodar, on the Black Sea. I gave her the ring when we returned from that trip. She saved my sanity, gave me something to live for in a strange and unfamiliar world where I was supposed to bring joy with my music. Everywhere we went she made the experience real for me.

My blessed sister made losing my son something I could live with, at least, even if I could not accept it. I could never accept it.

True Stories and Other Dreams

Valentine's Day, February 14, 1985 / Fargo, North Dakota

At the Holiday Inn, I receive a dozen roses from Louis, "Be my Valentine." I have no galoshes, so I walk across the snow-strewn highway in my Charles Jourdan black high heels, looking like an insect in the snow, to the mall. The stores sell jewelry and cheeses, gift wraps, microwave ovens, ice skates, baby clothes. I buy purple insulated boots, down and leather, comfortable and warm, and cheap at twenty dollars. For the first time in days, I don't work out.

I talked to Freddy DeMann, my manager, on the phone this morning, and remembered that winter of 1977 out here in the snowstorms of the Midwest. Freddy and Jerry Sharell were both promotion men from Elektra and had come with me to Fargo, St. Paul, and Madison to promote "Send In the Clowns" on the radio. The three of us spent an afternoon sitting in a limo that had broken down in the snow outside Minneapolis. It was freezing cold, the fogged windows were rolled up, and while waiting for the tow truck, we listened to "Send In the Clowns" on a tape recorder. Freddy was wearing his white wool coat, which reached below his knees. During that week we went to radio stations, had dinners with program directors, lunches with radio disc jockeys.

Two weeks before that trip, Freddy had split open the palms of both his hands in a freak accident with a container of bottled water, and the glass had gone to the bone. The healing scars were like stigmata.

In the music business, luck, survival, a sense of humor, and a tough skin are just the beginning, and one of the things they say you need is a manager. My first experience with managers was in 1960, when I was appearing at the Gate of Horn in Chicago. I had worked six weeks at the Gate that first summer, and was moving to our new home in Connecticut with Peter.

"You must have a manager and an agent," said Alan Ribback, the owner. "You're in the music business now, where politics count as much as art. I love your work, but you can't assume that everyone will have a first hand knowledge of you. You need someone to be your representative."

I had little more than a great belief that I had something important to say.

"What does a manager do, Alan?" I asked.

"A manager can be different things to different artists: a nursemaid, a friend, a parent, a business representative. I know a couple of people who would work well with you, and I think Danny Gordon would be a good person." I had met Danny and liked him. He was Odetta's husband, and that fall he became my first manager. Throughout the year, he found club dates for me and organized concerts after I made my first record. I wasn't all that sure I needed a manager after the first year, so Danny and I parted company in the summer of 1961.

A manager theoretically oversees the entire career; an agent books individual concerts. In 1961, Burt Block became my agent. When I moved to New York in 1963, Burt was running a company with Artie Mogal. Later, he became a manager and worked with Kris Kristofferson and Rita Coolidge. He tried to help me, but he wasn't able to get much work for me. I would go to his office, put my elbows on his desk, and cry.

"Why can't you get me more work?" I would say. Burt would light his cigar and shrug and say he wished I could do better.

"What you still need is a manager, Judy."

Burt said I should go see Harold Leventhal, who managed Pete Seeger, the Weavers, Arlo Guthrie and Theo Bikel. Harold had a round rosy face, glasses, and he constantly smoked a cigar; he looked like the classic image of a personal manager.

He was to become my mentor, my friend, and my professional guide.

I turned my life over to Harold, and for the nine years I was with him he did my bookings in clubs and for concerts and oversaw my record contracts and the relationship with Jac Holzman at Elektra. He kept my bank accounts. I had a faith in Harold that transcended his doing all the business deals and record contracts. He supervised my publishing, my finances, my investments. I trusted him with everything. After our initial contract, which was for a year, we stayed together without a contract. His word was enough for me.

I was working in clubs around the country, had two records out, and had begun to develop a following. Harold was a political mentor as well.

"Chopin was the mayor of Warsaw," he would say. "Art and politics must always mix." It was what I had learned at home.

Harold is one of the survivors of the old school of management. He always said we didn't need a press agent.

"If you're doing things, the press will be there," he would say. "If you aren't, it wouldn't matter anyway."

With Harold, I didn't think; I just did. I was free to be an "artist." But that kind of freedom has a price.

In the early seventies, I began to go to women's groups where the issues of money, men, business, and independence were talked about at great length. I felt a big hole where my financial responsibility should have been. I started to ask questions. Harold had done a good job and would have continued doing so. But there were things I wanted to find out about my business, about myself. At the end of 1972 I told Harold I wanted to manage myself. I asked Charlie Rothschild, who had done the actual concert bookings and road management for Harold, to continue booking concerts and going out as my road manager.

"You have to set up a corporation," said my friend Ed Bernstein. Ed was a lawyer from the West Coast and helped me incorporate my business into Rocky Mountain Productions. He was my lawyer for a number of years after the birth of my company.

As I began to talk with lawyers and accountants, I saw how much I must learn, and eventually realized I was learning more than how to run a business. The process would begin to teach me how to live my life.

In the years of being on my own, I have come to untangle much of the mystery. Since I have managed myself, I have had my biggest hits at Elektra.

This morning, I asked Freddy if he would sign a release, and he said he would. We have parted company. It was all very pleasant. I am a free woman.

Several days ago I was visiting Clark, and we spent some time with my old friend Terry Williams, whom I have known since the days of Central City and the Gilded Garter. Clark was a baby then, and now he is working and going to school in St. Paul.

I'm proud of him, he's working hard, and as Terry says, he's living practically like a monk out here in the Twin Cities. He's going to graduate, finally, in a year.

After Mandarin Chinese, semiotics, and building houses, Clark has found what he wants to do—computer electronics—and has been making great grades and loving it.

"You'll probably invent some successful game for adult children of yuppies that will make you rich and famous," says Terry. Since Clark has lived in St. Paul, he and Terry have become close. Terry lives in a stone house, on a hill near the cathedral, which overlooks the city. Last night he cooked dinner for his son Steven and Steven's girlfriend, Ryn, and Clark and me. We all sat around talking into the night. Mostly we discussed how what is important to us hasn't changed. Ryn is the age I was when Clark was nine.

"I took a little time out to rest," says Terry. "I began to see that the whole universe did not revolve around me, which made it easier to say I count, I can make a difference. That's what William James said, isn't it? To live as if you make a difference? When you're young you know you do, then you doubt it, and maturity is coming to believe it again, that you do make a difference."

I am glad to see Terry, he's a familiar and loved friend. He is sitting in the living room with his back against the stone wall, an empty plate on his knees. He continues speaking as he rises to put the dishes in the sink.

"It isn't so important anymore to be right. To get up in the morning and go on, that is the heroic act."

After dinner, the discussion has turned to abortion.

The *Roe* v. *Wade* decision was twelve years old last month, and the antiabortion groups are lobbying for its reversal by the Supreme Court. On *Donahue* yesterday there were pictures of sixteen-week-old fetuses and a discussion of when life begins.

"Men have always told women what they could do and could not do with their bodies, ever since they found out they had something to do with procreation," I say to no one in particular. "Kate Millett says that it was because women are born with power that men had to oppress them to make themselves more powerful."

"I think the choice should be personal. I don't believe that abortion would be an option for me now," says Terry.

"But wouldn't you want to have the choice?" asks Ryn.

"It is a question of choice, a personal matter each woman must decide for herself," I say, mostly for the benefit of my son. We have talked about sex only recently; I don't have a memory of much being said about it when he was growing up. Once again, I give him the only advice I have ever given.

"There is no such thing as impromptu, easy sex anymore."

"Funny, the only protection we have from AIDS provides the only protection we have from what Planned Parenthood refers to as 'unwanted pregnancies,' " says Clark.

"But what about the times it doesn't work?" I ask.

Silence in the room. The choice for motherhood is never painless and the choice for abortion is never easy. Like many women, I have made both.

In 1972, after one hundred women in France spoke out on the issue, I joined a group of American women who told the stories of their illegal abortions in an issue of *Ms.* magazine. We had to speak out so that we might give women who are not as visible the courage to choose.

There was a bright moon shining in the sky. I started up the borrowed Volkswagen and headed for Sterling, Nebraska, from Denver. It was November, with a wind coming off the Rockies at midnight, and I had finished the first week of a two-week booking at the Exodus. Mom thought I was going to stay up in the mountains in Gold Hill for my day off; the friend whose car I had borrowed thought the same thing. The wind buffeted the little car on the deserted highway as I headed north.

On the seat beside me was a map marked with the route I would take. I drove five hundred miles—first north on the interstate, alongside the mountains, then into Nebraska. It was early morning of a bright, cold day when I pulled into Sterling. I had only stopped twice, once for gas and once for a piece of pie in a diner in a one-mule town. I drove and thought, thought and drove, two hundred dollars in my handbag, an address and phone number in my pocket. The nurse had said, "Don't eat for three hours before you come here . . . and call us from the hotel. There is a reservation there in the name of York." I found the hotel, checked in, and called the number. The nurse said to come on over.

The shadows were long and flat across the fields outside the white house, which was on a ranch at the outskirts of Sterling. A picket fence surrounded a reassuring front yard, a screen door swung on a hinge of metal. In the doctor's office we exchanged no pleasantries.

"All right," he said. "Get undressed and put on this robe." Next he held a mask over my face. A sweet-smelling odor, the feel of cold steel stirrups, and I breathed out a sigh of relief—it was over, over. It seemed to be only a minute later that I got up, dug into my purse, pulled out the money, handed it to the nurse, and got dressed. The doctor disappeared before I could thank him.

Back in the car, I drove to the liquor store, bought Bloody Mary mix and a bottle of vodka. At the hotel I mixed myself a drink and took the pain pills the nurse had given me. I had planned to sleep, to get up at the crack of dawn, and drive the five hundred miles back to Denver to do my first show. But I was becoming more anxious by the moment. I turned on the television set, and the faces had enormous mouths, opening and closing with red lips, their eyes waving around, looking into my hotel room. I could not stay in the room a moment longer. I packed, put the bottle of vodka and the mixer in a bag, and walked out the door. I paid my bill and was back in the car by seven-thirty that night, on the road out of Sterling.

The trouble with the car began about three hundred miles from Denver. In the middle of a black highway, with the moon gone, I pulled over, got out, and stood in the dark road. There were no cars in sight. I lifted the hood and looked into the tidy maze of the engine. I had never looked at the engine of a Volkswagen before. I stared hard and slammed the lid shut. Back inside the car, I turned the key, and when the engine started I moved out onto the highway, going as fast as I dared. The road was a narrow, desolate ribbon. I thought of western boys in pickup trucks going back to their ranches from town, seeing a girl alone in a small car. I thought of the bottle of vodka—I would break the half-empty bottle and use the edge as a weapon. The sky was heavy with clouds, hiding what I knew was no longer a full moon.

The engine sputtered and died again. I pulled over to the side of the road, gravel crunching under the tires, my heart pounding. Gas—there was plenty. Water—no water-cooling system in a Volkswagen, I knew that. Battery—O.K. I turned the key and tried once, then again, and on the third turn of the key the engine started up. I pulled back onto the road and prayed, listening to the engine fight me all the way, but it got me into a town with a miracle—an all-night gas station. The man said it was the points, and what was I doing out there at that time of night. He showed me how to open the hood and file the points with an emery board. I should do that, he said, if it should stall out on me again. I didn't need to know any more, and I don't know anymore to this day about the inside of a Volkswagen. The miles went on and on, and when the sun came up I passed shafts of light shining on the Flatirons in Boulder and then finally entered Denver. I passed the stockyards and the gold dome of the capitol and rolled into the street where my parents' house is. I crept in through the back door and into bed, where I lay wide awake.

I couldn't sleep. I got into a hot bath, thinking that might calm me. After the bath, I went back to the bedroom and lay down, shaking with tension. Abortion was illegal, but I knew that I had had to make the choice I had made. I got up, walked around the house, took the pills they had given me in Sterling. I went back out to the Volkswagen and it started right up. There's a hospital on the campus of the University of Colorado in Denver; I drove there, went in, and walked around the corridors. I was afraid to ask anyone for help, to tell anyone what was wrong with me. What *was* wrong with me? I got into the car, drove back to my parents' house, and waited through the afternoon for the feeling to go away, but it didn't. When I went to the Exodus to sing for the show, I drank a lot of beer, and the awful feeling in the pit of my stomach began to lift. By the second

Ethel Booth and Frank Collins, Sr., my paternal grandparents, in 1918.

Agnes May Cope Byrd, my maternal grandmother, with my uncles Shannon and Robert in 1925.

John Oscar Byrd, my maternal grandfather, in 1925.

top left: My father, age nine, pretending to read a book while his brother, Frank, also blind, looks on. top right: My mother's high school graduation portrait. left: my father (far right) with college friends in front of his fraternity house.

My first nude portrait, age three.

With my mother when I was four.

Christmas in Los Angeles in 1947. David, Michael, and me.

Our family singing around the piano. David, Michael, my parakeet, Chris, on my shoulder, Denver John, my father, and my mother.

Performing at the piano for Daddy's radio show on NBC in Denver, 1951.

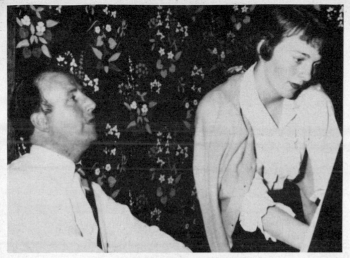

Learning "Laura" from blind pianist George Shearing.

Daddy using a typewriter. Next to him is his Braille writer with a half-finished page.

Dr. Antonia Brico, my teacher, conducting in New York in 1945.
Dr. Ralph Weizsäcker

Practicing with Danno Guerrero for our concert together.

My high school graduation picture. *Maynard Photo* Left: At sixteen I'm playing my first guitar, the National, at East High School in Denver. *Lowell W. Bauer*

Performing "The Gypsy Rover" in high school, 1956. *U.S. Army Photograph*

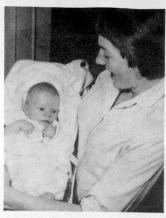

My husband, Peter Taylor, in his R.O.T.C. uniform shortly before our marriage.

With Clark when he was only two weeks old.

Playing at Fern Lake Lodge during the idyllic summer of 1958. *John Clark*

With Holly in Poland in 1965, the summer after I lost custody of Clark. © *1978 Arline Cunningham*

With Clark on the trail to Fern Lake in 1964. *John Clark*

Singing with Theodore Bikel at the Newport Folk Festival in 1963. *David Gahr*

Odetta, on my right, with her husband, Danny Gordon, my first manager, on my left. At the Newport Folk Festival in 1964. *David Gahr*

With Len Chandler and Tom Paxton at Newport in 1964. *David Gahr*

Sucking on a lollipop at the Philadelphia Folk Festival in 1964. *Mike Felix*

Harold Leventhal, my long-time manager, with his constant cigar. *Suzanne Szasz*

With Clark. *Suzanne Szasz*

Mimi Fariña, "Big Joan" Baez, and Dick Fariña in my Seventy-ninth Street apartment in 1965. *Suzanne Szasz*

(Left to right) Mimi Fariña, Dave Van Ronk, Joan Baez, Leonard Cohen, me, Chad Mitchell on the guitar, with Terry Van Ronk stretched out on the floor, at my friend Linda Leibman's apartment in 1966.
© *1966 Daniel Kramer*

Examining an African flute at a fund raiser in 1966 with Bill Crowfut and Adlai Stevenson. © *Henry Grossman*

Performing with Pete Seeger, Bob Dylan, and Arlo Guthrie at the Woody Guthrie memorial concert at Carnegie Hall in 1966. *David Gahr*

Recording "Hard Lovin' Loser" by Dick Fariña, with Harold Leventhal, Mimi and Dick Fariña, and Mark Abramson in 1966. *Suzanne Szasz*

In the recording studio. *Suzanne Szasz*

With Leonard Cohen at Newport in 1967.

With Clark, in front of my apartment on Seventy-ninth Street. *Rowland Scherman*

Michael Thomas

A 1967 portrait. *Suzanne Szasz*

With Jac Holzman, the president of Elektra Records, in 1967. *Elektra Records*

Singing in Washington, D.C., on January 15, 1968, for the Jeannette Rankin Brigade, which marched against the Vietnam War. *Djordje Milićević*

With Arlo Guthrie at a concert in Forest Hills, 1968. © *1987 Julie Snow*

With Joni Mitchell in her tree house in Laurel Canyon. *Rowland Scherman*

With Stephen Stills. *Rowland Scherman*

Mother, Denver John, Michael, me, Holly, and David in Denver in 1969. *Copyright © Stephen Stills. Used by permission.*

With Stacy Keach, dressed in our costumes for *Peer Gynt*, taking a break under a tree in Central Park in 1969. *© 1987 Julie Snow*

Stacy Keach and my brother Denver John on the set of *Doc* in 1970. *Brian Hamill*

With Pete Seeger in 1973 at the Clearwater Festival. *Coulter Watt*

Being led down the steps of the Capitol in Washington, D.C., after being arrested during a protest against the Vietnam War. *Sheldon Ramsdell*

With Melina Mercouri in Paris in 1973. *Coulter Watt*

With Josh Rifkin, Mark Abramson, and Jac Holzman (standing next to me), mixing *Whales and Nightingales* in 1971. *Elektra Records*

On the road with Charlie Rothschild, my concert agent, as he reads the *New York Post*. *Gayle Burns*

With Susie Crile at an exhibition of her paintings at the Fischbach Gallery in New York in 1976. *Mary Ellen Mark/Archive*

With my voice teacher, Max Margulis, in 1976. *Mary Ellen Mark/Archive*

Shooting "The Muppet Show" with Jim Henson in 1977 before my throat operation. *Copyright © 1977 Henson Associates, Inc.*

My co-stars on "The Muppet Show." *Copyright © 1977 Henson Associates, Inc.*

Louis Nelson.
Irene Kubota Neves

top: My brother Denver John, his bride, Allison, my mother, and my stepfather, Robert Hall, in 1979 at Denver and Allison's wedding. *Carol Kaliff*

middle: With Clark at my brother Denver John's wedding to Allison in 1979. *Louis Nelson*

bottom: My mother, David, Denver John, me, Holly, and Michael at Fern Lake, September 1978. *Allison Laird Collins*

Louis Nelson relaxing beside the Snake River in Idaho. *Holden Bowler*

Jogging in Brooklyn. *Gayle Burns*

On the road with my group in the eighties. Clockwise from upper left corner: Russell Landau, Warren Odze, me, Shelton Becton; Zev Katz (holding the cup) and Warren Odze; Ken Bichel, me, Lou Volpe (with the guitar). *M. Pizzuro-Cleary* With Maria Pizzuro. *Kevin Mazur*

Performing at Hampton Beach in 1982. *Jacque D. Maris*

With Clark at Bella Abzug's fund raiser in 1981.

With my friend Pat Schroeder, congresswoman from Colorado, whom I have supported for many years. *Bill Brown*

A "time to renew the faith" breakfast in the U.S. Senate dining room in 1985: (left to right) Ken Fritz, Peter Yarrow, Mrs. Howard Metzenbaum, me, Senator Howard Metzenbaum, Odetta, Mary Travers, and Harry Belafonte. *Courtesy Howard Metzenbaum's office.*

With Patricia McBride, Jacques d'Amboise, and Mary Tyler Moore at the Felt Forum in 1983. *Daily News*

With Rosa Parks, the woman whose bravery in refusing to give up her bus seat started the Montgomery bus boycott. *Copyright © Richard Gordon/ Archive*

With Marlo Thomas, Joan Mondale, and Gloria Steinem, my fellow board members, during a press conference for the Wonder Woman Foundation, which gave grants to women of courage. *Deborah Millman*

In front of the Metropolitan Museum of Art in 1985. *Jim Wilson/NYT Pictures*

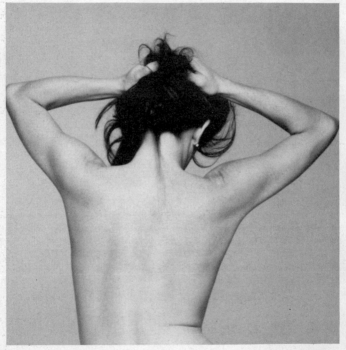

My second nude photo, for the cover of *Hard Times for Lovers*. Photograph by Francesco Scavullo

At Clark's wedding to Alyson Lloyd, March 1987. *Ann Marsden*

At Clark's wedding: (left to right) Peter and Sandy Bergen, mother and stepfather of the bride, Louis Nelson, Alyson Lloyd, Clark, me, and Peter Taylor. *Ann Marsden*

Today is a new beginning. *Allison Laird Collins*

show I was quite relaxed, feeling more as if I could sleep that night. I returned the car to my friend, who may have noticed the odometer but said nothing. I never told anyone where I had been. That night I went home to my parents' house, and I slept a long, long sleep.

". . . easy, abortion is so easy now," Ryn was saying. "It's legal, safe, fast, you can even get a solution that makes the process quite painless. This whole thing is political anyway, a big scam to make women breeders for the state." I tried to imagine what she might have felt like being in that car, on that dark road, a girl in a pair of jeans, a sweater, alone.

Clark goes to put away the dishes, and I stand up.

"It's late. I'm going to get Clark home and get back to the hotel." We all hug our good-byes, and Clark and I drive through the dark and quiet streets of St. Paul. As we drive, my thoughts are on the children I haven't had.

"What are you thinking, Mom?" A question only a son should ask.

"I like knowing that I might choose to have another baby."

"Men can try again until they practically fall over," says Clark, "but women can't."

"Yes. I have to decide before I get much older."

"Whatever makes you happy, Mom," says Clark.

"In any case," I say, "I got the best."

Monday, February 18, 1985 / En route, Fargo to New York

It snowed in St. Paul the other night, and when I left on the airplane the weather reports for the whole country were filled with warnings for flurries and inches. I got to Fargo with time to spare, and met up with my band. Weather has seldom stopped me, and I think in twenty-five years I have missed very few concerts. (God must really want me to work.)

The concert last night was in a hall that was built in 1915. Huge and barnlike, it is the scene of community functions in Fargo: the Chamber Orchestra, the school shows, the wrestling team—the Judy Collins concert. We dress in the motel across an alley covered with snow, so I tramp over ice and drifts from hotel to stage door, back and forth at intermission, my heels teetering on the slick, crusted surfaces. The concert is great, I feel nourished by the evening.

"Why do you still do it? Why do you keep on traveling, keep on singing? What do you get out of a night of singing? Bette Midler says it's for the money," he says. The interviewer for an Ohio television station points a microphone in my face and waits for an answer.

"It's for the heart, and it's great to make a living doing what you love to do," I say.

"Is it only a living, then?" asks the young, eager interviewer.

When did making a living and having a good job get a bad name? This young man, with his unblemished face, seems to harbor some hostility for work, as though—if one were really with it—one should have been able to find some way not to have to do it. I love to sing. I love performing. Singing is my life's blood. It gives me pleasure, it makes me happy; it's more than a job—it's a life in process. Work is vital. It gives me purpose, calls on me to do my best. You don't have to be paid for work. I work for free, and for fun, too.

"How do you feel about being called a singer's singer, Ms. Collins?"

"I guess it is a compliment," I say.

I wonder if my destiny is always to be a singer's singer as I try to change, transform, and struggle to break through into new things. I feel that inner push again. It is a familiar companion, this urge to go on to something new, something different. It crunches at me from within, like an awkward new life, demanding attention, demanding that I listen.

The concert in Fargo is with my trio, and when we arrive at the hall it is late in the afternoon, all of us having come in on the plane, gone to the hotel to check in and unpack. I do my workout and rest for an hour. My work day continues with the sound check at four-thirty.

I go to the dressing room with Maria Pizzuro, my travel assistant, where we touch up my makeup, adjust my hat, and pull out my book of lyrics. Then I go to look for the stage, which can be a journey unto itself.

Sometimes the halls are gymnasiums, or tents, or cathedrals. Some of the best sound I have heard comes out of school auditoriums. At times I dress in a trailer and at times in the opulence of carpeted rooms with full-length mirrors. Tonight's hall is perfect, set in the classic design with the dressing rooms in the right places. At the sound check I talk to the sound man who is working on the show. After I am comfortable with the sound of my voice (I carry my own microphones, having learned over the years never to trust what might be supplied locally), my lighting director and I talk to the personnel at the hall, and I joke with my musicians as we try a new song onstage, to see how it all sounds. Above us the local Fargo crew climbs over the light bars, balancing among the violet and green gels that dangle like space ships over our heads.

After the sound check and local press interviews, I go back to the dressing room, where Maria has set up our home on the road. It is two and a half hours before the show, and we have much to do. Out of the aluminum Halliburton cases, opened up on the floor of the dressing room, has come everything a touring singer could possibly need: needle and thread, gaffer's tape, regular and decaf instant coffee; iron, safety pins, mouthwash, iodine, scissors, slippers, Wash 'n Dri's, Kleenex, steamer, mirror, guitar picks, toothpicks, lipstick, tweezers, Swiss army knife, bottle opener, aspirin, Q-tips, straws, press photos, business cards, black pen for signing autographs, shampoo. I head for the shower that opens off the dressing room.

"Maria," I call, raising my voice to carry over the sound of the running water, "is the nailbrush there?" Maria brings it, handing it to me through the steam-covered glass shower door. I think I could ask Maria if there was a prefab log cabin in the Halliburton, and she would pull it out. When I have finished washing my hair, my dinner has arrived, and while I eat, Maria sets my hair in thirty rollers. I devour baked chicken and steamed vegetables (I have never gotten over being famished on the road) and drink sparkling water. Then I put cream on my face and do my yoga while Maria leaves to have her own dinner. I am alone to continue the quieting that has begun. When she returns, I am sitting in the chair under the hair dryer, meditating, and she begins my makeup. Peace. Centering. On the door, a sign in Spanish and English says DO NOT DISTURB. I am in another world. Maria does her work with competence, and a knock comes at the door, forty minutes before show time. Maria has transformed me, the meditation has centered me. The band comes in and we have a production meeting, determine the sequence of songs, joke a little, connecting before we go out on the stage to connect.

"Shall we do the order from the last concert?" I ask Shelton Becton, my pianist. He is a slim black man of indeterminate age, handsome and extremely talented, who can play Chopin, Marvin Hamlisch, or Collins with equal skill.

"I think we ought to add that new song of yours, 'Dreamin'." It sounded good in the rehearsals, and we haven't done it onstage."

"Fine, let's try it. And I want to ask you about the tempo last night on 'Clowns.' I thought I dragged it a bit. I'll pull it up a little." Warren Odze, my drummer for years, runs his hands through his black curly hair.

"The order was good last night. Let's put 'Dreamin' ' in, but let's keep the flow of it the same. It felt right."

We settle on a new set. Mike Sapsis, my road manager, writes it down, copying everyone, and as they leave the room, Zev Katz, my bass player, tells a joke. I respond with one I heard recently from David Braun about Gloria Steinem. Gloria thought it was funny when I told it to her, so it is all right, even in Fargo. Gloria is taking a plane on which the pilot, the co-pilot, and the flight engineer are all women. She asks the flight attendant if she can come to the cockpit to congratulate the crew.

"Of course, Ms. Steinem, but it is no longer called the cockpit."

The punch line eases our performance nerves, and they dare me to tell it on-stage.

"You know I might, if I feel relaxed enough." My band is a fine group of musicians. Tonight Shelton Becton and Warren Odze are teasing Zev Katz about something that seems to be confidential. I think musicians on the road must be just a little mad. I think I'm a little mad. It's a fragmented life, the life of a gypsy. These musicians are talented, and I tell them so. They leave at seven-thirty, and I begin warming up my voice. I do scales, I say clear vowels, run the voice up and down, a clear *Ah*. I warm up for a half hour, and by the end of that time I have on my lipstick and my stage clothes, my hair combed out. My energy is high and I am eager to be on the stage, doing tonight what I have trained all my life to do.

The moment when I step from the wings onto the stage is a

sacred time, a spiritual journey in which I plunge into an air of lightness, made of the energy of myself and the audience. The audience wants everything, and they deserve everything. They have been there for me from the first night at Michael's Pub, sitting in the dark, waiting to have their lives changed, touched. They have sat in the dark and stood in the rain, marched with me, cried and laughed with me; they greet what I bring them with willingness, never holding back when I have changed again and gone in a new direction. They have grown up and had children and brought their children to hear me—an audience dressed in blue jeans, dressed in silk. They have supported me, bought my records, written letters to me saying that I have changed their lives. They have changed mine. One must not take a night of singing for granted, for the gods may become jealous and take it away. I have my set of rituals and prayers: God, make me good, bless my audience, let me be an instrument. I bring everything I have studied to be and everything I am onto the stage. I am as vulnerable and as prepared as I can possibly be.

When I walk out onto the stage, the audience is usually invisible beyond the footlights; in the shock of light they see me, but I cannot see them. I depend upon hearing and feeling who they are and what they are willing to bring to me tonight. I learned from my father on those nights when I watched him on-stage in cities like Fargo and Butte and Carson City how to sense an audience without seeing them. I learned how to perform at the feet of a master dreamer and gypsy, and now I, too, go on, hauling my bags and my guitar and myself from hotel room to hotel room, from city to city, living out his dream for the joy of these moments on-stage when the actual becomes the mystical.

I stand on the stage in bright, bright light. I am singing "Shoot First," a song I wrote with Dave Grusin about violence and a child's game played in the park by two children. There is electronic music in the background, sirens and bombs, and then a lament by Thomas Moore, "The Minstrel Boy." If the audience is to go through an inner transformation during each song, I must go through it myself, and it is at this point that we are the same, the audience and I. Even from behind the bright lights, I can begin to see the faces, the eyes, the smiles, and I take energy from every pair of eyes. In the carbon arc light I am by myself, and the audience is out there, but we are together, united. I must make the song as fresh and as familiar as though the audience knew it by heart, yet was hearing it for the very first time.

When I sing "My Father," sitting at the piano, very often my eyes are closed, and I think of the vivid details of the song—the Seine, the girls dancing in the light of a dying summer day, chiffon curtains ironed by my mother's hand blowing into the room, drifting in and out, breathing through the windows.

Tonight I am energized. Light as an eagle, I am flying. On-stage, in the bright light of the carbon arc, sometimes I am Piaf, scrawny arms and a black silhouette; sometimes I am Peter Allen in sequins and silk; sometimes John McCormack's spirit comes over me, a clear Irish tenor in tails. I am all of them, none of them; I am myself. I am a singer alone on an empty stage—no guitar, no mike stand—singing a song a cappella from the whalers of the Scottish coast. I sing about the work they did, and the voices of the singing humpbacked whales, played on a tape, fill the auditorium. (In their poignant, calling voices you can hear the slap of the tails on the water and the wind in the big sails of the little ships that followed the Greenland, right, and humpbacked whales from Bermuda to Alaska and back again to Newfoundland.) Now, I am a lovestruck girl with just a guitar telling a story about a rodeo rider and how I would follow him anywhere. Then I sing "Marieke" in Flemish and French. At the piano I then accompany myself and sing in English the story of houses and lovers, then a song by Randy Newman. I love being funny on-stage. I love making people laugh and cry. I am the clown, I am the hero, I am all of these, none of these, I am the music. . . .

Off-stage, lights off, the show over, snowdrift and ice slush under my black high heel shoes (Where are my purple boots now that I need them!), we pack up the gear and change clothes. Maria has everything together now, Halliburtons packed, clothes in the hanging bags. The promoter comes to pick up the Halliburtons. He is absolutely deadpan and sad as he tells me it was a "lovelyshow." I wish he had let me revel in my own excitement instead of almost deflating me with his sullen mood. I am flying, and he sounds like he is on Quaaludes. Tomorrow he has a wrestling team coming in to Fargo.

Back at the Holiday Inn, one of the old motels with a court-yard square in the center, the swimming pool is full of snow, the doors to the rooms opening onto the snow-patched path. In the trees, sleeping birds are stacked, piled, layered. They are roused and begin to chirp and flutter as we pass them on the way to our rooms. I dump my sheepskin coat and my heavy purse, kiss Maria good night, and then I'm on the phone, cotton in my other hand, taking off makeup while I dial New York and Connecticut and wonder where is Louis, why isn't he in? It's late, what can he possibly be doing? I know he went out to dinner tonight with David Braun and Irene Cara. Did he fall in love with Irene Cara—fly the coop?

I try the number again and reach him before I go to sleep. It's so good to hear his voice.

Octopussy on the tube, then a chapter of St. Augustine in paperback. Life on the road. . . .

Living

Wednesday, March 27, 1985 / New York

Home from the cold northern cities, home to more cold. The heavy snowflakes are still falling as I make my way downtown to a lesson with my voice teacher, Max Margulis.

I met Max in 1965, six years after my first job at Michael's Pub and two years after I moved to New York. When I returned from touring Poland and Russia, I decided I needed to find a teacher because at times, if I sang a lot, my voice would become rough and sound tired. I had never studied singing, although the years singing in Dr. Brico's opera choruses and in the church choir had been good training. Max Margulis was recommended to my by Ray Boguslav, a guitarist and pianist who worked with Harry Belafonte, and by Mordecai Bauman, a friend who ran the Indian Hill music camp in the Berkshires.

I called him on the telephone, introduced myself, and he invited me to come by and see him. When he told me his address, I realized that he lived next door to me. Same building. Same floor.

The woman who opened the door was tall and beautiful.

"Hello, I'm Helen, Max's wife," she said. She had long dark hair that was wrapped in a braid on top of her head. She spoke in a clear voice, ushering me past a Chinese screen into a blue-carpeted living room, bright with sunlight. A small man came into the room. His eyes were gray behind his glasses, and he held out a tiny hand, shaking mine.

"I'm glad to meet you," he said. "Ray Boguslav has told me about you." He smiled at the mention of the other people who had recommended him, as though he knew a secret. He was noncommittal at first about whether he would teach me, but then he agreed we should make a start. What I did not know then is that Max does not teach by the hour, but by the lifetime.

Today, twenty years later, when I arrive for a lesson, Helen makes coffee for me while Max drinks his tea and we all stand in the kitchen together, talking (Helen looks so young—how old is anyone?) She leaves the room, and Max and I go to the piano.

"All right," he says, with a musical ring in his voice. At times, he has a crooked, enigmatic frown as he does now when I say I am thinking of going to hear a singer he doesn't particularly like. "Yes?" he says, the voice going up at the end into a question mark.

Max calls what he teaches "clarity." He has taught this clarity to many people, singers, actors, painters, writers. Laurence Olivier, Stacy Keach, Sigourney Weaver, Harris Yulin, Susie Crile. When Olivier came to the States to make *The Beggar's Opera*, he studied with Max. Louis studies with him, and it has changed his whole way of speaking.

This afternoon his eyes are dancing behind his glasses, as he holds his cup of tea in his hand. Papageno, the parakeet, is singing in his cage. "My name is Papageno, do you want to come out?" "Do you want to take a bath?" "Hello, sweetheart," sings the powder blue parakeet. I am trying to teach the bird to say, "Are you a singer or an actor or do you work for Hammacher Schlemmer?"

Max sits down at the piano and I stand in its curve, where I can see his face and the window behind him, with the roofs above Seventy-eighth Street and the birds flying by in snow or rain, on bleak days, or through skies of blue. An ever-changing canopy, they fold behind Max's head. When the sun is out it shines through Max's ears. A Willem de Kooning sketch of Max, finely drawn, hangs on the wall above the piano, a reminder of a long friendship that exists between the two men. The drawing was done when he and de Kooning were both young. De Kooning made the sketch on a dare, when Max told him all his expressionistic work was fine, but that somewhere along the way he had forgotten how to draw.

Max's father was an opera singer in Chicago, and Max came to New York, where he went to City University, wrote music criticism for *Mainstream*, taught singing, and helped start Blue Note Records. Max knew Arshile Gorky well, and a Gorky hangs beside the de Kooning, as do the works of Joe Solman and Susie Crile. There is a watercolor of mine on the shelf by the window. He told me it is good, and I try to trust him.

Max says, "You are singing now, all you have to do is open your mouth and connect with the sound, connect with the already moving tone, without interfering. There should be no noise, no other sound than the vowel that is clear as a bell."

I open my mouth to sing, *"O, mio babbino caro,"* but he stops me before I can go on.

"No, that is not right, try again, make it clear." I begin again, and he interrupts again. "Yes! That is it. That is clear! Can you hear the difference?"

It is a terrible strain to stand there. He has never ended a lesson first. I am always the one. I often feel that if I stay a moment longer, I will faint. I give credit to Max for the voice I have today. It was a long struggle and it still is going on. Clarity, like a Zen riddle, is a simple thing. It is the basis of the ability to move the voice in complete control from the top of the scale to the bottom, with fluidity and grace, without any interfering noise. Clarity ensures understandability of the lyric.

Once Max wrote out a paragraph describing what he teaches, and I came upon it recently in an old journal.

> My attitude—singing is a unitary act involving mental and physical processes efficiently operating as one. Good teaching is an instrument for bringing this about. Although the teaching of technique is basic and exhaustive, it is not an end in itself. Through it the teacher *guides* the singer to hitherto untapped resources of musical and dramatic expression. The singer thus learns technique in order to forget it as it becomes embodied in expressive singing.

It was three years before I was capable of making a simple *ah* sound without cluttering fuzz in the tone. Another five years, and I began to translate this into singing a lyric in which all vowels are clear and no longer stumbling into consonants along the way. When I first went to see Max, I had an octave and three notes of range, all in the lower end of my voice, and I was pushing the notes out, straining all the way. I have two and a half octaves now, with a smooth line from top to bottom.

It has taken every moment of the twenty years I have worked with Max to get me here. I am a better singer than I was when I was twenty because then I didn't know I had that kind of range. I have not been an easy student, nor has he been an easy teacher.

Max had a stroke years ago—before that, he had been a heavy smoker. By the time I met him he had quit smoking his strong cigars. When we work together I can often hear Papageno singing and Helen in the kitchen making dinner or cups of tea for us. Even if Max and I never spoke during these sessions, I would still remember all the lessons we have had together in this room. Max really does not have to say a thing.

At times we have had terrible arguments about my lack of total devotion, and they remind me of such arguments with Dr. Brico. Maybe the tug of war is the price of being the student of a teacher with a vision. I know Max has given me the tools to sing for a lifetime if I want.

Today he tells me, if I keep working, that I might do something spectacular.

I tell Max I am thinking about doing an album of the great sons of the British Isles—perhaps with classical arrangements. Max says, "I've been telling you this for years." I feel my back go up. I'm ready to fight because I resent being told what to do. But at the same time I come to him precisely for this genius. It is a wonder I was able to stay long enough to learn anything. All my life I have studied with people, and it has always been a fight to remain open to teaching. I've made peace with my father; I thought I no longer balked at authority. When will I make peace with Max? I must remember there is no contest here, no one has to win. "Oh, Max," I say, "you're sounding just like my father." And laugh.

Once, at the end of one of our arguments about how much more dedicated I could be if I were really serious, I stood out in the hall, so angry I was shaking. Max put out his hand, reaching for mine. We stood there in the hallway, our hands clasped.

Max said, "Do you feel that heart beating?"

I could feel it pulsing between our hands. Max smiled.

"Is that yours or mine?" he said.

Monday, April 1, 1985 / New York

Dinner with my friend, Virginia Dwan, at Hisae's on Seventy-second Street. Over baked eggplant and chickpeas, Virginia and I talk about her neighbors Yoko and Sean Lennon and about all of our lives in the sixties. Virginia was living her own legend then, and for many years she ran the Dwan Art Galleries in New York and Los Angeles. Virginia is very tall and good looking, with short black hair and long limbs. Eccentric. She comes from Minnesota, where her family was in the mining business. Both of our fathers were named Charlie. We both adored and lost them (too soon) before it was possible to live without them. The "two Charlies" loom in our lives.

After dinner I walk Virginia home to her apartment building, the Dakota, past the spot on the sidewalk in front of the doorman's post where John Lennon lay bleeding to death. When she had gone upstairs, I stood out in the wind on the pavement. It was cold, and I tried to imagine what John Lennon must have felt the moment before he was cut down by that maniac. A fan. A freak. I heard that Yoko ate nothing but chocolate for months after his death, and I was told she did not come out of the Dakota for a year.

People ask if I miss the sixties. I do not. I was filled with misery and pain for many of those years. I went places and did things in a daze.

There are people I miss who were alive then. I miss John Lennon. His mind and imagination were one of the driving forces behind a vision of music that reached out and changed the world. He was one of the Four Horsemen of the Apothecary, bringing "Lucy in the Sky with Diamonds" to us care of the acid express, telling of the joys of expanding our consciousness through love and chemistry. Perhaps it was the fame, or the times, but I was stung by the icy distance he put up; like many who are able to communicate on a universal level, on a personal level he appeared to be cold. But I listened to the music as though it were psychic medicine, and waited for the arrival of each album with great expectation. The Beatles were brilliant, he was brilliant. The music reached a height of creativity and we were all a part of it. But I wouldn't go back.

A year before I recorded the Beatles' song "In My Life," Richard Fariña died. Richard was one of the people I felt closest to in the music world. I felt that he understood the journey I seemed to be on. He didn't laugh at my confusion or my efforts to turn in new directions. I often find his letters scattered through my files, like beacons shining from the past. In one of his last letters to me, dated July 1964, he included these words:

> . . . the private terrors you speak of, stalk us all   the ones who, like yourself, stay on the razor's side of survival. One learns, takes strength, a certain degree of heart. When you've walked a little with death, you learn to court it, play with it, defy it if you choose, because having turned, you possess the choice. What I am saying is that you mustn't be afraid.

We first met in 1962 at a folk festival in Connecticut. He was married to Carolyn Hester then, and I to Peter Taylor. It was a night filled with guitars and banjos, a couple of hundred folk singers gathered in the chilly, rainy September night in a lodge not far from New Haven. The music went on all night, and around midnight, as Peter and I were heading off to bed, Richard corralled us.

"You must come and hear these songs that Carolyn has written, they are so good." He led us to his room, where Carolyn sat in bed, in her nightgown, the guitar across the covers on her lap.

"Hi," she said, smiling, and pulled the covers up over her chin. Carolyn had long reddish hair, and it fanned out around her Texas smile. Her soprano voice was delicate and definite. "Y'all sit down here on the bed."

"Now," said Richard, "isn't this better than standing out there in the rain listening to banjo pickers?" All four of us wound up crowded onto the little bed, and Richard and Carolyn sang us songs in the candlelight, while outside the banjos went on warring in the rain till nearly dawn. I sang a few songs as well, and Peter, although he never sang a note, was the best audience. Richard's pixie face was pleased we were there together, huddled in the room while the rain fell outside, and we were warm with one another's company and the music. I was to have many nights like that with Richard.

In 1964 he married Mimi Baez, and I saw him again when

they were living in Carmel, California. He and Mimi came to my concert there, and once again he spirited me off.

"Come with us, you'll bring your bags and stay overnight," said Mimi, hugging me. "We have plenty of room, you can sleep on the couch."

We drove down the coast to their cabin in the woods above Big Sur, drank California wine out of silver goblets, and I listened to Dick and Mimi sing their own soon-to-be-famous songs. They had a magical sound that was recorded later that year on an album called *Celebration*. In the woods around the cabin the dogs howled; in the fireplace the red and blue flames rose into spires. On the mat in front of the fire, Dick played the dulcimer, Mimi the guitar, and I listened, mesmerized. Then I would sing a song, and they would join me, or hum, or sing sweet, wild harmonies. I slept on the couch that night, and the next morning I left with their singing echoing in my heart.

Richard and Mimi moved to Cambridge, Massachusetts, in 1965, and it was wonderful having them nearby. When they came to town in those years they would often stay with me, and we would roam the streets and the shops of the city, go to parties, listen to music, and sit up talking till all hours of the night. They put me up in their little apartment when I went to sing at Club 47, and they held my hand through the years of my custody hearings, consoling me and talking all night if I asked. Richard wrote some good songs, very sad ones, and one or two funny ones. I recorded one called "Hard Lovin' Loser."

> *He's the kind of guy*
> *Puts on a motorcycle jacket*
> *And he weighs about a hundred and five.*
> *He's the kind of surfer got a ho-daddy haircut*
> *And you wonder how he'll ever survive . . .*
> *But when the frost's on the pumpkin and the*
> *Little girls are jumpin',*
> *He's a hard lovin' son of a gun—*
> *He's got 'em standin' in line,*
> *Just to tell him he's fine,*
> *And they call him a spoon full of fun.*

Once when Peter and I visited Carolyn and Dick on Martha's Vineyard, for what was supposed to be a rest, he met us at the ferry, picking us up in his old car, and drove us around town to look at the signs: JUDY COLLINS, RICHARD FARIÑA AND CAROLYN HESTEN IN CONCERT. I was upset; he was a cat that had swallowed the canary.

"But we always sing when we are together," he said. "I just thought it would be nice to get paid for it, make your expenses for coming here." I had to forgive him. There was something about his gaiety and his easy-wearing of life that charmed me, made me more willing, eager to experience the world and all it offered. I adored him, as one can only adore some people who are never lovers.

Dick was killed in a motorcycle accident in 1966. He had just finished writing his novel, *Been Down So Long It Looks Like Up to Me*, and was at a party to celebrate its publication. It had been a wild and drunken night in Carmel at a friend's house, it was three in the morning, and Dick went for a ride on the back of a motorcycle. Before he got on the bike, he gave Mimi his keys. Mimi never drove because she didn't know how; but he gave her everything from his pockets. The driver lived, miraculously. Dick died instantly.

He is buried in the graveyard in Carmel, in a plot surrounded by willow trees facing the Pacific. I flew out from Denver for his funeral, in a daze of disbelief. Mimi and her older sister Pauline and I spent the night before the funeral cutting one another's hair, half hysterical, in a sort of pagan rite of mourning. We slept little, and in the morning went out to the beach to run the German shepherd, Lush, who had been whining and looking lost; he ran in circles on the beach, barking into the wind. At Dick's graveside we threw white and red roses down on his coffin. It was 1966, the war in Vietnam was getting worse, the protests had begun, all the young singers were raising their voices, and Richard's had been a voice of beauty and sanity in the madness. The music had started and would go on, would have to go on. I knew a lot of those singers, and some were my friends. Richard had been one of the best friends I had among them, and I learned from him a little about courage. I walked away from his grave, chilly and lonely in the crowd of mourners. Good-bye, good-bye.

After he died, I had a dream about him. We ran into each other on the street, in New York. He was wearing a red and black sweater. We talked intensely about writing while we drove uptown in a bright yellow taxi. I told him I had finally started writing songs.

"I'm so happy for you," he said, hugging me hard. He leaped out of the taxi and vanished up the street, looking over his shoulder at me, smiling, his eyes twinkling. I miss him still.

Wednesday, April 3, 1985 / New York

It it still snowing in New York, and today I drove downtown to Greenwich Village, watching the white flakes settle, disappearing into the black water of the Hudson. At my friend Ilana Rubenfeld's studio on Waverly Place, I have a Rubenfeld Synergy session. Ilana and I have known each other for many years. She practices a method that is meant to relax and to realign the body, but she is a healer as well. Once I'm there on the massage table, I let her straighten out my spine and feel my tensions go. In her studio, crystals hang from the ceiling and cast diamonds on the walls, on my face, on Ilana's face. Buddhas sit poised in silence, squat on their pedestals. The room is full of healing and silence. When the session is over, I feel relaxed, refreshed.

Back out on Waverly, I walk down to Washington Square Park, where the wind is bending the trees, blowing the snow into drifts. Last year my old friend David Blue dropped dead of a heart attack while running around this park. He was a singer in the old days of Bleecker Street clubs and West Coast dreams. If we had met today, we would have laughed, and he would have pounded me on the back in the snow and taken me off for a beer at Minetta's, where we would gossip about everybody and not get nostalgic for the old days. Joni Mitchell wrote a song for him; he wrote songs for us and sang them in bars in Greenwich Village when we were young dreamers. Once I visited his little house in Laurel Canyon, and I peeked into the bedroom where he had a narrow single bed. "You're a pessimist, David," I said. He laughed.

"Anyone who stays the night with me has to be able to sleep tight," he said. I don't think David ever lived with anyone very long, with his worn engineering boots that held a gallon apiece, his long curly hair and teddy bear figure. He was very tall and sang in a rich, deep voice.

"You and I are survivors, we just have to keep on singing our songs," he would say. "Nothing can harm us then." I will always think of David Blue as a survivor, even though he is gone.

The same year I met David Blue, 1966, I met Michael Thomas in England. By now I had been divorced for two years and lost custody of Clark. Michael came to the cocktail party given for me by Elektra after I released my fifth album in London. He was a Welsh writer who had spent time in Australia. He had curly hair and the smile of an imp. He told me that he had come to hear my Conway Hall concert the night before.

"You are the best there is at what you do, and that is as much as any of us can expect," he said. Flatterer. That was the most he ever said about my work. We woke up together at the Strand Palace in London, on Passion Sunday, March 27, 1966. We went to the Tate Gallery to look at the Blakes and drank strong tea with his other Down-Under expatriate friends, walked miles around London, ate Indian food in tiny restaurants on Piccadilly Square, saw plays in the Haymarket, and met a famous forger in the lobby of a West End theater. We drank pints of bitter and laughed on the trains to the English Midlands, where I did concerts in halls for cheering audiences of distant relatives.

I could never get a straight story from him of who he really was—a writer, a vapor, or a dream I had materialized.

"That is so American, to want to know the details," he would say as he fabricated yet another version of his parents' life in Wales. Once they invented the seat belt and once they were simple farmers. We went to a tiny suburb of London to visit his grandmother, who was sweet and had a garden. She was the only family member I was to meet.

He took me to the airport after my two weeks in England. As I waved back at him, smiling and holding my bouquet of flowers, my bags of books, by the customs gate, he yelled across the heads of my fellow travelers, "I'll see you in a few days." I came home from London with a taste for bitter and his promise to follow me. I was sure he would not come to America. But he did. In two weeks he was in New York and in my life.

Although I wouldn't describe our situation as living together, Michael settled himself into my apartment. He was a vagabond, always on the move. I didn't really intend to live with anyone after having finally disentangled myself from my marriage. But Michael and I got along well, and at a desk in a huge cedar closet of one of the bedrooms, he set out his dictionary and began to write his novel. When we were both in town, we roamed New York together, as we had London, and went to parties and laughed and drank. He said he hated New York, but he didn't leave.

"New York is like a vaccination against Western civilization. The filth and decadence will make me a better person," he would say.

Michael made his living writing about the New York music scene for newspapers in London and Australia. Often when I was home from touring, we went to the Fillmore East and hung out in Greenwich Village, at the Bitter End, the Café Wha, the Gaslight, and Max's Kansas City. We listened to Phil Ochs and Tom Paxton and Joni Mitchell and Dave Van Ronk and Frank Zappa. We went to the Newport and Philadelphia music festivals.

In May 1966, as I was working on my album, *In My Life*, I came down with hepatitis and had to spend three weeks recuperating in Lenox Hill Hospital. I put the typewriter and the tape recorder on the bed and worked on the songs from Peter Brook's production of *Marat/Sade*, which I planned to record. Michael visited me, bringing blank tapes and typewriter paper.

When I was well, I went to Los Angeles to do a concert with Arlo Guthrie at the Hollywood Bowl, and afterward Michael and I went to Colorado and lived in a cabin on a ranch in the mountains for six weeks. Clark came to stay for the better part of the summer.

In 1965 Peter had taken a job teaching at the University of British Columbia in Vancouver, so my visits with Clark had become less frequent, and phone calls were the most regular contact we had. When we did have our vacations together, I would sometimes lie awake with the thought of myself as an inadequate parent gnawing at me. Even more than I had been before, I was the "other parent."

But the visit with Clark that summer in Colorado was one of the best times. Clark rode horseback like a real westerner, taught in the summers by his father and me, with his skinny fanny glued to the saddle, his body at one with the animal, as though he had been born to it. He was really growing up, with his gangly arms and legs getting longer, and his freckles more dense with the summer sun. My love and my feeling of closeness were always there for this boy growing up away from me, in another city, and now another country. In spite of our distance we were always close. Having him with me was wonderful. It eased my feelings of unworthiness. And despite our less frequent visits, I was more aware than ever of the connection I had with him.

Linda Leibman came out from New York to be with us, and all of us hiked, taking Clark on trips into the wilderness. Michael Thomas had never been on a horse and he learned to ride well, and John Denver came to stay with us for a week. Sitting in front of the potbellied stove at night, he and I sang duets, Beatles songs, old love songs. We had a good version of "Here, There, and Everywhere" that we still promise to record someday. John Denver, Clark, Michael, Holly, Linda, and I all rode horses together. We had a western interlude, and pretended to be Welsh, Irish, and Jewish cowboys.

My brother Michael, who was now twenty-seven, was married that year. He came to the mountains to visit with his bride, Susan. He was studying to become a doctor of speech pathology in Denver. Brother David, twenty-four, was living in the mountains, skiing and building houses. Denver John, my youngest brother, had moved to New York to seek his fortune. They all visited us that summer. One day Denver John and John Denver stood out in front of the cabin and laughed very hard at their reversed names.

That summer, we went backpacking in to Thunder Lake and the Lake of Many Winds. We drove to Trail Ridge and stood at the very top of the continental divide, looking down on the lakes that lie in the arms of the mountains like so many emeralds in the pines, trying to decide which one was Fern Lake.

At the end of the summer, when Clark had gone back to Vancouver and everyone else had scattered, Michael and I took a trip to Aspen, where we stayed with my old Colorado friend Lyle Taylor, who was working at the Aspen Institute for the summer. One night, after coming home late with Lyle and his house guest, David Hockney, we heard a woman being murdered across the street. Her screams ripped through the mountain air as we stood on the porch, our heads bent in the direction of the jagged sounds. It was over in a breath.

Lyle ran to the phone to call the police.

"Too late, she's dead," said Hockney.

We started down the stairs, heading for the house opposite, where the silence now roared. Before we reached the road, the police car pulled up, its red and white lights turning while the sirens poured out their own mangled sound across the town, waking everyone under Ajax Mountain. We saw the police enter the house. It was three in the morning, and we went to bed not knowing what had happened. The next day, over coffee, we read the papers. The woman had been in bed with her lover, and her husband had surprised them in the room. He then stabbed her to death, and wounded the other man and himself.

"Love is powerful in America," said Michael. He told me he would write it into his novel. He finished an article on Susan Sontag and his paper in London sent it back, asking him to revise it. Maybe that night wouldn't make it into print after all.

Michael went around the world that year on a trip that lasted for months, and I went to Japan with Arlo Guthrie and Mimi Fariña on a concert tour. It was Mimi's first trip out of the country after Richard's death. Mimi and I sang Pete Seeger's song, "Oh, Had I a Golden Thread":

> *Oh, had I a golden thread,*
> *And needle so fine,*
> *I'd weave a magic strand*
> *Of rainbow design,*
> *Of rainbow design*

Mimi was a dancer as well as a singer, and she twirled in a flying silk skirt while Bruce Langhorne played the guitar for her. Bruce played for me and Arlo as well.

Dressed in a long white shirt and pants, Arlo sang his own songs and played the harmonica, and the Japanese seemed to love us. In Tokyo the audience went absolutely wild—the university students understood that Americans love to have a lot of noise from their already loving audiences. They spoiled us for the tranquility of the audiences in the smaller cities whose appreciation was more sedate. Irene Zaks, my friend and Harold Leventhal's assistant, traveled with us, arranging transportation and meals and talking to the Japanese promoters. We visited Nagasaki and Hiroshima and went to the peace museums. We met survivors of the atomic bomb, valiant workers for nuclear disarmament who wage their war of hope against hopelessness. I found their cheer, their warmth, uncanny in light of their experiences. Arlo, Mimi, and I sang our songs of peace for them.

"Would it be possible for us to have seats by the window?" Irene would say to our Japanese guide as we boarded the speeding train from Tokyo to Osaka.

"*Hi, hi,*" Tats-San replied, bowing nearly to the platform outside the train. *Hi* means *yes* in Japanese. Once on the train, we would find we were seated on the aisles.

"Can you arrange for the women to have a tour of the mountain this afternoon, please?" Irene's beautiful jaw began to set in a hard line.

"*Hi, hi,*" our guide would say, bowing deeply, and Mimi, Irene, and I would sit for the afternoon, waiting for our guides, who never materialized with the promised tour. It was the same for many things, and we began to understand that yes can mean no at least half the time. I thought the problem was that three of us were women who thought we were in charge. I later came to think that it was partly cultural politeness; they did not wish to offend us or embarrass themselves by saying something was not possible.

I adored Japan, despite the cultural difference between yes and no—like yin and yang. Our guides had a plan, and we were dutifully shown everything that was in the schedule or on the itinerary. Next to the Imperial Japan Hotel, a creation of Frank Lloyd Wright, was a Zen garden where Mimi and I wandered in mutual silence between the black rocks on the combed white sand. We ate sushi and Japanese noodles in little shops in Tokyo, the very best at the very cheapest prices, and slept on tatami mats in Matsuyama-by-the-Sea. We took hot baths in the stone quarries near a palace in Tokyo, where Irene amazed me by stepping unembarrassed into an integrated hot tub, along with a dozen old Japanese men, without batting an eye or attempting to cover her very Western, voluptuous body. I struggled with the towel, making do with a soak to the knees until the Japanese left, giggling openly at the Americans.

We met a man named David Kid and his friend Muri-Moto, who ran a Japanese cultural school and collected Oriental art. They prepared a traditional meal for us in the royal carriage house in which they lived, and let us dress up in the costumes of ancient Orientals. Mimi looked splendid, like a Japanese princess, in her headdress and three-inch fingernails; when Arlo donned the embroidered silk robes of a king, he assumed the stature of a fourteenth-century Japanese and spoke with royal authority. I was sure he would have been a fierce balladeer to his royal subjects.

Mimi, Arlo and I stopped in Hawaii for a few days on our return trip. Alone on the beach, the water washing up on my legs, I thought about the dark dreams I had started to record in my notebook. It was the first time I had written since high school, and I decided that these somber poems might be songs. I was determined to set them to music when I returned to New York.

When I returned from my trip, I didn't begin writing songs until after the bizarre sensations I had one afternoon on Long Island, in 1967, when I took my second acid trip.

I had taken acid once, in 1963, in New York's East Village at John and Michelle Phillips' tiny apartment. That time had been a frightening trip. I watched the lamp make spiders on the wall and Michelle's fingers turn into spaghetti. I drew a picture of a dog that looked like a painting by Munch. I had to drink a quart and a half of bourbon to come down and swore I would never take another acid trip.

But here I was again. I was like a rider on a horse that I know has had a bur put under the saddle; knowing it seemed to make the event more frightening but exciting. I wasn't very sure of my sanity, as it was, and the acid might put me over the edge. On the other hand, perhaps this time it would turn out differently. I was always willing to gamble for the ride.

Michael, John Cooke, and I drove out to John's family home on the north shore of Long Island. I had known John, "Cookie," since the first few times I had gone to Cambridge in 1960. Cookie used to play the mandolin and guitar with the Charles River Valley Boys. He's a writer, a connoisseur, a raconteur, and the son of Alistair Cooke. He's also quite a good photographer. The Cooke family home, with its forests of pine and beaches of stones and silvery water, was a perfect place to take my psychedelic journey. It was in the middle of February, the beaches were cold and deserted, the air was crystal clear. I cooked a roast for dinner and dropped my capsule.

In the afternoon light the stones and the birds spoke to me and told me everything I would need to know in life. They promised the bougainvillea would become so impossibly purple in the spring. I wandered through the woods and stood in the open fields. It was very cold. We drove to the main beach near Orient Point and walked down what seemed a million steps to the sea, and sat there till the light left every stone. The darkness became so black that we could not see the water moving and we felt our way back to the car. We had lost our keys somewhere on the beach below, so we walked back to the house on the dark roads with our eyes blinded by the headlights of the oncoming traffic. When we reached the house, I was going mad again. I began yelling and ran out on the lawn in front of the water. I sat with my head in my hands and my arms wrapped around my body for a long time. Perhaps all night. I was afraid I might never come back.

After that I wrote my first song, when I was twenty-seven. It was called "Since You Asked."

> What I'll give you since you asked is all my time together;
> Take the rugged, sunny days, the warm and Rocky weather,
> Take the roads that I have walked along,
> Looking for tomorrow's time, peace of mind.
> As my life spills into yours, changing with the hours
> Filling up the world with time, turning time to flowers,
> I can show you all the songs
> That I never sang to one man before.
> We have seen a million stones lying by the water.
> You have climbed the hills with me to the mountain shelter,
> Taken off the days one by one,
> Setting them to breathe in the sun.
> Take the lilies and the lace from the days of childhood,
> All the willow winding paths leading up and outward,
> This is what I give,
> This is what I ask you for;
> nothing more.

I am so grateful that I don't have to take another acid trip as long as I live.

John Cooke later went to work as Janis Joplin's road manager. It was he who found her dead from a drug overdose in a Los Angeles hotel room in 1970. I only saw Janis Joplin once, in the bar of the Troubadour, a folk and rock music club in Los Angeles, on a night when she and I were both very drunk. Janis's raw energy and stretched, pained agony both repelled me and drew me in. She was on a wild wire like mine, but her act was very different. Like Karl of the Flying Wallendas she was way out there, with no net. Janis once said in an interview that of the two of us, she thought I would be the one to make it. I wondered if she meant I would just stay alive. She sang herself hoarse and was known for swilling Southern Comfort. She shouted her story and spilled it out into the world with an abandon that had genius in it, barring no holds. Every secret was laid bare, every hair on her head belonged to us. I sought a far more private hell and haven from the storm.

She once said, "Don't compromise yourself, you're all you've got." I pinned her words up on a bulletin board, and for years they caught my eye as I came up for air from my own troubled journey, passing them on the way to coffee in the morning, catching them out of the corner of my eye as I plunged toward another night of tangled drama. Though Southern Comfort was the last thing I'd drink, by the time Janis died I was doing whatever I thought I needed to get me through the night. It was fashionable, perhaps even required, for the interesting lives all of us were leading. I have often thought that Janis knew we were the same and were both burning out, she at the greater speed and with a bomb, not an inferno. I was lucky and lived, I was touched on the shoulder, I was pulled from the wreck before it blew.

Whales and Nightingales

Friday, April 5, 1985 / Boston, backstage at Symphony Hall

Concert night at Symphony Hall in Boston. Sound check goes well. The piano is great, the hall sounds marvelous. Symphony Hall is in the tradition of Carnegie Hall in New York, built the old-fashioned way, with the right ideas about materials, design, and sound.

We are nearly sold out, there are only a few tickets left. Tonight is Passover, and Good Friday as well.

I had the same room at the Ritz last night that Louis and I shared the night of a great snowstorm in 1983. Our separate planes had both been diverted to Boston from New York. I was bound from Austin, and he was headed home from San Francisco. It was a fairytale weekend. The whole New England coast was under snow, and outside the windows of our corner suite, the old gas streetlamps in the Public Garden looked like jewels in the flying flakes. All the trees were hung with winter wraps of swans' down, like Queen Anne's lace, or opals.

But now spring is here, and that same park is a garden of yellow forsythia, pale greens, and white and pink dogwoods.

Wednesday, April 10, 1985 / New York

Dinner with the Romes tonight. Nedda and Josh Logan are there and Joe Machlis, Kitty Carlisle Hart, Philip Hamburger, and Regina Resnik. Harold Rome is one of the great writers of American musical theater. He has written wonderful songs and the shows for forty years. *I Can Get It for You Wholesale, Wish You Were Here, Fanny, Pins and Needles, Destry Rides Again, Call Me Mister.* Josh Logan, his friend and producer, was one of the great theater and film directors of his time. He is seventy-eight and has been very ill. Nedda Logan is eighty-five. They still go on the road together, traipsing around the country to do shows. If they can do it at their age, I cannot have any complaints.

Florence Rome is my second mother, my New York mother. Harold is in rare form tonight, telling theater stories and jokes. He and Florence look younger than ever.

The friendship of the Romes and the Logans has survived some difficult times. Josh Logan once took Harold's musical score for *Fanny* and turned it into a movie. After he finished shooting the picture, there was a big cast party to celebrate the event. Harold was sitting at the piano, playing and singing the songs from Fanny. Maurice Chevalier, who was one of the stars in the movie, put his arm around Harold and said, "Monsieur Rome, it is a terrible tragedy that those beautiful lyrics of yours will not be in the movie; they are so elegant, so descriptive, so, *Je ne sais quoi*—so good!" Harold went on playing the piano, so as not to spoil the party, and then left. He didn't speak to Josh Logan for two years. Tonight Josh and Harold are telling stories like old warriors who have lived through the toughest battles and survived as friends. I need to hear that friendships can suffer and recover from such wounds.

Thursday, April 15, 1985 / New York

"It's what you learn after you know it all that counts," I heard recently. This morning I found a letter in an old and dusty box, tied with a lavender ribbon, from my first shrink, Ralph. The letter is addressed "Dear daughter."

Ralph Klein practiced what he called the Sullivanian therapy, and I fell into the Sullivanian "group" quite by accident. One of the top singers in the radio and television jingle business in New York in those days was a friend of Walter Raim's, a six-foot, barrel-chested man named Bob Harter, who was the voice of Ajax, the foaming cleanser, and sang about floating the dirt right down the drain, ba-ba-ba-ba-ba-ba. Bob mentioned Ralph Klein and recommended that I talk to him.

When I started therapy with Ralph in 1963, I wouldn't have known a Freudian from a botanist or a Sullivanian from a scream therapist. I only knew that I was in pain and wanted out.

Sullivanian therapy is an interpersonal therapeutic approach developed by Saul Newton and his wife, Jane Pierce, in the fifties in New York, and is based on the work of Harry Stack Sullivan. Jane and Saul's book, *Conditions of Human Growth*, put forward ideas of nonconformity: get away from the nuclear family, develop your interpersonal relationships with your peers (including sex, if you feel like it), and get out of the box that society puts you in, whatever that might be. At the beginning, the Sullivanian colony of therapists patterned itself after Sullivan's early thinking, but as time went by, the colony developed its own clear and distinct outline. Although the therapy may have owed something to Sullivan's work, in the end it would probably have caused Sullivan to roll over in his grave.

"Why have you come to see me?" Ralph Klein asked at my first session, sitting in his Mies van der Rohe chair.

I was experiencing severe anxiety attacks and had been given a prescription for Miltown by a general practitioner at New York Hospital. But my depressions had increased.

"I'm terribly depressed."

"We will find out about your relationship with your mother and father, we will look at your childhood, your dreams. Anything else you can tell me?"

"I think I drink too much." I liked to drink, plain and simple. But I had already realized that I had a different relationship with alcohol than most people seemed to. I used it more regularly than I thought might be healthy.

"That, you shouldn't worry about. It can't hurt you." He smiled. I was relieved. "Sometimes a drink can relax you, and it's better than taking drugs. Let's get started on who you are, where you came from. We will solve these temporary problems." We were to have the same conversation for another seven years.

Michael Thomas, with his disdain for things American, thought therapy was absurd, another one of those U.S. inventions of which he was always suspicious.

"You're addicted to therapy, Judy," he would say. I suspected he was right. I had to solve a problem, and I didn't know what it was, but maybe Ralph did. I hadn't spoken to anyone about the turmoil I was in—leaving my marriage, making a choice that was so different from the choice my mother had made. Peter's taking Clark had left me vulnerable emotionally.

I hadn't yet established those dialogues of the heart with women friends that have now become nourishing, the stuff of friendship and living. I needed to talk to someone, and gradually, as if he were telling a child how to spell or to add numbers, Ralph instructed me in the process of making friends, reaching out. I did it, feeling awkward, as I had when I tried to dance at the Sweetheart Prom. I wasn't very good at it, but I did it because he said it would make me feel better, and after a time, I didn't hurt as much.

In Ralph's waiting room, I would often meet other patients. Many of them were painters, and I asked him who they were and if he had been seeing them for long. He said he had, and that Jackson Pollock had been one of the people he had wanted most to help.

"Creative artists have many problems, and sometimes they must relieve the psychic pain in which they find themselves," he said. He told me about Jackson's death. "He ran his car into a tree on Long Island, killing himself and wounding the passenger in the car." Ralph shook his head angrily. "He had great resistance to therapy, but we were making progress!"

Ralph encouraged his patients to get to know one another, introducing them without embarrassment. I met other therapists in the Sullivanian community and became friendly with a number of them, including Saul Newton and Jane Pierce, who were in their sixties. The Sullivanians challenged social codes, attracted talented people, and gave a support system to the lives of people who were breaking society's rules; I found them supportive of my own political viewpoints. They all deplored the war in Vietnam, were nonconformist and antiestablishment.

While undergoing treatment, it is common to become emotionally attached to one's therapist. I had a very strong transference with Ralph, although I wouldn't have known what "transference" meant at the time. He was a good-looking, comfortable man, who dressed in soft jackets and courduroy trousers and wore no tie at the necks of his washed-out, checkered shirts. In 1964, after I had been seeing him for a year, he was leaving for the city for his summer vacation.

"Why don't you come out to the beach for a couple of sessions in August?" He would be at his Amagansett house, with his three children and the housekeeper. On my way into the office, I would often see two young children playing in the other part of the house. Ralph was Jewish, but the two babies were Mexican. He didn't seem to be married, and had another son of his own who was about five at the time we started therapy. "You could take the bus out, have your sessions, stay for the weekend, and go back to the city on Monday."

It sounded fine to me, and I made my plans for my first trip to Long Island. I can think of few things less inviting than getting a suntan with your shrink. But that summer I was desperately lonely, so I traveled out to Ralph's beach house on the bus, convinced he had invited me there to have his way with me. It would have been fine. I was crazy about him, new to therapy, and under the impression that behind his very professional, serious manner toward me in the office he must be attracted to me as well. As I rode past the potato fields and the duck farms, I fantasized a Tom Jones weekend, lots of lusty sex, intense discussions of *The Story of O*, and becoming the adopted mother of three children, two Mexican and one Jewish. By the time Ralph picked me up at the bus station in Amagansett, I expected him to sweep me into his arms and say, "Darling, you're finally here!"

"Hi" was the extent of his greeting, accompanied by a chaste handshake. We hefted my small bag into his car, and I said hello to the children.

The rest of the Sullivanian colony, and many of their patients, had summer places all along the beach near Amagansett, and Ralph pointed them out as we drove. The way they were living, in a community, had a great appeal to me. All over the country, people were looking for ways in which they could come together. Living communally was one way to help counteract the isolation of living in a city. I thought the Sullivanians had solved the problem rather well.

"I think we'll go get settled at the house, have some lunch, and then I'll leave you to your own devices for the afternoon. We can have our session before dinner, if that will be all right." Heathcliff he wasn't, Rhett he wasn't. I had my session that afternoon and slept alone in the guest room. The next morning, he took me over to show me the beach and we rowed to a little island in the Amagansett Sound, and I thought there might be still a reprise of my lovely dream, but he simply got out of the boat, pointed to a building on the opposite shore, and said, "I always wondered why they called that the fish factory. They don't make fish, it's a cannery, they process fish. So why do they call it the fish factory?"

Even with therapy, my anxiety attacks would often leave me shaking and sweating, convinced I was going to die from food poisoning, or loss of sleep, or from the fear itself. Ralph couldn't prescribe drugs, but there were always doctors who would. He told me pills didn't mix with alcohol, and probably saved me from an overdose.

By 1966, I was twenty-seven. My career was going well: Harold Leventhal was managing me, I was doing dozens of concerts a year. I was on the road a lot, hustling from Los Angeles to London to Calgary, doing concerts and television shows and making records. At home in the city, Dahlia, my housekeeper, cooked big batches of peas and rice, cleaned the apartment, took care of my cats, Jam and Moby, and loved fussing over Clark when he came for visits. He and I roamed the city at these times, haunting the Museum of Natural History and going to the Empire State Building. Clark and Ralph Klein's son Josh, who was just the same age, became friendly, so Clark had a buddy in New York. I began to have some friends in New York and really felt that it was home.

I met Leonard Cohen in 1966, when my Canadian friend Mary Martin arranged for us to meet. Leonard had been a published and successful writer and poet for many years, and had recently written his first songs. He came down from Canada one night, and I listened to his songs in my living room. He sang "Suzanne" and "Dress Rehearsal Rag" that night, sitting on the couch, holding the guitar on his knee. I was moved by his singing voice, and by the songs, and by his whole presence. There was something very ethereal and at the same time earthy about his voice. When **Leonard sang,** I was entranced. I became immediately devoted to him, and we soon were friends.

I often saw Leonard when he came to New York. He would check into the Chelsea Hotel on Twenty-third Street, and we would have tea together and walk around Greenwich Village. I recorded "Suzanne" and "Dress Rehearsal Rag" on *In My Life* in 1966, and it went gold in 1967. With the record's success, Leonard became known as a songwriter. I suggested he make his debut and sing in public, but he was terribly shy. I knew once he got over his fear, he would be powerful on stage. I was going to appear at a concert for Sane against the Vietnam War at Town Hall, on April 30, 1967. I asked Leonard if he would sing "Suzanne" there.

"I can't do it, Judy, I would die from embarrassment."

"Leonard, you are a great writer and a fine singer, people want to hear you." He finally agreed, reluctantly.

When I introduced him, he walked onto the stage hesitantly, his guitar slung across his hips, and from the wings I could see his legs shaking inside his trousers. He began "Suzanne," with the hushed audience leaning forward in their seats; he got halfway through the first verse and stopped.

"I can't go on," he said, and left the stage, while the audience clapped and shouted, calling for him to come back.

"We love you, you're great!" Their voices followed him backstage, where he stood with his head on my shoulder, my arms around him.

"I can't do it, I can't go back." He smiled his handsome smile. He looked about ten years old. His mouth drew down at the sides, he started to untangle himself from his guitar strap. I stopped him, touching him on the shoulder.

"But you will," I said. He shook himself and drew his body up and put his shoulders back, smiled again, and walked back onto the stage. He finished "Suzanne," and the audience went wild. He has been giving concerts ever since.

I have loved and recorded so many of his songs—"Sisters of Mercy," "Joan of Arc," "Priests," "Hey, That's No Way to Say Goodbye," "Famous Blue Raincoat," "The Story of Isaac," "Suzanne," "Take This Longing," and "Dress Rehearsal Rag." His songs carried me though dark years like mantras or stones that you hold in your hand while the sun rises or the fire burns. They kept me centered as I stood in front of thousands of people, my eyes closed, my hands around the neck of a guitar, my voice singing his ethereal lyrics. The audience responded to his writing, the songs were like water to a person dying of thirst. They were songs for the spirit when our spirits were strained to the breaking point.

I met some extraordinary people through Leonard Cohen, some of whom became close friends. He introduced me to Yafa Lerner, a woman who was an actor and became a potter and edited my *Songbook.* And Leonard introduced me to Nancy Bacal. Nancy is a redhead; a writer and an adventurer, she had studied acting at the London Academy of Music and Dramatic Art, produced radio shows, and when I met her had just produced *Raga,* a film about Ravi Shankar. In 1966, Nancy was moving to New York from London, where she had emigrated after leaving Canada. We became neighbors on the Upper West Side, sharing our love of cats and conversation, our traumas and our tears, and continued to do so for years. While she was living in London, Nancy had become friends with Michael Malik, who was called Michael X and was one of the leaders of the black civil rights movement in the British Isles. Michael was from the West Indies, and I had Nancy introduce me to him. I was interested in his civil rights work in the United Kingdom, and how it related to what was going on in the United States. I met him on my second trip to England.

We had tea in the Northumberland Hotel one rainy afternoon. I found him to be a ruggedly handsome and gracious man. He told me he expected, like the man whose surname he had taken, to die a violent death. Even some blacks in England were against him, as they were against Malcolm X. Michael Malik, like Malcolm X, had discovered in his spiritual journeys that he was dedicated to humanity.

"Our problem now is to understand that we are all the same color under the skin," he said, "the color of blood."

Michael's charismatic voice spoke for the civil rights of West Indian blacks in England, but he became the bad boy of English black-white relations. He was the scapegoat, and soon, according to the press and the government, he was to blame for anything that went wrong in race relations. In the early seventies, he was arrested on a trumped-up charge while visiting Trinidad. Leonard Cohen, John Lennon, I, and many others were writing letters and campaigning to save his life, but a jury in Trinidad convicted him, without defense, of political treason and sentenced him to death. The day of his execution, as dawn approached, I was on the phone to the jail from New York, trying to talk to the guards, then to the administrative personnel. Just before daybreak, I was put on hold. As dawn came in Trinidad, Michael Malik was hanged by the neck.

I continued my therapy with Ralph Klein, seeking continuity in my otherwise fragmented life. Talking to him about my fears and my emptiness seemed to help. That year I took Clark to Expo '67, Montreal's World Fair. We rode the sleek high-speed train out to the fairgrounds, stood ten deep in line, watched five-story-high movies, bought cotton candy, and wandered among the exhibits, treasuring our precious time together.

At home in New York, Ralph and I often agreed that if one could do something for other people, one's own inner world would be healed as well. My friendships with women began to fill the gap of loneliness in my life at this time, and the political work I did eased my own sense of isolation.

Woody Guthrie died that year, after being hospitalized for ten years with Huntington's chorea. Since Harold Leventhal was very close to Woody, I was often with Arlo, his son, and Marjorie Guthrie, his exceptional, energetic wife. She formed a foundation to combat Huntington's and to continue the fight against the disease that had killed her husband and threatened the lives of her children.

The war in Indochina intensified, and in 1967, Hanoi was bombed by the United States. The largest demonstration against the war so far took place that year in Washington at the Lincoln Memorial, gathering 50,000 people who were of one voice against our continued involvement in Vietnam.

The impact of women singers made up an enormous part of the popular folk music in the early sixties. As I look back, I can count fifteen women folk singers, and have probably forgotten a dozen more. We were doing many kinds of music. In addition to Ethel Raim, with whom I and others made a fund-raising record for Women Strike for Peace, I knew Cynthia Gooding, who was on Elektra when I made my first record; I had been buying her records and learning her songs since my days in Colorado. Bonnie Dobson, with her gentle voice, was a quiet singer of long, beautiful ballads. I would see Carolyn Hester before she was married to Richard Fariña, and afterward as well. We shared gossip and drinks after shows in the Village and at festivals. Jean Ritchie played the dulcimer and lived out on Long Island with her husband, George Pickow. Joan Baez was from Boston and had made her first record in 1960, and her sister, Mimi Baez Fariña, had also become known.

There was Jo Mapes, Judy Henske, and of course, Ronnie Gilbert, who had been with the Weavers for many years. Ronnie embodied our idea of the passionate female singer; she sang in a vibrant and personal way, inspiring me with her thrilling alto voice. Later on, Joni Mitchell came down from Canada to add the poetic luster of her songs to our musical lives. I heard Miriam Makeba at the Shadows in Georgetown; she was dressed in an elegant muumuu, singing in the "click" language of her native South Africa. Janis Ian was the baby, whose songs of growing up a dreamer and female were to make "Seventeen" a call of feminism and yearning; there were Lucy and Carly Simon, and Maria Muldaur, who had such zest when she sang!

Joan Baez had the first really commercial success, getting public exposure, followed by Mary Travers, as she sang and spoke out in the trio with Peter and Paul. And Buffy Sainte-Marie became quite well known. The essence of our individual presences, our diversity, provided a richness to the folk music revival.

One of these women who had a great impact on my writing and my musical sensibilities was Joni Mitchell. Hers was a lyric background, infused with the western familiarity of the Canadian Rockies, echoing my own memory of the speech and music of Colorado and the West Coast. Her experience as a woman came through in her writing, and this autobiographical form affected me deeply and served as a catalyst for my own work.

The first time I heard "Both Sides Now" was on the phone in 1967 during the middle of the night. I got a call from Tom Rush, who was very excited. Tom, a great fan of Joni's, had earlier introduced me to her and to her fine song "The Circle Game."

"Joni has a new song, and I want you to hear it. I think you'll love it." He put Joni on the phone, and she sang "Both Sides Now."

I immediately fell in love with the song and knew it was a

classic. I had to sing it. On September 28, 1967, I recorded "Both Sides Now" at Columbia Studios in New York, with Josh Rifkin conducting his arrangement and playing the harpsichord.

My producer, Mark Abramson, and I had made a very unusual decision about *Wildflowers*, my seventh album, on which I recorded "Both Sides Now." We had used a couple of Josh Rifkin's arrangements on the preceding album, in addition to Richard Peaslee's arrangement of "Marat/Sade," and now we decided to do an album that was entirely orchestral.

"Both Sides Now" became my first hit single, going onto the pop charts in 1968, and *Wildflowers* received the second of my Grammy nominations.

One night in April that year, Joni and I had dinner together in her apartment on the East Side and talked about triumph and disaster.

"Both are imposters," she said. We had been in the music business since the early sixties, and each of us had complex and painful things in our past lives, before coming to the big cities and the bright lights. Joni had been living in New York for about as long as I had, having come down from Canada to find her fortune after separating from her husband, Chuck, with whom she had done a lot of singing in folk music clubs in Canada and the United States. Joni's apartment was filled with candles and crystals and velvet tapestries, a long way from log houses and mountain winds. She prepared chicken and salad, and we ate our meal sitting at a low table.

"How do you live in this filthy city? I can't stand it anymore, I'm going west." Her face was pale and lean, and her fingers held the long-stemmed glass in front of the candle so that the light shone through the wine, making patterns in the room and on our faces.

"New York is all too tight, too crowded, too cramped," she said.

"What saves me now is writing," I said. I had just written my first songs, "Since You Asked," "Albatross," and "My Father."

From the pages of my diary, out of the painful poetry I had begun to write, came the lyrics. The most natural place for me to write music was not on the guitar, but at the piano, where I had spent my childhood seeking comfort in the melodies, and the day I wrote my first song, I sat at the piano, looking for surcease. As my fingers wandered over the keys, the thoughts from the deepest part of my being filtered out into melodies and words that came at the same time. "Since You Asked," from visions of the sea on Long Island that day during my acid trip; "Albatross," from a visit I paid to friends in a house by the sea in Carmel. The sound of iron wheels rolling down the hills into the sea had come to me there, the view of the trance and the isolation of the troubadour, images spilling out from years of Mozart, from thoughts of my marriage gone awry, from the view of the world outside and what I knew of inner loneliness.

I always seemed to relate to Canadians. When I met Leonard Cohen, I showed him my dark poetry with great apprehension.

"If I can write songs, so can you," he said. I trusted him. He didn't tell me how painful it would be at times, but he never lied to me.

"Nobody would believe you could live in New York City and write those songs," said Joni. The cover picture of me on *Wildflowers*, in a field of yellow blossoms, would perpetuate the idea that I still lived in an acre of daisies somewhere in the West.

"I have the feeling that if I moved to the West, I would lie down and never get up," I said. "New York keeps me moving, running, looking behind me to see if I am still in the race."

Joni smiled and pulled out her guitar, wrapped her long fingers around its neck. "My newest song is about that feeling of being chased, and not knowing by whom, or by what, but just having to stay as far in front as possible, trying never to look back. It's called 'The Midway.' "

Joni's songs are delicate and tough and feminine and strong, like she is, and they always reached the part of my western soul that all these years of living in New York have left intact. I cried, as I usually do when I hear her songs.

"You can break my heart anytime you like," I said. "Just open your mouth and sing."

When Joni moved to Los Angeles that year, I was sad to see her go. I'd spend time with her in Laurel Canyon when I visited Los Angeles, and I gave her my calico kitten, the first kitten from Jam's litter, because Joni believed that calicos are good luck.

Joni and I often had shared our thoughts on work and lovers, and on one of my visits to Los Angeles she sang for me "Jealous Lovin' Can Make You Crazy," a song about the price of freedom, and I responded by singing her my own latest song, "Houses." Up above the New York streets I had sat at my piano writing this song of mountains and meadows. I escaped into an interior place of beauty and peace.

You have many houses
One for every season
Mountains in your windows
Violets in your hands . . .

Through your English meadows
Your blue-eyed horses wander
You're in Colorado for the spring

When the winter finds you
You fly to where it's summer
Rooms that face the ocean
Moonlight on your bed
Mermaids swift as dolphins
Paint the air with diamonds
You are like a seagull,
As you said.
. . .

"Come," you say. "Come with me,
I'm going to the castle."
All the bells are ringing
The weddings have begun.
But I can only stand here
I cannot move to follow
I'm burning in the shadows
And freezing in the sun.

There are people with you
Living in your houses
People from your childhood
Who remember how you were . . .

You were always flying
Nightingale of sorrow
Singing bird
With rainbows on your wings.

When I finished, she looked at me with that beautiful, wide smile and shook her head.

"Judy, after all the shit you've been through, how can you still be so romantic?" she asked.

It was true that I sustained a romantic ideal. Though I'd been having great success in my public life, I longed for some inner contentment that could not be shaken or ever lost. I had what every girl wanted, so I should have been happy. At my therapy sessions, I talked to Ralph about why I wasn't.

In December 1967, during the Christmas holidays, I got a call from Peter, in Vancouver. He sounded upset.

"Judy, I'm sure you know that we've been talking about Clark's coming to live with you." You could have bowled me over with a feather.

"I had no idea," I said.

"Yes, well, Clark could come to live with you in two weeks."

I knew there had been difficulties. Clark had a new sister and was finding it hard to adjust. Later, Clark told me that his father had put it this way: "It's either your mother or military school."

On January 27, 1968, I met Clark at the airport and brought him home to New York. I applied immediately for sole custody, and soon I had the official-looking papers, signed and stamped with the great gold seal of New York State. I was not going to lose him a second time.

Clark was nine years old, tall, freckle faced. His honey-blond red hair was cropped short.

"Can I grow my hair long, Mom?"

"You can do anything you like, within reason." I had not been a full-time mother for years and I had a lot to learn. I was out of practice. My first lesson had begun.

I enrolled Clark in the Professional Children's School in Manhattan, and he did fine that spring. When I was away, Dahlia took care of him. He made new friends and had after-school dates and sleepovers. I was thrilled to have him with me at last.

All his life, Clark had been exposed to the antiwar movement through both his father and me. One of the reasons Peter took a job in Vancouver was the war, and Clark's stepmother, Sue, was a Quaker. I had been actively protesting the war for years by singing at rallies, and Clark would often join me. He knew Dave Dellinger and Joan Baez and Pete Seeger, and had grown up around people who regarded the war in Vietnam as unconstitutional, an abomination.

In April, the brother of one of the children in Clark's class at school was killed in Vietnam. Clark was very emotional about this, and cried inconsolably. The teacher sent him home. The next week the principal called me.

"Ms. Collins, we're very worried about your son. He seemed so distressed over the death of the brother of this girl in his class."

"Why wouldn't he be distressed?" I said. "I'm distressed, too. Clark has very strong feelings about this war, and if his friends' brothers are dying, that's terribly upsetting."

"Yes, well, be that as it may, we think Clark should have some outside help."

"I think Clark is doing well. His reaction to this man's death is something I consider healthy."

I didn't like the school's reaction, and they didn't like mine. We were at odds, so I began looking and found a small school on the East Side, where I was able to get Clark accepted for the fall. Meanwhile, I thought that maybe he did need someone to talk to. That year, with a Sullivanian named Mildred Antonelli, he began his own therapy.

That summer of 1968, I was working on the songs for my eighth album, *Who Knows Where the Time Goes*, at the Elektra studios in Los Angeles, and met Stephen Stills for the first time. I knew his reputation as a fine musician and singer. He had been in the Buffalo Springfield and was forming a new group with David Crosby and Graham Nash. My producer, David Anderle, suggested Stephen play on my album, and when the sound of his guitar was added to the songs, magic happened both on and off the record.

One night during the recording sessions we were driving back to Hollywood from Malibu Beach. He was singing, his steely, sweet, heartbreaking voice rising and falling in the car, a cappella, perfect. Our noses were sunburned; we were spent from the day at the beach, yet exhilarated from being together. It had been one of the best of our days.

"There's a young man that I know, his age is twenty-one," he sang, and I found I knew all the words, and joined his silvery voice. The duet lasted all the way back into town on the freeway. "Someday soon, I'm going with him, someday soon." All the romance we knew, all the bitter sweetness of what we had, and what we would lose, was in those lyrics. The next day we recorded the song. It was mysterious that I knew every line, as though I had always known the song that the Canadians, Ian and Sylvia Tyson, had written when they were lovers, married and happy. I sang, and later that week Stephen's guitar found the notes that were always to be the right notes for that song. Though I have sung it with other musicians over the years, his guitar told the story perfectly.

Stephen was brilliant, but we had a volatile relationship from the beginning. Clark was in California with me for part of that summer, then went to camp in the East, and then spent a week with his father in September. We both came home, Clark to start school, and I to untangle myself from my relationship with Michael.

"Why don't you see them both?" said Ralph. "Why don't you date?"

"I'm too traditional," I said. "But I don't want to live with Stephen."

"Here, here," said Ralph.

Stephen and I continued a coast-to-coast romance between our concert dates and careers. Crosby, Stills, and Nash were working on their first record and Stephen was living in Malibu. He played with me at my Carnegie Hall concert on December 22, 1968, and the following spring he joined me in concerts in other parts of the country. In May 1969 *Life* magazine did a cover story on me, with photographs taken at concerts all over the country and with Stephen, Joni Mitchell, and Clark back in New York.

When Stephen and I made music together, the magic continued, and when the music stopped, Stephen thought he knew best.

"I hate shrinks like I hate bad gasoline in my car," he said that winter. "Are you secretly married to your analyst?" he would ask, and then tell me he thought I was really still in love with Michael.

"I want us to live together," he would say.

"I can't do that, just walk away from my life in New York and move out here."

"Sing your songs and be your sweet, sexy self, Judy. That's all you have to do." We were in a hotel in Santa Monica, overlooking the ocean. It was my birthday, and Stephen had brought me the little Martin guitar that he had had reworked for me, and a bunch of roses. I walked into the bathroom, slamming the door behind me.

"And don't slam doors in my face, goddammit. You know I'm right!" Stephen's voice was half covered by guitar notes. He had picked up his Martin and was playing the blues, as he often did when we were together, bending the notes into those heartbreaking sounds that flew from his hands on their own wings, like birds. It infuriated me that I had so much respect for him musically. I wished our romance was not mixed up with the feelings I had when I heard him sing. It didn't matter whether he was right or not, I hated anybody telling me they knew best what I must do. I had to trust my inner voice, I had to trust my heart.

"And your analyst, you trust him more than you trust me! And don't worry so much about your career," he said. "Just relax, and be what you are, a beautiful singing bird."

I felt like a trapped bird. His idea of intimacy was my idea of bondage. Part of me yearned to lose myself. The other part knew that if I gave in, I would be lost.

For a year, we continued our romance. There were days when I flung myself into his arms, and days when I fled, knowing that on Tuesdays and Saturdays it was possible, and for the rest of my life it would have been impossible. I was afraid of being absorbed by him. The words my mother had spoken about my father, "I knew he was my fate, and there was nothing I could do about it," haunted me. I would have died in the cage, I never would have made it out again. I could not be free and be his; I chose not to be his, but I still was not free of him.

Even after Stephen and I broke off our relationship, there were times during the coming years when he would welcome me. For a day, or two days, he would give me what he could and hold my hand. And I found that he knew when to let go. In 1975 I went to Florida to stay with him for a week and heal the wounds from yet another romance that was not working. He was always there for me as a friend, and gave me the best he could.

There were flowers in the hair of the hippies in Haight-Ashbury and at Woodstock in the sixties and seventies, but I found there were thorns as well. We were free to love, but sexual bondage still grew like weeds among the flowers, and I often found myself at odds with the men in my personal as well as my business life. I was making my way in a musical world in which men and women alike are treated as though they are children and belong in the nursery. If you are a musician, you have to fight to be a full person, and if you are a woman and a musician, it is a double struggle.

Our gifts and our burdens as women singers were very different from those of the men, whose wives, if they had them, or their sweethearts were sure to be in the wings, bringing solace, often following on the road or taking care of children at home with no conflicting feelings of "differentness." Quite naturally they had other difficulties, but a woman performer has certain matters of protocol and opinion of which a man might never have to think. I felt prey to agents and managers in a way I am sure men did not, not only because I was afraid of sexual conflict, but also because there was always some inner agenda of wanting "Daddy" to love me as well as get me work, represent me well, and do for me the things that had to be done. Sometimes I felt a yearning to be "taken care of" that astonished me, the girl who wanted to be independent when she was little, the child who had not wanted to ask for anything from anyone. It took a long time for me to become my own person in the business of music. Men feel pressures as well, but the second wave, the feminist movement of the late sixties and early seventies, came none too soon for me. I needed all the help I could get.

I knew some strong female role models in the music business who had forged a path through the briars. One of the strongest of these women was Odetta. I saw her often on our gypsy journeys. I remember her shining face on the stage at Newport, and under the lights at the Gate of Horn in Chicago; it was exhilarating to be near her warmth and to hear her huge, rich voice wrap itself around you in its embrace. One night at the Gate, as I sat out in the audience, catching her last show the night before my own opening, the lights went down, the voice came through the dark room.

"Ladies and gentlemen, please welcome Odetta."

The spotlight followed her as she walked through the audience, her dress rustling close by me, a sound of silk, the scent she wore reaching my nostrils. I remember thinking how interesting it was that she wanted not only to look good and to sound good, but to smell good.

I ran into her recently at a book party for Howard Fast. I

asked her how Danny Gordon was doing. "Do you remember that he was my manager for a year in the sixties?"

Odetta engulfed me in her arms and laughed her laugh that sounds like a baby earthquake.

"Of course I remember. He was my first and only husband. We were married then. He adored me, but he didn't understand about certain things. We were married for three years. Once, he wanted me to cook dinner for his family on a Sunday. He knew I had to sing that night. I resisted, he insisted, and I gave in, made chicken and all the trimmings, and sat down to eat with his mother, sister and aunt; after the meal, I washed the dishes, took off my apron, picked up my guitar, and went to Carnegie Hall to do a solo concert that night. I left him the following week."

By 1969 in Manhattan, as well as around the country, women's consciousness-raising groups had begun to spring up. There was a reason I felt as I did, and I started to talk about it with other women who were working through their own ambivalence about sexual and social mores.

I met Gloria Steinem in the late sixties, and she continues to be a solace, a heroine, and a friend. Shortly after we first met, I went to a conscoiusness-raising group at Gloria's. She had begun to look for funding for a new magazine devoted to feminist issues. I went to some meetings with Gloria, Marlo Thomas, Margaret Sloane, and Florynce Kennedy. It was a diverse group, and we gathered once a week to talk about ways in which we could grow as people.

"I don't understand why it makes me so anxious not to play the role that is expected of me," I said. "I feel I am violating some kind of pact, and I'm not ever sure I know what it is."

"But you are violating a pact!" said Margaret. "The deal is, you can be free, but not so free as to break the stereotype. You can be talented, but not so talented that you are a threat." Margaret is a black woman who was a social worker. "There are certain pacts that must be broken. For instance, one of the things racial discrimination does is to make black and white women think they are enemies. They shouldn't be enemies. They are fighting the same thing, economic and sexual discrimination. If we can get together, we can win."

That seemed very clear to me. But sometimes the issues were not that clear, even for these strong and determined women. We talked a lot about how our own friendships with women, our children, and men meant so much to us.

"Part of what is essential to my happiness is being able to bare my soul to a friend," Florynce said. "Men are deprived, they seem too busy networking to bare their souls." Florynce and Margaret had both been speaking partners with Gloria at universities around the country.

"If they bared their souls, they wouldn't have time to build their power muscles. Or missiles," said Margaret, laughing. We all laugh, but it isn't funny.

"Men are radically different from women," said Marlo. "Men are born knowing they are above-average people who deserve to be waited upon, and usually are, by their mothers, and then by us. Sometimes I think I would be able to handle everything in my life if I only had what some men have, a wife." Laughter again, with no humor.

"I am afraid of losing a lover if I don't do things his way," I said.

"We are not afraid of losing men or of single womanhood. We are afraid of becoming who we really are." Everyone nodded in agreement at Marlo's words. She continued: "Feminism is not about who opens the door when you are getting out of the car, it is about who will hold your hand while you are opening up your own life."

"It is very frightening for most men to be present and not suffocate another person, particularly a woman, while she tries to find out who she really is." Florynce's beaming smile filled the room. "Women are called on to do that as their birthright; any man who can do it is a real feminist."

Wednesday evening, April 17, 1985 / New York

An impromptu dinner last night with Joyce Ashley. She has gone back to school full-time and is becoming a psychotherapist at NYU.

"I feel like we're adolescents out for a study date on a school night," she says. We are at Diane's restaurant on Columbus Avenue having hamburgers, Cokes, and french fries.

"Thank God we're not," I say. "I don't think I could bear to go through it all again.'' Joyce and I have seen each other through many anguished and exuberant times.

"How's your book going?" she says.

"Well, as Red Smith always said, it's easy to write. You just sit down in front of the typewriter and open a vein."

A rare visit with my old friend Ned Rorem, the composer and another writer of journals. We meet up at his apartment on Seventieth Street, and eat the dinner of quiche and salad he has prepared. In my honor, he is wearing a multicolored scarf I gave him for his birthday two years ago. On the walls around us are watercolors by Nell Blaine, Helen Frankenthaler, and Jean Cocteau.

"If I were to write a book about my life, I would start with twelve presents people have given me over the years," he says. "Millefiori paperweights, and those boxes I love of stone, marble, slate, or turquoise; scarves of silk, paintings of flowers—this scarf, that you gave me. I would hold each present up to the light, and as I turned it in my hand, I would remember what each present meant, and what the person who gave it to me meant to me. Twelve chapters, twelve presents."

I tell Ned I am going out to do concerts until the end of the summer.

"Do you keep your journals while you travel?"

"Yes. Notes that tell of my search for something solid, permanent," I say, remembering one particular entry from the late sixties.

It is late in this town on the road. Somewhere between Cincinnati and Miami . . . room service quits, so no dinner . . . nobody thinks of the late-night minstrels. Fried chicken and margaritas. Rain is falling outside. Inside me storms produced by tension and worry are preparing to burst . . . always in the back of my mind is the trip to the next concert, anxiety. Lately when I wake up alone, at home or on the road, I have to put together a flimsy, loosely constructed craft to launch my day on. Put the pieces together, sort out some meaning and some reason from my loneliness . . . I ache sometimes, head to foot, inside pulse to eyelids, afraid of opening on the newness, the againness, of the day. In the silvery aura that surrounds and isolates me on the stage, I sing trips and dreams that are the only way I can affirm my life. So often lately I feel lost, struggling to pin down some reality, some connection to the source of my life forces. For so many years now trains and planes and cars have been the places of meditation, for quiet probing into reasons, motives. Most often the landscapes soothe me, lull me and awaken some secret voice of promise. . . .

Perhaps because I came from a very large family I always seemed to be looking for something that would connect me with people. In 1968 a group of about a dozen of my friends and I made plans to discuss living communally somewhere outside New York. We longed for sky and water, acres of open space, and easier contact than was possible in New York. We thought we might pool our money and buy land, where we could live and work together.

That same month, I went to dinner at the home of Tom and Nancy Hoving. Tom was the director of the Metropolitan Museum of Art, and his wife, Nancy, was involved in community work with drug addicts in the city. Through her work she met Candy Latson, a very tall and handsome black man. Candy came out of Synanon in Los Angeles. Synanon was a closed society for the treatment of drug abuse. Some have called it a cult, for it excluded much of the outside world and asked total devotion from those who joined its ranks, as do some religious groups. Some said Candy had escaped from Synanon. In the late sixties, he moved to New York to set up the Phoenix House drug programs, using the encounter technique that he had learned and polished in Los Angeles.

"Why don't you come to one of the sessions at the facility, see what it is I do?" He sparkled all over, even his teeth.

"You would love it. I went to a session and I was very impressed." Nancy Hoving had been raising funds for Phoenix House. Tom just smiled. I somehow couldn't imagine him going to an encounter at a rehab center.

"Maybe you could encounter my board of directors," he said to Candy, "see if they can tell each other why they're so pig-headed." Tom had been trying to bring the Metropolitan Museum into a more contemporary, active role in the arts and was frustrated.

"Well, I'll come. It will be interesting," I said. And that fall, I did. Candy was the leader of the group that night, and afterward we went out for coffee. I told him how impressed I was with what he did, and I told him about my plan with my friends to look for land outside the city. Before I knew it, he had invited himself and his partner in addiction rehabilitation, Sandy Jackson, to come to the meeting.

One hot, autumn night, the group had its first meeting at my apartment. After I served the drinks, food, and introduced everyone to Candy, we had barely begun to talk when he interrupted the conversation.

"You must encounter each other before you try to live together," he said.

"All we want to do is get some land together in the country, maybe build a place together," someone replied.

"But before that happens, you must honestly confront each other with who you are, otherwise your experiment will fail," Candy spoke with calm authority.

"You run groups with drug addicts. We're just people who want to find a way to have a communal living situation together," I said.

"Addicts are people with problems, who have to learn to live with each other, and you are people whose living problems should be addressed before you try to live together. It's the same principle. You're all people."

Before any of us knew what had hit us, we had committed ourselves to a series of encounter groups.

The weekly meetings, with Candy presiding as our leader and Sandy as his second, started hot and stayed hot. We began practicing honesty. The sparks flew; Candy and Sandy were doing for free what they did for pay at Phoenix House. They taught us to tough it out, to grit our teeth and take in the hard truth about who we really were. "Encountering" was humanism, feminism, and reality applied with a sledgehammer.

We met at a different apartment each time, and soon we decided we should pay Sandy and Candy. The group conscience voted to start with ten bucks per person per session. We were happy to do this. They were tearing us apart.

Sandy and Candy quit working for Phoenix House to run this new breed of therapy. Gradually, the price went up.

The basis of the encounter group was supposedly open sharing. It was the late sixties, a heyday for free speech, free love, and tough talk. Some friendships faltered on the honesty, many never recovered. Confidences that had been held sacred were violated in public, explosive emotions were aired in a group that was supposed to be supportive, but was basically confrontational. The method taught us to be tough (cruel), open (brutal), sincere (hurtful). In the name of honesty, my one-night indiscretion years before, with a man who happened to be in the group, was shared by him in the presence of my current beau. It was a typical exchange. Another time someone shy and vulnerable was confronted with all her professional deficiencies by the man who paid her salary. One woman became so graphic in her criticism of her lover's sexual habits that he stood up, said he would not take this ever again, and walked out of the group and out of her life permanently.

Encountering was supposed to be beneficial for our egos. Healthy. Eventually the numbers grew until we had to split up into three or four groups. It was a game, and God help us, we all got good at it. After a couple of years, I was revolted to find I liked playing the game. Soon afterward, I left the group for good.

Monday, April 22, 1985 / New York

Finally, it's really spring, and the city is full of people in the park, dressed in short sleeves, hoping the weather holds warm. I'm reading *Memories, Dreams, Reflections*, Jung's autobiography. He says the people he knew, their significance, the traveling he did, are unimportant, that it is the inner journey that counts. I know this is true, and yet there have been catalysts for my inner journey, people and places that have contributed to my journey in a way that is memorable.

I think of Stacy Keach this morning. Stacy was always a talented, driven man, a good companion, and a friend. How are his mornings? How is his heart? Once I was close to his heart, or thought I was. But we know so little of each other's dreams.

In April 1969 I got a call asking me if I would be interested in doing a role in *Peer Gynt* for Joe Papp's Shakespeare in the Park. I would be playing the part of Solveig. New songs had been written by John Morris, who thought they should be sung by someone who sang like Judy Collins.

"Why someone who sings like her? Why not ask her?" said Joe Papp.

When the call came, I hesitated. "No, I don't think so, I'm going to be on tour, doing concerts." But then I hung up the phone and thought, Why not? I called back. "Yes," I said, "I would love to do the part if I like the songs." I went to see Jerry Friedman, the director, to hear the songs. Stacy Keach walked in while I was singing, and when I was finished he came toward me, clapping and smiling.

"That was beautiful, I am a great fan." I shook his hand. He had a high forehead, a wide face, a smile that went from one side of his face to the other. It was a handsome, open face. A friendly face.

Ibsen's *Peer Gynt* is one of the great romances written for the stage, and I was cast as the patient, all-loving, all-forgiving Solveig. Stacy was Peer Gynt, who storms about the world, sinning, creating havoc, orating, searching for God and good and the answer to life. At the end, when he is an old man, Solveig is still there, singing "I will wait," and holding him, at last, in her arms.

We rehearsed at the New York Shakespeare Festival's building in the East Village in May and June, and by the beginning of the summer Stacy and I were romantically involved both on and off the stage. We performed the play at the Delacorte Theater in Central Park to full houses. Stacy was a man who appeared to have knowledge of himself, of where he belonged and what he wanted. After the summer and the play were over, our drama continued.

Clark was doing well at school and seemed happier, well adjusted. He was naturally a very sensitive child who could have moments of exhilaration as well as of deep sadness; he was quick and intelligent and seemed to be addicted to excitement; he had a short temper, like mine. I was trying to be an understanding parent, but I suppose that, like most parents, at times I felt less than adequate. But he and Stacy got along well.

In the fall of 1969, Stacy bought me a four-poster bed and a Husky puppy with a red bow around its neck. I met his brother, James, his parents, his fellow actors. Stacy had grown up in the West and gone to the London Academy of Music and Dramatic Art. At the time we met, he was considered one of the finest actors on the American stage. His film career was just beginning. Many New York actors were his friends, and we spent nights with Raul Julia and James Earl Jones, Cleavon Little and Harris Yulin, Diana Davilla and René Auberjonois, nights of wine and roses and good food and good talk. It was during this time that we became friendly with Melina Mercouri, her husband, Jules Dassin, and their children, Ricky, Julie, and Joe.

I introduced Stacy to my brothers and my sister, Holly, and by the end of that year, we had entwined our friends, our families, our lives. He had an apartment that he kept, but we were spending a lot of our time together, and I was softening in my resolve not to live with anyone. Perhaps living with Stacy was a good idea.

"Why don't we get married?" he said to me one day.

I was thirty, and single, and why in the world wouldn't I want to marry this man? I had been divorced for five years. I got along well with Stacy; he seemed to be the whole, complete human being I had been looking for. He loved Clark, I could tell that. But as much as the idea of being his wife attracted me, as soon as we would discuss marriage, my heart would pound, my breath would come in short gasps. I felt I had had one too many marriages already.

"Let's think about it for a while." I couldn't even think about it, let alone talk about it. But then my opinion of marriage would thaw briefly.

"Stacy, let's do it, let's get married," I would suggest.

"I'm not sure I'm ready for marriage quite yet," he would respond.

Sometimes when we were together I had a strange feeling in the pit of my stomach that was totally counter to what was in my heart and my head.

"I think there is something missing in our relationship," I said to Stacy one night, "but I don't know what it is."

"I know what it is, Judy," he said. "It's you." I fought my stomach, listening hard to my head, and my heart, and we went on. When doubts would rise, I put them down, thinking they were foolish. How could this not be right?

In early 1970 Stacy was doing Arthur Kopit's *Indians* on Broadway. Stevie Phillips, Stacy's agent, who had become a friend of mine as well, was working on getting Stacy movie parts. She also represented Robert Redford and Liza Minelli at that time, and was very excited about Stacy's film potential. I was making a new album, *Whales and Nightingales*. Clark seemed to be adjusting to his new school, and I felt calm for the first time in years. It was, in comparison to other circus times, rather a tranquil time for me personally.

Both Stacy and I were ambitious about our careers and supported each other's work. He was determined to be in films and to do quality roles on the stage. Arvin Brown, the director at the Long Wharf Theatre in New Haven, was talking about directing Stacy in *Hamlet* and bringing the production to New York. I didn't look for another role in theater after *Peer Gynt* because I was absorbed with recording, doing concerts, and writing more songs. With a new album in the works, I had to do a great deal of traveling again in the spring, and I went to Los Angeles to be on Glen Campbell's show in February.

Under everything we did, the antiwar movement pulsed. It was with us at every moment. I got to know Dave Dellinger and Rennie Davis and Abbie Hoffman that year, and in January 1970, I went to Chicago to testify at the Chicago Seven conspiracy trial.

William Kunstler, who was representing the Chicago Seven, stood in front of me in the witness box.

"Miss Collins, you were present at the meeting of the Yippies in 1969 in New York City?"

"Yes, I was."

"Will you please tell the jury what happened at that meeting?" Kunstler paced the floor in front of the jury.

The memory of the press conference filled my mind; it had been exciting, a huge gathering at a hotel in New York, the crowd's imagination fired by the thought that the Yippies would bring an attitude of loving and caring to the Democratic convention.

I opened my mouth to sing.

"Where have all the flowers gone, long time passing, where have all the flowers gone, long time ago—" Before I finished the first verse, the court officer put his hand over my mouth, and I was ushered from the courtroom, not allowed to complete my musical testimony.

On a television show after my appearance at the trial, ABC censored my comments. Everywhere sides were being taken, anti- and pro-Vietnam. In the spring, there was a Moratorium concert in New York, featuring many artists who were by now known to be against the war. On May 9 I went to Kent State to appear with Ramsey Clark, Ted Kennedy, and Averell Harriman, to honor the student protesters who had been killed earlier that week by the National Guard.

The country was in turmoil, and while my anger against the war seethed and I searched for ways to speak out against it, I fought my own guerrilla war on an inner battleground. I hated the war, but I had the feeling during the sixties and seventies that people expected me and others in the antiwar movement to have the right answers to everything, the solution to "it," to have a firm, unqualified position on every issue. I was not as sure of myself on many issues as other people seemed to be.

Certainly by now, I thought, I should have settled my ambivalence about marriage. One of my worst disagreements with Stacy started because I had said on *The Dick Cavett Show* that I was not looking for "a man on a white horse, a Prince Charming, to come and save me." I said it innocently enough in response to a question about my independence, but Stacy seemed to take it personally. I had a fear of being muzzled, prevented from fulfilling my own life, my own dreams. At times when we talked of marriage I could only see the pain that had come from the one I had already had.

I was still working on *Whales and Nightingales* in early 1970, recording live at Carnegie Hall and St. Paul's Chapel on the campus of Columbia University.

It was there, in the chapel, that I recorded "Amazing Grace." Stacy sang in the chorus, and many of our other mutual friends joined me. "Amazing Grace" seemed the perfect prayer for peace, some kind of answer to the madness that plagued the world. The song was to become a hit, an anthem of hope, a salve for the times and the feelings, its timelessness a balm for our torn lives.

It was during this time that Stacy and I decided to get a bigger apartment. I finally felt that I was ready to take the big jump and really live with him. As soon as we began looking for a place together, Stacy got a part in a movie, *Doc*. A remake of *Gunfight at the OK Corral*, *Doc* was being shot in Spain. Stacy's friend Harris Yulin was cast as the sheriff, Faye Dunaway as Kitty. Frank Perry, the director, was looking for someone to play the kid. One night at dinner I told him I thought my brother Denver John would be perfect. Frank auditioned him, and he got the part.

Before Stacy went to Spain that summer to begin filming, we settled on what was to be our new place, this big, sprawling, light apartment I live in today with Louis. I was almost finished with the new album. I got Clark off to camp, moved my piano and the rest of the furniture to the new apartment, and flew to Spain in early July. Stacy picked me up at the airport, all smiles and glad to see me. Everything was going well, he said.

"And your brother is a real actor." After Denver John's experience that summer, when he did so well, he decided to make his living on the other side of the camera, and eventually became a cameraman and a director of cinematography.

We drove to the white stucco house Stacy had rented and sat in the cool living room, drinking wine and watching the fading light of the sunset. It was as good as the best of the western sunsets, rivaling Colorado and Arizona's. I was glad to be there, and I should have been happy. The situation had all the makings of being perfect, but no matter where I went, there I was. The uncertainty that I felt underneath all situations was with me, a personal discomfort. I felt there was no security anywhere.

Standing around in the sun, I watched the movie being made. There were gunfights, barroom brawls, swinging-door bravado, and love scenes between Stacy and Faye. Stacy and I were together, my brother was there being a movie star, and Clark came to Spain with his friend Josh. Squinting into the Spanish sun, I had the photo for the cover of my new album taken on a brown hillside. On the weekends we drove from Almería to a small town by the edge of the Mediterranean, where we stayed at a resort, partying and laughing and splashing in the sea. At night we ate by candlelight and danced on the terrace. But often in those weeks, just as we would be feeling our most intimate, our happiest, an inner terror would seize me. I would find that I couldn't stand the hard look of the Spanish hillsides, and something unreal would come over the whole scene, like a poisonous gas. My heart would beat faster, my breath would become difficult. I thought, at those moments, that I was going crazy.

When the lights were out and the sets were dark, when the others were sleeping, my terrors began. I could not stand for a moment to be alone, lest the terrors came to face me. I was gay and carefree in the daylight, but at night I watched the full moon crack and split, shattering into a million pieces. The beautiful bright dream had to be put together again at dawn. Outside was romance and beauty; inside, I was falling apart.

I had to leave before the film was finished because my fall concerts were beginning and Clark had to start school. When

Stacy came home, we tried our plan of living together, but it didn't work out very well. Soon, Stacy had his own apartment again. That winter I worked with Blood, Sweat, and Tears and had another concert at the Hollywood Bowl with Arlo Guthrie. I went to Detroit for the Windsor war crimes trials, continuing my tour in the autumn. I had decided I definitely didn't want to have another child at that time, but the decision hadn't seemed to change things, and Stacy and I were as involved as we had ever been.

In November, *Whales and Nightingales* was released, and Stacy, Clark, Josh Klein, and I went to Mexico for a vacation to try to get away from everything and spend some time together. Continuing in my struggle to find out about myself, I was seeing another Sullivanian now, Julie Schneider. In Cozumel, Stacy and the kids swam and basked in the sun while I sat on the beach with my arm in a bandage from an injury I received on our first day. While riding a motorized bike, I had fallen, and the skin was stripped off my entire right arm. The doctor who smeared yellow antibiotic cream on me and gave me antibiotics to take by mouth had had some words to say about motorized bikes.

"Yes, we lose about one person a month on those bikes!" he said. I wound up feeling lucky instead of deprived. But the same inner terror had followed me to Mexico.

When we returned, Stacy and I tried to repair our relationship. We took a country house in Greens Farms, Connecticut, and bought Volvo station wagons, red and blue, to haul potting wheels and furniture and people back and forth between the city and the country. The house had high ceilings, dozens of rooms, stained-glass windows of mountain scenery, and room after room full of shadow and light. Grapevines twisted over the trellises on the porch, a studio invited us to sculpt, to play. I put a grand piano in a windowed alcove that looked out on the tree-shaded lawn. Stacy and I wrote "Easy Times" there, the theme song for his movie *The Repeater*, which was about recidivism in prisons. There was laughter and parties with friends who came from the city for weekends. At this house we cooked mammoth meals, had holiday celebrations. In the kitchen there were utensils for doing anything you might think of to every vegetable, fruit, meat, and dairy product you could come up with. We were playing house and garden.

My anxiety increased.

One night we were having a candlelit birthday party for one of us—I don't remember who: mine is May 1 and his is June 2. We began to argue and shout at each other during the dinner. (I can't for the life of me remember what we were arguing about.) The table was flung over, the wine, the plates, the glasses, and porcelain all smashed into the wall behind me. The chairs were flying around the room. When things finally settled, it was as though a scene from a movie had just been cut. We were quite rational. I apologized, he apologized. We picked up the plates and wiped the wine off the floor, swept up the glass, and went on talking as though none of this had happened. One of us was a year older the next morning.

For me, the center of our country house was flying apart from the very beginning, like a handful of jewels, unstrung, all the wrong color, unmatched, not meant to be a part of the final necklace.

As the months went by, we still talked about marriage, but only occasionally and with less real interest. Sometimes I wanted to run away completely, and the next day I would beg for resumption, absolution.

How like all my relationships this was. How much like my whole, ambivalent, careening experience with men. I never wanted to be with them, I never wanted to be without them. I could not find myself without them, I could only find myself without them.

Before Christmas, Clark was caught smoking pot at school. He was eleven by then and had grown up fast living with me. I smiled and looked confused if he drank, and was furious when one of our friends turned him on to pot. As a result of my feelings of frustration, he either did pretty much what he wanted or we fought about what he couldn't do. Whether I let things go or not depended on my ability to cope at the moment. He was quick to remind me that I was practicing a double standard.

"How come you and Stacy and your friends can do this stuff and I can't?" said Clark, almost looking me in the eye. He was tall, weedy, growing every day.

"Because," I said, "I'm your mother, I say so, you're too young, and that's that." Only I didn't feel it. I was a child of the sixties mentally in both its positive and its destructive aspects. I thought he had a point about the double standard.

Through Clark's therapist, the core of the Sullivanian principles began to emerge: they truly believed children and parents do not belong together. I have often puzzled over the strong relationship I had with these doctors. Their power had a great deal to do with their understanding of the "creative personality" and their perceptions about struggling with a life that was different from society's norm. During the time my own career and discipline as an artist were forming, their input was invaluable, and I believe that painters and other artists were attracted to them for many of the same reasons. Saul Newton was, I think, quite brilliant. I had admired his politics and thought him brave for having fought in the Spanish Civil War. His disciples, the younger Sullivanians, had apartments together, then buildings together, then suggested strongly that their patients move into the community, then used peer pressure, and in one case the custody of children, to assure adherence to the rules.

I have known people who feel they have "lost their children" to the Sullivanians, one man who hasn't talked to his daughter, who became a Sullivanian patient and later a therapist, in fifteen years. I have also heard that they think of parents and ex-patients as people from whom money can be borrowed. The Sullivanian doctrine, I was to learn through Clark's and my experience, is separation so that the neurosis caused by the family doesn't grow. I was Clark's mother; I had to be the problem.

"Clark is in a total rage at you!" said Saul. I was frightened by his strong language. Saul was always extreme in his diagnoses. He told my therapist, Julie, and Clark's therapist, Mildred, that Clark must get away from me immediately and go to boarding school.

I moved, as though I had touched a hot stove. Saul Newton's words sent a spasm of panic through me. I didn't want to be the cause of Clark's troubles.

Stacy, Clark, and I started hunting for schools and settled on one in West Virginia, the Richard Moss School. It was run by a woman who seemed to be very capable. The school had a good reputation for academics, healthy food, and an outdoor, country atmosphere. Clark seemed to like it, and although I hated its being a boy's school, I felt I was cornered; it was the only school we had seen that was remotely the right sort of place. In January I took Clark to West Virginia and the rigors of country life, convinced it was the solution to a crisis.

He called me at the end of the first week.

"I hate the food, this woman is a Nazi," Clark said. "She made me cut my hair." I gasped. I loved Clark's hair. It was strawberry red, and during the three years he had been home it had grown down to the middle of his back. He sounded upset, and I was upset.

"Oh God, I'm sorry. Are you doing all right in the classes?" I asked.

"I hate the teachers, too."

"Please, Clark, give it a little longer. I'm sorry about the hair, I really am. I'll talk to her. Give it a few weeks." I was afraid to have him come home, afraid of Saul's warning. The next day I made a call to give the headmistress a piece of my mind, but couldn't reach her.

I got home late that night, January 19, 1971, after having dinner and a painting lesson with Susie Crile. There was a message from a telephone operator in West Virginia. I was to call the head nurse at a hospital in Hagerstown, Maryland, right away.

"Yes, this is Ms. Collins. What is the matter."

"Your son has had an accident. We need your permission to operate. I'll put the doctor on."

A foreign-sounding voice came on the line. I was standing in my bedroom, with the telephone in my hand, the sweat beginning to run down from my armpits.

"Ms. Collins, your son was in a sledding accident. He is unconscious. We must operate. Clark's skull has been fractured. If the ragged edge of the bone moves, it may puncture the brain sac. We must operate immediately to prevent his further injury. It is life and death."

"Is he going to live?" I asked, unable to stand up, sitting down, collapsing.

"Clark could die, or have permanent brain damage, even if we operate," said the doctor, "but we must operate now."

I said, of course, do the operation. Stunned, I hung up the phone, packed my bags, and was on the next plane to Washington. I rented a car and drove to Maryland in a daze. When I walked into the intensive care unit at three o'clock that morning, Clark lay with wires hooked up to his entire body, harnessing him to equipment that regulated his heartbeat, his breathing, his blood pressure, his brain waves. His head was covered completely with bandages except for his closed eyes, and they were circled with purple.

I kissed the bandaged face and thought, He can't die. He mustn't die. It can't end here.

The next day, he opened his eyes and smiled at me.

"Hi, Mom. What's happened to me?" He couldn't remember. His memory of the day before and of the two weeks before that was gone.

"I remember being in Mexico," he said.

Clark's life hung in the balance for a week. The doctors couldn't tell me if he would live. He looked terrible. When the bandages came off part of his face, there were the raw-looking scratches on his cheeks and forehead. His teacher told me he had been running into the walls for a week, banging himself up. Stacy came to spend a few days with me at a nearby motel, where I and my faithful friend Linda Liebman were staying. My shrink, Julie Schneider, came for a weekend. Harold Leventhal, who had canceled all my concerts, joined us. I was grateful for them all.

There was a day when I went to see Clark in the morning, and he looked so awful that I thought he would die within hours. When I came back that afternoon, he looked at me and smiled.

"I had a dream that a white veil was passed over my face, and I saw the sun on the other side of it," he said. I knew he was going to live.

On January 30 I brought Clark back to New York in an ambulance, Stacy and I sitting by his side. He was admitted to the Neurological Institute at Columbia, where he was to remain for two more months. He had therapy for his aphasia, and gradually his short-term and long-term memory came back. There was no permanent damage—the stitches in his scalp were cleanly placed, the sac around the brain intact. He was 4-F.

"My father will like that, I don't even have to dodge the draft," Clark said.

For two months I spent nearly every day at the hospital, watching Clark become himself again. When he was really well, we tried another school, this one in Vermont. Glenrock was a school where you didn't have to go to class if you didn't want to—very much a school of the liberal mentality. It was based on A.S. Neill's experimental Summerhill school in England. I had tried to get Clark into Summerhill the preceding winter, but he was too old to be accepted. The trouble with Glenrock was that A.S. Neill and Summerhill were in England. But Clark liked Glenrock and did well there for the next year, before the school, with its ideas and nonideas, folded.

When it did, Clark and I went to look at Windsor Mountain School, up in Lenox, Massachusetts. We both liked Heinz Bondy, the headmaster.

"Adolescence sometimes resembles temporary insanity," Bondy said. "The symptoms will pass if we give it understanding. We recognize that teenagers have problems that are part of growing up." Clark and I looked at each other, smiling. They certainly did.

"We here at Windsor Mountain are prepared to talk about these things, whether they are sex, or drugs, or behavior problems. All teenagers have them. We as a school are willing to recognize that and deal with it."

In the stone building, with the big leaves in the maple trees outside the window blowing gently against the panes, the summer ending and the sun still warm, we felt comfortable; it looked good. The headmaster was smart. Clark liked him. We would try again.

It wasn't a great situation, but it worked for a while. He went there for a year, until there was more trouble in "behavior" problems. Then he went to a school in Maryland, where he and I were able to do some therapy together for eighteen months during 1972 and 1973. We got through a lot of the anger and trouble that had brewed between us and were able to re-establish communication.

In June 1973 I got a letter from Clark from Baltimore.

Dear Mom,
   I love you, don't ever doubt that, but there's a time when a young man has to make it on his own. My time has come, I can sense it in my bones. I can't live up to the expectations of other people. I want to live my own life. I hope you understand me, please, don't waste any effort on looking for me, if I can't make it I'll never try again. Don't worry, I'll keep in touch. Love always, Clark

Clark didn't belong to me or his father, and never had. He was his own person, finding his own way. At that time I wrote a song for my son, who had grown, been on his own, and was becoming a man.

I was only nineteen,
The morning you were born,
With your hair fine and red,
And your eyes like my own.
I've seen you stumble,
You've watched me fall,
You know we've got nothing,
You know we've got it all.

Sometimes there were roses,
Sometimes there were thorns,
I know you're going to make it
As sure as you were born.
And I hope from what you wanted
You get what you need,
And I know you're going to make it,
You were born to the breed.

In 1974, after living on his own for a year, Clark decided he would come home to New York, live with me, and finish high school.

During this time, my relationship with Stacy had undergone many transformations, and Stacy's film career had become a reality. After Clark's accident, Stacy got the lead in *Fat City*, a story about a prizefighter that was being directed by John Houston and filmed in Stockton, California. Stacy invited me to come out and spend some time with him there. I felt insecure and troubled about my relationship with him. Stacy was moving fast, doing a lot of films, and was away from New York often. I wanted to get as close to him geographically as I could, and was glad we would have the opportunity to be together away from the city.

It was already hot in the Stockton desert. Stacy and I rented a house with a pool, and I rented a grand piano. I worked as much of the day as I could; it was there that I wrote my "Song for Judith," one of the first happy songs of my writing career. After I had worked on my own writing for the morning and part of the afternoon, I would join the cast on the set. Susan Tyrell was in the movie, as well as Jeff Bridges and Candy Clark. There were always parties at one house or another, and on some nights the crew and actors would come to our house, and I'd cook massive dinners.

The set of a movie is a world within a world. There were parties on the barges that floated on the canals—a lot of drinking, a lot of laughter. While doing a film, everyone is very close to one another, very much like a family, and when the film is finished, that experience, that particular "family," parts forever.

I was twenty-five pounds overweight, still smoking, and I couldn't breathe. I began using the swimming pool at the house and doing the Royal Canadian Air Force exercises. I decided I would stop smoking, so I switched to little cigars and smoked three a day, allowing myself one after each meal. I was smoke-free in a year. But I went straight from the cigarettes into an eating disorder. I started throwing up. I didn't know anything about bulimia, certainly not that it is an addiction or that it would get worse. My feelings about myself, even though I had been able to give up smoking and lose twenty pounds, were of increasing despair.

For the next two years Stacy and I both continued to be involved in actions against the war in Vietnam. We often went to rallies and fund raisers together. In April 1972 we went to Washington to appear with Daniel Ellsberg and Donald Sutherland at a reading, on the steps of the Capitol, of a play about peace in Vietnam. Ellsberg had released the Pentagon Papers to the press earlier in the year. That night he was hooted at by people who called him a Communist. I was sure, as I watched these agitators in the crowd, that they were thugs; they didn't look like people who belong at a rally to celebrate life and plead for peace in Vietnam. It turned out that they were part of the same organization that was behind the Bay of Pigs incident in the sixties and that would work for the Committee to Re-elect the President. They tried to humiliate Ellsberg and caused a dangerous situation in the crowd. The police swarmed; those of us on-stage—peaceniks, they called us—were pushed to the back of the stage and shoved about by the police. There was shouting and scuffling. Stacy put himself between me and one of the aggressive, shouting men, who had come onto the stage and, brandishing a stick, approached Ellsberg. Nuns were on-stage with Elizabeth McAlister, Donald Sutherland, and Jane Fonda; all of us had had parts in the play, singing and pleading for peace. The incident passed, but inside I was shaken by the violence. Both my inner world and my outer world were fraught with turbulence that frightened me. Nowhere, it seemed, was there any peace.

Stacy and I continued to spend time between New York and our house in Connecticut. Sometimes we had wonderful days, but at other times we would bicker and argue. Although something about the relationship was lasting, I also knew that its center was falling apart. In my life some wrecker seemed to be at work, ripping out every seam, smashing into every close encounter.

By the beginning of 1974, Stacy and I had been together nearly four years. We had started seeing other people—me in my panic, Stacy with whatever devils are his own. As our lives pulled apart, we spent less time with each other. We were free "to come and go, to see other people."

I thought I had wanted to be in an "open" relationship. But then I turned around, and surprise, there was no relationship at all.

Judith

Tuesday, April 16, 1985 / New York City

Anniversary day, anniversary day of my meeting Louis, and the house is filled with flowers. At Tiffany's I bought a pair of polished stone cuff links for him, red and amethyst, blue and moonstone, each set in a gold oval. "Who deserves them more than he does," I said to the salesgirl, and immediately felt that rush of pleasure in finding the right thing at the wrong price.

All the tender and loving feelings I have had about men, my father, my great-grandfather, all the trust, all the caring, I feel intensely for this one man. With him I have had seven years of something wonderful.

I'm off to do concerts with symphony orchestras in four cities, starting with my hometown of Denver. I'll be gone a week.

I called Freddy yesterday to learn how the single "Shoot First" is doing, and found out that we have "picked up a couple of stations." "Shoot First" is a good song, perhaps the best I have written. I am not holding my breath.

Wednesday, May 1, 1985 / Denver

When I was a child, people hung bunches of lilies of the valley on their doors to celebrate May Day; mayday is also a nautical term for ships in distress. Communists and socialists call it a holiday; it is a day of fertility and joy. Maypoles with bright ribbons falling from the tops of their pointed poles, the girls in ribbons and silk dance in a circle with boys in knee pants, neat caps on their heads. Everything is blossoming and blooming and swelling to the bursting point. May Day, my day, Taurus, with flowers in my horns, bells on my hooves.

I flew to Denver this morning. I'm missing spending my birthday with Louis, I had hoped this concert date would move to another time. In other years, Louis has often flown to be with me in cities around the world, as I have done to be with him for special holidays, but this year he is designing five new subway stations for the MTA in New York and working on the AT&T museum project. Instead, dozens of roses in my hotel room and his card, I LOVE YOU, HAPPY BIRTHDAY, LOVE LOUIS. Today is my birthday, I feel young at last.

My father died in St. Luke's Hospital here in Denver, May 4, 1968. I was in London the morning I got the call that he was dead. My nineteen-year-old brother Denver John was there with me. This trip was my treat to him and was to have been an adventure for both of us. He came into the room where I lay sleeping, and leaned over me in the dawn light.

''Daddy is dead, we have to go back.''

Although he had been ill, there was no way my father could be dead. The shock was almost too much to absorb. The adventure became a funeral journey home.

We had to stay over that night in London, waiting to get a plane to Denver. I canceled the concert at Albert Hall and we left the following morning. I was distraught with grief. I couldn't think, couldn't eat, couldn't sleep. The only thing that made it at all bearable was that my father was at peace now. I can't shake him out of my mind today. His powerful, strange personality.

I dreamed of him last night and awoke feeling remorse and sorrow. In the dream he was lonely and frightened of what was becoming of his life. He was so tough, so delicate, so musical, so much of an enigma to me, and so indelible on my own life.

Tonight in Denver I had dinner with my mother and stepfather, my godfather, Holden Bowler, his wife, Ann, my brother David, and his wife, who is also Ann. It was good to see my mother, who looks younger than she did when I was a girl. She is happy with Robert, her husband of fifteen years. Holden and Ann also look well. They live in Bliss, Idaho, on the Snake River. When Louis and I visited them two years ago, we rode the whitewater rapids on the Snake and swam in it as it lapped beside the long front lawn of the Bowlers' log house, the house that was built by Holden's hands. The river is beautiful and deceptive—wide and smooth as glass one minute, the next studded with treacherous white water. Last night Annie told me that three people drowned last year.

"Weren't they wearing life jackets?"

"They had them on wrong, and they were taking chances." Holden has never ridden the river.

"I've always said that river is totally unpredictable and dangerous," he said. When Louis, Ann, and I rode the river two years ago, we put our life jackets on the right way. With the wind blowing his beard and his eyes filled with pleasure, Louis faced the roughest rapids in the river.

"You see," he said later, "if you point the raft into the very center of the rough water, you are safe." I still had my heart in my mouth and spent the whole trip on the bottom of the raft, screaming with what I hoped sounded like delight.

"You better get to the Snake this summer. I know what's gonna happen, I'm gonna die, and you'll say, Oh, Louis, I knew I should have seen more of that man while he was alive."

Ann and Holden have three children who are grown. Bookie, Sarah, and Bindy; they lost their fourth child, Timmy, twenty-six years ago, when he was shot and killed in a hunting accident in Colorado. I don't think Holden has ever really gotten over Timmy's death. Timmy was fourteen when he died in 1959, the same year Clark was born.

"I've been fishing, caught your Christmas salmon already, Judith." He goes up along the secret tributaries above the Snake, where he catches fish that he smokes and sends off to us Collinses around the country at Christmas time. They come in the mail and the scent tells us it's our godfather thinking about us, doing for us what Dad would do if he could, and what he couldn't do but wanted to. They were friends in the young, noisy years, and in the present years of silence their friendship echoes. Daddy is with us tonight, as he always is, as we talk of his singing, of his extraordinary, strange life.

"Charlie would turn over in his grave, aghast. My God, he would say, isn't this just the most bloody boring crowd you ever saw!" We howl with laughter, and my sides ache and my mouth hurts from smiling. My stepfather, Robert, listens to the talk of my father with what Louis refers to as the patience of a saint.

Tomorrow I will rehearse with the Denver Symphony. I remember the first time I played with an orchestra, with Dr. Brico. In 1972 I was sitting in the lobby of the airport in Buffalo, talking to my pianist, Richard Bell, about Dr. Brico when the idea to make a movie about her life came suddenly and irrevocably into my mind. The next day I called Jill Godmillow, a filmmaker I had met through friends, and invited her to become my codirector. I hired a cameraman, Coulter Watt, and instructed my financial manager to write checks. I became a movie producer and director overnight.

I called Antonia Brico to tell her she was going to be my movie star and that her story was going to be a film.

"Oh sure, and I'll believe that when I see it," she said.

I laid out the scenes I would put in the story: there must be interviews with her, scenes of her teaching piano students, giving master classes, and conducting rehearsals with the Denver Businessmen's Orchestra. I wrote an outline of the movie, which I had learned from watching Stacy work. Film is so much like making music. Everything is in the phrasing, I discovered, and it became the means I used to tell a story that had been vital to my life.

In the winter of 1972, Jill, Coulter, and I showed up in Denver for a week of filming. It was then that I learned the true story of Dr. Brico's life.

In 1903, Antonia Brico was born in Rotterdam, where her mother had come from Amsterdam after a falling out with her family before Antonia was born. When the baby was due she went into a convent for the birth. Baby Antonia lived with the nuns during the first year of her life while her mother, also Antonia, worked at a menial job, trying to put enough money together to make a home for herself and her infant daughter.

When Antonia was two, her mother was destitute, and the child was placed with a foster family. Antonia's mother tried as often as she could to see the child but the foster parents, the Grosses, did not welcome the visits.

Grandfather Brico became extremely ill, and on his deathbed he asked to see his daughter and his little granddaughter. Antonia's mother went back to Amsterdam and was welcomed with open arms. The dying father asked her forgiveness and instructed the family to go to Rotterdam and retrieve his grandchild. The grandparents hired a lawyer, the foster family was contacted, and the date was set for the judge to arrange to have Antonia returned to her mother's care. The day before the hearing, the foster family slipped out of Rotterdam with the baby on a boat bound for the West. They left no forwarding address, and they left with everything they owned.

The grandfather died, never seeing his granddaughter Antonia, and a few months later Antonia's mother died, her health gone, her hopes gone, her father and daughter gone. Everyone in the family assumed they would never hear from baby Antonia again, that she was lost forever.

The Grosses migrated to San Francisco, where they established a bakery business. Mrs. Grosse was something of a spiritualist, and Antonia was taken to seances, where a white-haired visionary would put a hand on her head and say that Liszt or Beethoven was standing behind her. The foster parents recognized Antonia's great musical talent and they got her a piano as well as sending her to music lessons in Berkeley. But there was another, violent side to Mrs. Grosse, and Antonia vividly remembers the emotional abuse she received from the woman who she had to assume was her mother. She remembers sitting under the piano after being disciplined, crying, and saying to herself that if she ever found her way out of the situation she was in, she would never hurt little children, but be kind to them.

When she was sixteen she left the house, vowing never to return. She went to live with a schoolmate, and when her promise began to look like more than just a threat, Mr. Grosse finally came one day and tried to patch things up. He showed Antonia her birth certificate and told her the real story—that her own people were back in Amsterdam.

Though it was unheard of for a woman at that time, Dr. Brico's ambition to be a conductor began when she was eleven and saw a band concert in Golden Gate Park. Paul Steindorf was directing the orchestra, and she saw the "little stick" in his hand become a magic wand. She, too, wanted to make the wand speak. She went to his concerts every Sunday afternoon, and began following him home on the bus and bumping into him on purpose. Steindorf became curious about this shy girl, now fourteen, who dogged his footsteps. Through some mutual friends he found out about her great musical talent and invited her to dinner, where he asked her to play the piano for him. He taught her for free, and when she got older and told him she wanted to be a conductor like he was, he shook his head.

"Antonia, that is just because you love me," Steindorf said.

"It is not because I love you, it is because I must do this!" Antonia told him.

"Antonia, that just cannot be. It is impossible." His words made her more determined than ever.

A great pianist, Count Sigismund Stojowski, heard her play in Berkeley, and when she was nineteen brought her to New York, where he, too, taught her for free. Though Antonia was planning to be a conductor, everyone else thought of her as a pianist because she practiced eight hours a day, plus going to the Steinway showroom every night to practice six more hours until Stojowski put a stop to it.

While she was living in New York, one of her teachers at the old Juilliard School told her she should look up her family in Holland by tracing the name Brico through the birth certificate Mr. Grosse had given her. She wrote to a newspaper in Amsterdam, inquiring for "the family of a child named Antonia Brico." After a few weeks she received word from the overjoyed family in Amsterdam, who had given her up for lost or dead. After many letters back and forth, she set off to see her real family.

The reunion was unlike anything she had experienced in her life. Nothing had prepared her for the emotion, the kindred feelings, the warmth, the open hearts that she found around her in Holland. She took her mother's name, Antonia Brico, and went back to New York to finish her degrees in theory, piano, composition, and harmony, and continue her attempts to get to Berlin to study conducting, the dream which she had never given up.

Even when Stojowski, Steindorf, and everyone else said Dr. Brico couldn't be a conductor, she was still determined and found the means to go to Germany to study at Bayreuth. Finally, through friends, she obtained an introduction to Karl Muck and applied to the Master School of Conducting at the Berlin State Academy of Music.

In 1927, Dr. Brico was the first American student to be accepted at this distinguished institution. On January 10, 1930, she conducted the Schumann piano concerto with the Berlin Philharmonic. The concert was a triumph, and she received great acclaim in the press. She was photographed in the newsreels and in the papers, the "rotogravures." At home in the States, the University of California competed with the Los Angeles Symphony to have her make her debut with their orchestras. The argument was settled—she would conduct in both cities. At the Hollywood Bowl, with the Los Angeles Symphony, and at the Greek Theatre in Berkeley, with the San Francisco Symphony, she had triumphant concerts. The papers called her "Cinderella."

Dr. Brico conducted orchestras all over the United States and in Europe, and for a while her artistic success made it seem that she was one of the few exceptions to the rule that women could not be conductors.

After the first wave of enthusiasm for her work, the shock came for Antonia when there were no more jobs. People didn't want a female conductor; they wanted a man, the symbol of community authority, power, and prestige. In the next ten years she struggled and gained the support of people all over the world, musicians, conductors, composers, who had seen her work and knew her to be a first-rate conductor. She begged these people to write her recommendations, which they always did, and once she announced to Arthur Rubinstein she would pay for a rehearsal and conduct in Carnegie Hall so he could hear her work and write recommendations for her.

"But I can't do that, I can't make that decision on my own," said Rubinstein. "Why don't you ask Bruno Walter and some others? I don't want to be the only one!" She invited Walter and other conductors and led a rehearsal on a Saturday afternoon two weeks later in Carnegie Hall with an orchestra she contracted and paid for herself. Bruno Walter, Rubinstein, and the others, after they heard her, wrote letters to orchestras all over the world. On their recommendations, concerts were booked for Antonia Brico around the world and she was a huge success once more.

In the United States, however, prejudice was greater against women than in Europe, and during the war, it was almost impossible to find work in New York. In 1940 she had a brainstorm. She would start her own orchestra, a women's symphony.

Dr. Brico was able to get funding because people were interested in this novel idea. She founded the New York Women's Symphony in 1940, and until 1945 it played regularly at Carnegie Hall, doing the major repertoire of her friend Jean Sibelius as well as Mahler, Beethoven, and the rest of the classical literature. The orchestra was very successful.

After the war, men were returning to their jobs in all fields and replacing the women who had assumed these roles. Dr. Brico felt it was time to integrate her orchestra. Her board of directors then told her that they weren't interested anymore, since it was no longer a curiosity. She was out of an orchestra and out of a job.

In 1972, after a week of filming Dr. Brico and her life in Denver, my crew and I were all exhausted. We had a great deal of footage on Helen Palacus, the young pianist who was to be the focus of our story. She was fifteen, a girl whose life closely mirrored my own when I had studied with Dr. Brico. Helen was studying the Schumann concerto. We filmed her private lessons with Dr. Brico and shot the concert in Phipps Auditorium, where I had played Mozart with Danno Guerrero.

But the hardest part of our story was still to be filmed. We had to tell the audience why, if Dr. Brico was really so wonderful, she was still in Denver. On the last night, she and I sat in the kitchen of her little house on Pennsylvania Avenue, with the cameras rolling. Jill asked the question from off camera.

"Antonia, what are you doing hidden away in Denver?"

There was a deep sigh. She was exhausted from the week, the attention, the lights with which we had disrupted her rehearsals, her studio, and her routine. She turned to me a face filled with fatigue and determination.

"What could I do? I was here, you see. In 1947, after my great success with the New York Women's Symphony, I was offered a concert here in Denver, conducting the Denver Symphony. The orchestra hadn't gone professional, they were just forming a board of directors; they were going professional literally in a few weeks. The concert here was a great success, and they asked me if I would think about coming here to be their conductor."

"Were you living in New York then?" I asked.

"Yes, and I had such awful sinus infections, I had the whole inside of the lining operated on. Denver is a mile high, dry, and pollen free, the perfect place for me to live. I accepted their invitation; they said they would give me first consideration when they went professional. This is why I never believe anybody, even you, beloved Judy, when you said you were going to do a movie about me! I put my two Steinways into a moving van and brought all my earthly belongings to Denver. And then, wouldn't you know it, I sat.

"They hired a man to be their conductor instead of me—Saul Caston—and I was in shock! The reason they didn't hire me, they said, was that as a woman, I would not be able to become a member of the Cactus Club." The club is a very exclusive male club in Denver, where men get together, and theoretically, where the politics of the symphony business and the fund-raising for the orchestra would take place.

"Here I was, in Denver with no job and no money to move all the statues and the Steinways back to New York. How would I live? Well, I would find a way, let me tell you, I would find a way. I have my own orchestra now, and I teach, and I conduct, four, five, six times a year. I have made a good place here, but I want to be conducting, I am capable of conducting, four, five times a month!"

The emotional scene broke the ice. We felt as though we had finally gotten what we had come to find out. It was late at night, everybody was hungry, we ordered out for hamburgers. I knew Dr. Brico was exhausted, she would never have agreed to eat a hamburger otherwise! We sat in the living room with our dinners on our laps, the klieg lights still bright around us. Antonia (I was still calling her Dr. Brico) sat down at the piano. I sat beside her and she took out her long scissors and cut my fingernails as she had done when I was eleven. I laughed and took the scissors and pretended to cut her nails, as well. Then she began to play rousing, jazzy pop songs.

"I don't want this in the film!" she said, and ran off an impressive version of "Alexander's Ragtime Band" with a killer left hand, stride piano, the whole works. I was shocked.

"This is a side of you I've never seen!" I said to her.

"These are the songs I played in the music store in San Francisco to make a living when I was seventeen."

Aha, I thought, I wish I had known that when I was seventeen and she was giving me a hard time for learning "Laura"! Coulter never took his hand off the start button, and we had it on film.

Back in New York, Jill and I sat in front of the Steenbeck, editing the film for four months; every frame of the movie was a collaboration of our ideas. As in producing records, collaboration, when it works, is wonderful. In the winter of 1973, *Antonia, A Portrait of the Woman* was finished. *Sixty Minutes* bought it and Mike Wallace went out to Denver to interview Antonia. The PBS station in New York, Channel 13, bought three showings, and when *Antonia* began to win prizes in film festivals, we were able to put it into independent theatrical distribution. *Antonia* opened the Whitney Museum's New American Filmmakers series in September 1974. Jill brought an old friend to the screening.

"Antonia, I'd like you to meet a fan of yours," I said to her. She put out her hand, smiling, beaming.

"I'm Robert Redford, Dr. Brico, and I want to tell you how much I enjoyed the movie. You are an amazing woman."

I had never seen Dr. Brico at a loss for words. She stood with her mouth open and couldn't believe her eyes.

"You're not! You mean you're the one who plays in all those movies on the ship?" She always took the *Queen Elizabeth* or the *France* on her trips to Europe. I knew she never went to the movies in Denver. "I don't believe it, but you really do look like him!" Meeting Robert Redford was better than being on *Sixty Minutes*, better than opening the Whitney film festival. It was the tops for her; I could do no wrong from that moment on.

That year, *Antonia, A Portrait of the Woman* was nominated for an Academy Award as Best Documentary and named as one of the top ten films by *Time* magazine. As Antonia's disbelief turned to acceptance, she blossomed. From the oblivion that had descended on her in Denver, she began to experience a resurgence in her career that energized her, and she proved once again that she was a fine conductor, which is what I had always known, what had driven me to make the movie.

The movie's release led to her being hired again by symphonies all over the world. She conducted the San Francisco Symphony once more, the Mostly Mozart concerts in New York, the Los Angeles Philharmonic at the Hollywood Bowl, the London Philharmonic at Queen Elizabeth Hall. There were raves in newspapers everywhere. Antonia had been rediscovered and was once more on the road conducting, being photographed, being interviewed, revived. At the Mostly Mozart concert *Antonia* was shown, and then Dr. Brico walked out to conduct Mahler and Sibelius. At the end of the concert, she brought me on to thank me. Cinderella had awakened to find herself standing in front of the orchestra again with a little stick, a wand, that made magic.

An international concert promoter, Kazuko Hillyer, became Dr. Brico's worldwide agent. She believed in Dr. Brico and took a real interest in her career, but couldn't do much.

Things haven't changed a lot. There are few women conducting today. Nadia Boulanger, who conducted in Europe and the United States, is dead. In New York, there is Eve Queler, and of course there is Sarah Caldwell, but she is not a symphony conductor, she has an opera company in Boston. I once met a woman conducting one of my symphony concerts in the South. Another Antonia, she had named herself after Antonia Brico. But things haven't changed a lot.

I remember a conversation with Antonia a few years ago when I was in Denver.

"It's still the same. They want a man who can be politically powerful. My movie [I love the way she refers to it as "my movie." It is, by God, her movie] was playing during the Year of the Woman, 1975. Do you think the Year of the Woman is over? They still won't let me join the Cactus Club."

Wednesday, May 8, 1985 / Washington, D.C.

Louis and I have come to Washington to be arrested on the picket line at the South African Embassy this morning. We arrived on the Eastern shuttle from New York and met today's group of "arrestees" at a Baptist church near Embassy Row. Today there are eight of us in the group, including Mickey Leland, a congressman from Texas, three black students, the president of the student body from Georgetown University, and the president of the university as well.

"I want you to be calm and follow our plan as closely as you can," say Randall Robinson. We are well instructed by a group of lawyers who are giving their time to set up this protest. It has been going on for months, and has drawn increased attention to the issue of apartheid. Randall has been handling the protests for the group called TransAfrica, and he is articulate and filled with good humor.

"Is everybody ready?" We all nod, and he smiles.

"I want to thank you in advance for your participation today."

"Does that mean we will never see you again?" jokes one of our group, a young high school student named Dennis.

"No, I'll be there when it's all over," says Randall.

Everyone laughs, but there is an undercurrent of uneasiness. Nobody really knows what will happen, even though the arrests have been going smoothly for months. It could all change in the twinkling of an eye.

At the South African Embassy, we walk calmly in single file to the door, knock, and ask to be let in. We are refused entrance, go to the sidewalk, and the police read us our rights, telling us we must leave immediately.

"You are advised that you are in violation of the law, and if you don't move within one minute, you will be arrested." Three times the police warn us, with the bullhorn, that we must move. As planned, we stand in line together, singing "We Shall Overcome."

When we are arrested, each of us is handcuffed, and we are put into the paddy wagon and hauled away. Louis is on one side of the van with the men, and Celia, a Washington lawyer, and I ride on the women's side to the station, our hands tied in front of us with plastic handcuffs.

"Ever been locked up in a police wagon before?" Celia asks. The paddy wagon bumps along the street, and I wonder where we are going, down to the central station or one nearby.

"I have been locked up before. How about you?" The main thing I feel is terribly hot; the handcuffs are wet with sweat and would slip off if I worked at them. I wonder about criminal security.

"I've been arrested on a number of actions," Celia says, "but it always feels the same. Frightening!"

I laugh, I'm glad I'm not the only one who is nervous. At the station, the police are men and women and black and white.

"All right, just sign here," the arresting officer says to me, and clips off my plastic handcuffs with a pair of scissors. The officers are polite and organized as they process us for disobeying a police order to disperse.

"Is that all we have to do?" I ask. "Aren't you going to put us in a cell?" The officer laughs

"No, ma'am." The police are efficient and cheerful, and for every one of us, there is one of them.

The officer processing my papers finishes with the work and looks at me, smiling.

"We're all on the same side today!" he says. We are released, and our cases are dismissed.

This is the first time that Louis has been arrested on a political action, though he came close in some of the anti-Vietnam War protests.

"I'm glad we did this today," he says as we stand outside the jail with our fellow arrestees. "This issue makes one feel so helpless."

To this date, four thousand people have come to the door of the embassy of South Africa, stood before it asking to be let in, and been arrested. There are demonstrations all over this country against the regime of apartheid. We must all go to the wall for each other.

In the afternoon, after we are released from the police station, Louis and I visit the Vietnam Veterans Memorial. People are wearing Easter bonnets; children with bright voices call in the sunlight. The sprinkler throws water between the wall of names, black granite slabs arranged in graduating heights and embedded into the ground, and the bronze statues of the Vietnam vets in uniform with their guns. People bend and stare, blinking their eyes at the memorial to the more than fifty-eight thousand people killed in the war. There are red and white carnations stuck between the slabs of stone, and I run my fingers over the letters, a bitter Braille. On the hill above the wall are three young men in uniform, one with a trumpet in his hand. Today he plays taps in the bright sunlight.

The peace has come, the war is over, and yesterday there was finally a parade for the Vietnam vets who returned, the ones whose names are not on that wall. But our national history is written on that wall in shame.

The first time I went to jail to protest the war in Vietnam was May 24, 1971. I was arrested in the halls of Congress, where I had gone to participate in a "Redress of Congress" action that I had helped organize. I had spent several months on the phone, calling, cajoling, finally begging people to come with us, to exercise the right of "redress" guaranteed by the Congress. Out of literally hundreds of calls, I got few responses. The antiwar movement was becoming a popular cause, yet people's resistance sent me into a rage of depression. What was the matter with them? But Francine du Plessix Gray, Cynthia Macdonald, Joe Papp, Barbara Harris, Kenneth Koch, Robert Brustein, Benjamin Spock, Grace Paley, Tennessee Williams, Larry Rivers, Barbara Rose, Martin Duberman, Dick Gregory, Dr. Robert Jay Lifton, Paul O'Dwyer, Dr. J. William Ward, and a lot of others came to Washington, our common feeling of revulsion at the ongoing war drawing us together. One hundred and fifty of us stood outside the floor of the House of Representatives while Congresswoman Bella Abzug read our appeal to Carl Albert, the Speaker of the House.

"We respectfully request that you take all appropriate measures to permit the legislative branch to exercise its constitutional responsibilities for bringing an end to this undeclared and immoral war. . . ." Carl Albert refused to recognize our petition. We stood outside while the police warned that we were to clear the halls as soon as possible. With one breath, in one moment of decision, we sat down and stayed put. We were warned we were trespassing and would be arrested unless we left the floor of the hall. I began singing "Where Have All the Flowers Gone," and everyone on the floor joined me. We were arrested one by one and led by the police from the building.

In jail that night I shared a cell with Barbara Harris. I emptied my purse in the open toilet bowl in the cell, fearing that my loose pills would be found by the guards. Later I realized I had dumped my great-grandmother's amethyst ring into the toilet along with the Miltown and Dexamyl and Gantrisin and Valium and Lomotil. Barbara Harris wrote a long letter to her mother on the toilet paper, telling her why she felt she had to protest against the war. The cops heckled Benjamin Spock, calling him a Communist. To my mind, Dr. Spock is as near a saint as you can get on earth. I read his book when Clark was a baby, and here he was, joining the people who wanted to save those babies' lives. I was released that night at two in the morning by a friend who came with bail money. Once outside, we arranged for the release of some of the others, and the next morning all of us appeared to plead nolo contendere. That same day I went to jail in Washington, in 1971, the following men were killed in Vietnam:

> Francis Brockman III
> Gary D. Sarris
> Daryl R. Kunzler
> Jamie Pacheco
> Robert F. Wilcox
> Henry H. Strong, Jr., Missing in Action

The last man to die in the war in Vietnam, whose name is carved on the granite wall, is Richard Vande Geer, who died on May 15, 1973.

Saturday, June 8, 1985 / New York

A lot of work lately "for fun and for free." Last night was the benefit for Jacques d'Amboise's National Dance Institute, an annual performance by the children from the classes in New York and outlying areas. Sunday night and Monday I joined the thousand children, together for the first time the day before the performance, and the dozen New York City policemen, who join us every year. I wrote two songs this year for the performance and learned the finale. I danced and sweated, sang and stretched, along with inner-city kids, black, white, poor, middle class—some of them have never been involved with anything like this in their lives. Jacques is like a Pied Piper, a wild-eyed, whirling child himself. For years he was a principal dancer in the New York City Ballet and a close friend and associate of Balanchine, who was also a founding member and on the NDI's board of directors. Jacques spins and shouts and laughs. Every year for eight years we have had a few other "celebrities" who join us: Baryshnikov and Bujones, Jason Robards and Kevin Kline, Colleen Dewhurst and Mayor Koch have appeared at the evenings at the Felt Forum in Madison Square Garden. Cloris Leachman and Ann Reinking are in the show this year. Florence Rome said that the NDI night makes her feel, once a year, proud to be a New Yorker; for one night, hope prevails. No car chases, no drugs, no dismantled social programs, no heroes with clay feet, just an amazing, directed energy. Jacques makes everyone feel like dancing.

Sunday, June 9, 1985 / New York

Overheard the other day, "Now I don't have secrets, I have a history."

I ran into Dr. Don Weissman at Carnegie Hall this spring at a concert by Jean-Pierre Rampal and Ransom Wilson. Like many doctors of the voice, Don is also an amateur musician, has studied flute for years, and is a great fan of Jean-Pierre and Ransom, as am I. Don is my ear, nose, and throat man. All singers have one of these magical people in their lives. We greet each other fondly; he knows my deepest secrets.

"My God, you look healthy!" he says.

I first saw Dr. Weissman in 1975 when I felt something strange happening in my throat: as I sang, a note would disappear from my voice. It would suddenly drop out as though someone had plucked it from the middle of a song. When this happened I would turn pale with panic, and my heart would beat wildly. I knew it wasn't nodes; nodes are caused from strain, and I knew I wasn't straining. I feared it was cancer.

At my first appointment, Dr. Weissman put a mirror down my throat and then sat back and wiped the mirror clean, looking at me.

"You have a slight swelling on a capillary; a tiny flaw, something called a hemangioma. I want to tell you, since you are an intelligent woman, that this problem can be fatal to a singer."

"You don't think it's cancer?" I asked, relieved.

"No, it's definitely not cancer. But a hemangioma might be

fatal to the voice if it gets big, because it interferes with the production of sound, and it may rupture.''

I sat in my chair, my head spinning, in shock.

"Is there anything to be done?'' I asked. I made myself say the words.

"Yes, if it doesn't absorb, we can take if off surgically, but I wouldn't want to do that. Let's wait first, and see what happens. I'd like you to go on complete vocal rest for a while. No singing.''

I would do better than that, I wouldn't talk at all. In ten days, when I returned, he said that it was still there, although he saw some improvement. He thought we should watch it, that with rest and continued silences, it might heal itself.

At the time Dr. Weissman found the hemangioma, everything seemed to be going my way. The press conference for the opening of *Antonia, A Portrait of the Woman* had been at the Whitney the week before. I had finished making my fourteenth album, *Judith*. Elektra was enthusiastic and David Geffen, Elektra's president, told me it was the best album I had ever made. The single from the album, "Send In the Clowns,'' was going to be released soon.

These successes in my career didn't make a dent in the nightmare that pursued me, the fear that I would finally not be able to sing. If I couldn't sing, I didn't know if I could live.

Stacy and I had been apart for two years. I had dated Coulter Watt, my cameraman on *Antonia*, for a while, and now was seeing a man with whom I thought I might be happy. My relationship with him was all right, but it had not made the difference I had thought it would. An addict to romance and excitement, I was forever running from one lover to the next, hoping to find something that would take away the pain of living.

I was singing forty to fifty concerts each year, more than most classical singers do, a strain for even the most healthy solo singer. In addition, there were interviews and press benefits, one for WNCN, a classical music radio station in New York, others for the peace movement, for good social causes; there was a trip to London to do television, as my latest album was in the top ten records there; there was my first appearance on *Sesame Street*. Through all of it, the worry about my voice was my constant companion.

In the fall of 1976 I started playing the piano again, hoping it would bring a kind of sanity and peace into my life that was slipping through my fingers everywhere else. Every December, following a tradition begun in the sixties, I sang one or sometimes two concerts in New York, usually at Carnegie Hall. I decided to play the first movement of a Haydn piano concerto in my Carnegie Hall concert that Christmas. My violinist friend Arnold Black contracted a chamber orchestra of about fifteen pieces and wrote a small opera for me around an old Yiddish story. I did two concerts that year; the Haydn and the opera were a great success. My audiences had come to expect the unusual from me; they were enthusiastic, and both of the concerts were sold out.

"Send In the Clowns" had become a very big hit, introducing people to my singing who might otherwise not have bought my albums or come to my concerts. I performed in Symphony Hall with the Boston Pops, with Arthur Fiedler conducting. This concert initiated the symphony dates I have been doing in the years since then.

Bread and Roses was released in 1976, and *So Early in the Spring*, a fifteen-year retrospective, came out in 1977. "Send In the Clowns" was reissued as a single and became an even bigger hit than it had been, going onto the pop charts in the United States and again in London.

In spite of everything, I could not help worrying about that little spot, that place on my vocal cords that made me so utterly vulnerable.

I had gone to Richard Avedon to have my pictures taken for the retrospective album, just as he was preparing his own thirty-year retrospective at the Metropolitan Museum. The day he photographed me, on Fifth Avenue, I was wrapped in shawls and layers.

"The look you yourself developed so all the women in America would wear it," said Richard. One of the shawls I wore was Holly's, for luck. We had to move the shooting schedule around my six o'clock appointment with my shrink, about five blocks away.

"It doesn't matter how much better you get from analysis, as long as your doctor is convenient," he said, and we both laughed. The pictures were very good and made me look better than I felt.

In 1977 I was scheduled to appear on *The Muppet Show*, which was shooting in England during May. I caught the flu and had to cancel the trip. Jim Henson and the puppeteers in London sent me a huge Kermit get-well bouquet, with balloons of every color, filled with helium. They rose to the ceiling, where they stayed for a week, the cheeriest thing in my life.

During this bad bout of flu, Dr. Weissman looked at my throat and told me the hemangioma had gotten worse. He said I should rest my voice, but that now we would consider surgery.

In my journals and datebooks through this whole time are notes saying "No Talk Day." In order to have the singing, I had to give up part of my life. I went on silences of ten days at a stretch, got in bed for weekends, resting, resting. I roamed the streets of New York, had dates with my friends and wrote them notes instead of talking to them. The "silences" became retreats, of a sort, in which my thoughts were free to turn inward in such a way as to reflect upon my chaotic life. The search for something outside myself began to turn into a deeper quest. The past loomed in front of me, for I was beginning to go backward in time.

I tried to talk to my lover about my fears, but I was unable to verbalize my terror at what was happening to me. We had arguments—why, I don't even remember. I sweated and had nightmares. I was afraid of losing everything I had ever hoped for or had.

Dream from my journal, May 1977—

I am watching a performance by a famous and renowned singer. She is hanging over the heads of the crowd, suspended by ropes from the height of the room. A man holds the ropes; the woman swings in circles, tying the rope around her in adventurous loops, sometimes about her legs, her waist, her upper torso. She is wearing a black-sequined top that glistens as she whirls in the air; she has dark hair and a red skirt that flies about her legs. Then she begins to scream, holding her hands to her throat. The rope has caught and strangled her. She grabs at the rope, trying to free herself, and the man cannot do anything, for if he drops her she will be killed and he cannot reach the ropes to free her neck from the knots. I waken while she is still screaming and tearing at the ropes, in the lights of a great stage.

The Muppet Show was able to reschedule me in October 1977, five months away. Meanwhile, I had a summer tour and a dozen concerts to do. All of this seemed overpowering. I was becoming terrified of doing what I had been learning all my life to do.

In August 1977, I went out to the first stop on a month-long tour. In Oklahoma City, I sang carefully, preserving the voice I had been silently protecting for months. That night was fine, but a few nights later, in Oakland, California, my voice was tattered. I knew I couldn't finish the concerts without doing more damage. Backstage after the concert, I saw the face of a childhood friend, Margo Michaelson, floating toward me in a daze. She was holding out her arms, and she had tears in her eyes.

"Oh, God, Judy, what has happened to you? What is the matter with your voice?" she said. Margo had known me as a little girl. I let her arms wrap around me.

"I don't know, Margo" was all I could say.

The tour was canceled. I went home to New York and straight to Don Weissman's office from the airport. I was becoming so used to opening my throat while he poked the mirror down it that he grinned and told me I had a throat like an acrobat. He showed me in the mirror that the hemangioma was now very big.

"How much can you sing if you are totally rested?" he asked me.

"I think I have about three days in me after a really good rest." My God, it seemed incredible. This is what I had been learning to do all my life, and now I was counting minutes, hoarding hours, hoping for three days before I fell apart again. It was madness.

"How much singing will you have to do with the Muppets?" I said I thought about two to three days.

"What we'll do is: you'll stay put, rest for six weeks, go to England and do that show. When you come home, we'll put you into Mount Sinai and take that sucker right off."

I kept silent for almost a month, and then went to London. I sang "Send In the Clowns" and "There Was an Old Woman Who Swallowed a Fly"; the voice sounded fine, but I knew I couldn't have kept on singing much longer. As soon as I came home from England I went to Dr. Weissman's office.

"Let's do it," he said. I checked into the hospital under an alias. During the surgery Don took a picture of my vocal cords. The left cord was smaller than normal and had a red swelling that stuck up like a biceps across its midpoint. The right cord was healthy; it had become twice as large to compensate for the damaged left cord.

The operation was a complete success.

Dr. Weissman warned me against fatigue, cigarettes, and alcohol. By March 1978 I had split up with my latest lover, and I had to face myself alone, at last. My voice was fine. I would rest. I knew how to do that, and I didn't smoke anymore. The problem was, I couldn't stop drinking.

I finally had to admit to myself that what I could not control for fifteen years was alcohol. Up until that year, I had been able to wait until my concerts were over to drink. Now I was drinking while I was on-stage. It was a disaster.

There is a song of Dylan's that I used to sing, "Just Like Tom Thumb's Blues." One of the verses says, "I started out on burgundy and soon I hit the harder stuff." From the time I started drinking at fifteen, there had been a gradual increase in the amount I found it necessary to drink. Although most Irish singers got warmed up with a few drinks, I found I couldn't sing when I drank; my voice would close up, shut down, cease to make music. So in the years between 1964 and 1975, I did not drink if I had to sing, and I never drank during the day. But by the time Dr. Weissman found the problem on my vocal cord, the need for alcohol was controlling me and I was often drinking a quart of vodka daily.

One morning soon after Dr. Weissman found the hemangioma, I lay in bed with my eyes open, my thoughts on the day to come. There would be a band rehearsal in the afternoon. On the weekend I was going to see Benny Goodman, to talk about making a record of my song "My Father." He loved it and wanted to play the clarinet while I sang it. That morning I thought about my fear of losing my voice. I had always waited till five in the afternoon to drink. This morning I asked myself, Why? Whose rule was that? I walked to the kitchen. It was still early and my housekeeper was not in. I poured a beautiful French wine glass, from Lutèce, full of vodka. I added ice. I drank, refilled the glass, and went about my chores in the apartment. By eleven I was headed for the pool. Before leaving, I poured myself another drink. In the dressing room of the pool, I looked in the mirror and saw blood running down my face.

"What have you done to yourself?" a woman in nothing but a towel asked me.

"It's nothing." I laughed. "I guess I must have bumped into the wall." I put a cold cloth on the cut and went into the sauna. I had my swim, and when I got home I realized I would have to cancel my rehearsal with the band. I slept, and woke up to have another drink while I was getting ready for a dinner party that evening. I thought I was in great shape. For two more years, this was the pattern of my life. People told me I had never looked better.

My anxieties increased no matter how much therapy I had, and I saw different therapists, looking for an answer. One of them would hand me a prescription for pills, some of which I took. Another said, "What you need is to go through analysis." A third doctor, who was quaint and had known Freud and Jung, said, "You have so many artistic things going on in your life, it's enough to make anyone anxious, so drink a little."

During this time I continued my busy concert schedule: I seemed to keep going faster and faster. I have always known that the mystical contact that is part of a concert spared me, held me, protected me. In those two hours, in the concerts I did around the world, I was safe. The music surrounded me. I was singing, but I was absorbing healing from the audience as well. A concert was like a session at Lourdes for me. If I could make it up to the stage, I could be touched, because as long as I could sing, I could in some way be healed. That mystical thing that had begun so long ago had not deserted me. I stood stock still, often with my eyes closed and my guitar clutched in front of me, and I could absorb the healing spirit of the audience.

I have heard it said that there is no pain in change; there is only pain in resistance to change. Everywhere I looked I was losing ground, there was nowhere to stand. I was going to have to change, and I both didn't want to and didn't know how.

This agony went on for another six months after the surgery. Then I was told by friends about a doctor who might be able to help me.

In April of 1978 I went to see a physician I'll call Dr. James. It was a spring day, sparrows were singing in the bright sunlight, fluffing their feathers on the posts of the traffic lights. Once I thought hope was cheap, until I had none.

I told Dr. James the history of my increasing use of alcohol and of my search for solutions with different therapists.

"Having therapy when you are drinking is like trying to learn navigation on a sinking ship or studying interior design on the *Andrea Doria*." I laughed. It was the first real laugh I had had in a long time.

Dr. James smiled behind his glasses, leaning toward me over his desk in his white jacket. "Total abstinence is the only treatment for this illness," he said. There was a silence in the room. The clock ticked, the sun came through the blinds, falling in yellow slats across the mahogany desk. It had never occurred to me that this problem could be an illness; I had always thought it was basically a moral issue. If I could just be a good girl, I could handle it.

"There are places you can go to get well," he said.

Down on Fifth Avenue, the traffic roared south, going to midtown Manhattan. I could hear the cars moving in the street, my eyes not focusing, my brain not cleared.

"I'm different, I don't think anything will work for me."

"You're just like anyone else with this physical problem. I can get you a bed at a treatment center on a farm in Pennsylvania, and they can help you to get well."

"I have a benefit for the ERA I promised to do on the sixteenth, I can't possibly go now."

"Have you ever realized that *no* is a complete sentence?"

I was bewildered, but he looked at me kindly.

"Look," he said, "It's your choice. You have a life to live if you want to live it. If you don't, that is your decision."

I wasn't sure I trusted him, but I felt relief, as though I had come running from a very long distance and thrown myself down on the finish line.

"I'd like you to call the place in Pennsylvania," I said, "and get me a bed."

Holly had come to New York with Kalen, and I went home and told her I had decided to go away, but I would do it after my ERA benefit at the Ginger Person. If I hadn't gone to that benefit I might not have met Louis.

I arrived at the airport in Reading, Pennsylvania, at seven-thirty in the morning on the nineteenth of April, 1978. It was raining. The countryside was budding, the flowers were just about to burst into bloom. I hardly knew where I was, except that I had nowhere else to go. It was the end, the beginning. No flowers. No crowds. Just me and my assistant, Janet Matorin, and my accountant, Saul Schneider, who had come on the plane to give me courage. But they would be going home to New York, and I would be staying. Whether you are by yourself or not, there are some places you have to go alone.

A bright-faced young man named Bob picked us up and drove

us to Wernersville. Riding through the Pennsylvania countryside in the back of the rattly station wagon, listening to his cheery voice, I thought I had come to the end of my life.

A big sign, sitting in the middle of the green grass behind the fence, said: IF YOU WANT TO DRINK, THAT'S YOUR BUSINESS. IF YOU WANT TO QUIT, THAT'S OUR BUSINESS. How tacky, I thought. It reminded me of my cousin Morris Caldwell's neon cross, the sign for his church, on the top of a hill in St. Louis. I had made fun of him for having such a corny, lit-up thing advertising salvation.

We rattled through the wooden gate and up a long hill to what looked like a cozy farmhouse at the top. Bob brought my suitcases up the stairs, past the nurses' desk, and set them down in a small, green room with one glass wall. I waved good-bye to Janet and Saul.

"Boy, these are heavy!" he said. I thought I would do a lot of reading. One of my bags was full of Camus and Sartre, Thomas Wolfe and Erica Jong, and Jung—I must read Jung. Find out what my dreams meant. In the other bag, among my robes and sweaters and silk shirts, were my tranquilizers, vitamins, and a vial of Gantrisin for bladder infections. I hadn't had any cystitis lately, but I always carried the medication with me just in case.

Only one thing compelled me to unpack my bag and hang my clothes in the bare closet, put my makeup out on the wooden dresser; one thing made me stay and not walk back out into the rain, onto the highway, out to the airport and home. I knew I could not go on living the way I had been, and that if I went back, there was a good chance I would die. I unpacked my bags and lay down on the bed.

The nurse came in, smiled, and said, "You can stop driving now and let us take the wheel."

She took all the pills from me and said I wouldn't need them. I told her I was terrified I wouldn't be able to sleep without something.

"Nobody dies from not getting enough sleep," she told me.

I was sure I would be the exception. The first night, I was given a low dosage of Valium, which I was told would prevent any seizures. When I closed my eyes, I saw a sea of gaping faces that mawed and yanked their mouths into grimaces; men screamed my name and the bottom dropped from the pit. Each night I slept better, and when I finally slept through the night, it was a deep, restful sleep.

But during the days I wanted to drink, I wanted to scream, I didn't want to let go, I wanted to run. Every morning I thought I might check out, and every night I thanked God because I had stayed another day. Part of what kept me in place was that I was so tired, so deeply tired, as if I had been pulling a semi down the road with my own hands. The steam had gone out of me. I didn't have the energy to fight, and though I wanted to, I didn't leave. The next morning always found me still there.

As the days passed, I found I was in a twenty-bed hospital off the main buildings of the treatment center. There were about sixty people at the farm. After five days, I joined the regular routine with the other patients, was given a daily schedule, and was sent off to be part of the community of people who were learning to live healthy lives again. We all participated in the lectures and group therapy, designed to inform us and help us to get well. Sometimes as I was enveloped in cigarette smoke, it reminded me of the lectures on TB when I had had tuberculosis in Denver.

In my group there were teenagers with sullen, sad faces, who slumped in their tattered Levi's and scowled at me from under their eyebrows; there was a very put-together lady who looked as though she had stepped out of *Vogue*, hair done just so, face made up. There was a television producer and a housewife. There was me, and I didn't know who I was anymore.

The only thing any of us really knew about one another was that we had come to the end of one road and were trying to find our way to another.

After my initial shyness, I started talking at meals and socializing, and after a few days these people seemed less like strangers. The books I had brought stayed in the suitcase. I went to the lectures and group sessions, and during our meetings, as I looked out the windows to where the hills of the farmland were covered with a soft green fuzz, it seemed to me that I was in a dream. I was telling these people things I had never shared with anyone. I knew them not at all, yet felt as though I had known them all my life.

As the days passed, the flowers began to push up through the Pennsylvania mud, and soon the farm was covered with red and yellow tulips, their deep centers coal black, their petals drenched by the rain. I experienced my first spring in years with my senses clear. I saw colors again. I began to smile, and one day, while I was in the bathroom brushing my teeth, I looked at the reflection of my face. I looked straight into my own eyes. I hadn't done that for years.

My roommate was a woman named Ruth. Every night she got down on her knees beside the bed to pray. She would bend her face over the pillow, and there she stayed for a long time. She was a little older than me, a kind and shy woman. I was appalled that she should get down on her knees right there in front of me, with the lights on. But silently, on both feet, upright and walking, or sitting, or lying in bed, I began secretly and fearfully to pray, to some flower or the sun or some tree, as I had heard people say they did.

One day in my therapy group we were all sharing our most spiritual memories from childhood, and I told mine.

"It was a moment when I was a teenager, riding in a car in the mountains with my friend Patti Gwen and her mother. We were driving alongside the Feather River, which runs down from the town of Nederland, Colorado. As we passed Idaho Springs, and the sun lighted upon the water as it flew down the mountain between the highway and the pine trees, I felt a sudden thrill of happiness go through my whole body." I realized I had held that memory, like a shining thing in my pocket, for years, wondering if I would ever feel so intensely happy again. I did now, and it was not about a hit album, or a romance, or a successful concert. It was because I was healthy and clear.

I turned thirty-nine while I was at the farm. It was May Day, and all the flowers were finally in full bloom.

I drove home to Manhattan with my brother Denver John on a day in late May that sparkled with sun and hope. I had started another journey. I was not the same woman who had left Manhattan the previous month to find help.

The idea that I have a choice to live a healthy life was given to me by the caring people I began to meet at the farm. My clear day today is their triumph. I thought when I went to Pennsylvania that I was at the end of my life. But I discovered that far from being over, my life had just begun.

Hard Times for Lovers

Thursday, June 13, 1985 / London

Louis and I flew to London two days ago, where it's forty-eight degrees and raining, as it should be. Bumbershoots, raincoats, and galoshes. Our biggest decision yesterday was whether to spend the day in the British Museum, go to a matinee of *Starlight Express*, or drive out to Longleet in the rain.

On television the newscasters are talking about Bob Geldof's Band Aid concert and the concert he plans for the States, Live Aid. Geldof's conscience will bring our minds back to the eyes of those children, with their bellies out and their arms hardly arms at all. Most of our problems are privileged, and fade quickly in the light of famine.

No singing last night, my first real vacation in Europe, and we had dinner with John Martin and his wife, Valerie, after going to the theater to see *The Caine Mutiny*. John has produced some of my concerts here in London.

"You need a new record, Judy. I can't get the kind of tour I want for you without it."

I had promised myself that I wouldn't talk business on vacation, even with him. But in the back of my mind, I hear a voice saying, Judy, business is done over dinner, don't you know that? That voice. I suck in my breath and say out loud, "Nobody knows better than I do that I need a record, but right now I don't have a record contract.''

'' 'Amazing Grace' is still one of the biggest-selling singles the United Kingdom ever had. There ought to be a company here that could record you. I'll see what I can do, the audience is here for you, they just need to be reminded.''

Back at the hotel, I run a bath. I had not wanted to think about making records on this vacation, this was to be a time to get away from all if it, to think about kings and queens and crown jewels and Caine Mutinies. Not about the pain I feel about not having a record contract. I try to forget everything in the bath, lean my head back, but I want to scream.

"Judy," Louis says, "the good thing is that John is positive about getting you a record deal. I think that is wonderful. Hold on to the thing that makes you feel good." I want to hear him, but I seem to be almost deaf. It seems impossible after all these years that I am unable to do as I have done, just go on with my recording career. Every bone in my body aches to get on with another record, another piece of work. Even when I am resting, or sick, or at a standstill, I feel that urge, as though I can never stop to think, but must go on. It is important to go on.

After my stay at the hospital in Pennsylvania, I settled back into New York in the summer heat of 1978, determined to pull my life together again. I hadn't seen Louis since our first meeting in April, but we had talked a few times on the phone, and although I didn't tell him exactly what was going on in my life, I told him a lot, considering he was someone I had just met. For some reason, I trusted him totally.

In July we made our first formal date. By then, I had told him exactly where I had been and what I had done.

"That sounds very courageous," he said on the phone, "and very exciting. It means your life will change a great deal." How did he know that? I thought at the time that I would simply go on as I had, with a slight difference. I had no idea what kind of changes were in store for me, but he seemed to sense it immediately.

"Let's meet for dinner, and we'll fill each other in on what's happened since we met at the Ginger Man a lifetime ago," he said. On the phone, his voice was wonderful. He named Orsini's, a restaurant I had only been to once or twice. It was to become one of our haunts, a place of memory, of importance.

When I walked into the restaurant and saw him sitting at the table, waiting for me, I was shocked by how handsome he had become, almost as though I were seeing him for the first time. He was wearing a suit and a tie of violet silk that set off his sparkling blue eyes. The smile on his face was brilliant, splendid, promising, full of spirit.

"Hello, you look happy," he said. "Much happier than you did last time we met." I agreed. We ordered drinks, Perrier for me and a spritzer for him. Louis never drinks much, and then without much zeal.

"Basically, I'm a cheap date," he said. It was seven o'clock, a summer night, the restaurant was filling up, and the waiters eyed us with looks that reflected an awareness of the romance they saw in the making.

"I want to know the story of your life," I said.

"That's only fair. I suppose I know more of yours than you do of mine, having been a fan of your music for a long time."

We talked about our lives.

"Mom was a rebel," Louis said. "She came over here from Norway at sixteen, alone on the ship, following her brother Nick. She intended to go out to Montana and settle near him, but she loved the pace of New York and stayed. She then met my father, who is also Norwegian and is still an engineer. I was born in 1936." He was three years older than I—and many times wiser about many things, I was to learn.

"I have a sister, Dorothy, and when I was in high school I found I loved to draw. I was very good at watercolors, so of course I wanted to do drawings from life models, at which I was not as good."

At Brooklyn Technical High School, Louis realized that he wanted to be a designer, so after graduating he attended Pratt Institute's School of Design. There he studied with Rowena Reed Kostellow, who was a pioneer in design and was to become his mentor. After being in the army, he returned to Pratt to do graduate work and became her assistant.

"Everything in life is design, really," he said. He picked up the cup that held his decaf coffee. It was Italian, a flowered pattern we would come to know well.

"This is designed beautifully," he said. "Look at the way it fits into your hand, the beauty in the pattern that pleases your visual senses while you are pleasing your culinary senses.'' His hand was beautifully shaped, and I wanted nothing more than to put my hand on his. We were only at dessert, but as far as I was concerned, I was staying for the next meal. I was enchanted by his voice.

"Raymond Loewy, one of the greatest designers, designed the Coca-Cola bottle; Charles Eames designed elegant chairs. Each object you touch in life—a silk dress, an airplane, the path through a park, the elevator in a skyscraper—is designed.'' I asked him how he thought of the ideas for his designs.

"I go through a process, investigating every possibility I can think of.'' That seemed beyond me. I was intuitive, jumping to conclusions, never able to read the directions.

"But you must follow your inner instinct about what you finally choose,'' I said.

"Oh yes. And like Oscar Wilde, I have the simplest of tastes— I am always satisfied with the best.''

"I go on raw, animal instinct,'' I said. "I see what I want, and move.'' At least I always had. That night I was cautious, like an animal camouflaged in the forest, waiting quietly, watching closely. Louis fascinated, attracted me. He was talking about things I understood, but in a way I had not heard.

"Actually, I could use more raw instinct in my work,'' he said.

"And I could use more planning.'' We looked at each other.

"Opposites attract,'' he said, and we both laughed. My heart was beating very fast.

In the army, Louis was stationed in Germany as a helicopter pilot and instructor. He once wrecked a helicopter, knocking off the undergear, while showing a student how to land with no power. Fortunately he brought both the student and the helicopter in for a safe landing. Louis was just two hours shy of the air time needed to be sent to Vietnam in 1961.

We had been talking with each other for four hours.

"You have such a musical voice,'' I said.

"Thanks. So do you.'' We both laughed nervously. I was beginning to feel as though I were in high school again.

"I had a radio show in high school, so I learned to speak English without a Norwegian accent. My secret desire, after all the design work, is to be an actor.'' I told him my secret desire was to be an artist, making beautiful things, leading a quiet life, like his. He laughed.

"Well, that is a nice thought. But my life is far from quiet. I travel a great deal to do my work. Probably almost as much as you do. At the moment, I have to share my time between projects that I am designing and supervising. We just finished a world's fair in Okinawa, where I spent a couple of months working with the Japanese on the lighting and the final design. I'm going to Virginia this week to do a big exhibit with a national park there." The thought of Louis alone in some hotel in Japan or Tennessee was interesting. I wondered if someone traveled to meet him there, around the world. We had already settled the most important question, letting each other know we were open to dating. But I didn't know if there was someone waiting for him in the wings. I didn't yet know about the Norwegian designer he had been seeing. I myself was free as a bird.

"I'm going to Europe this week, to do some work on the design for a wine import company," he said.

My heart sank. I wondered whether I would see him again and, looking at him over the table, whether he was feeling the same things I was. It was as if I had stepped onto some strange planet, whose air was very thin and whose altitude was much higher than the moon.

"Do you have a house in the country?" I asked. I knew he did. Jeanne had told me that she could envision me in that house.

"Yes, a house on a lake in Connecticut. And I have a boat in Manhasset out on Long Island. Do you know how to sail?" I didn't, but if he sailed, I would make an effort to learn.

We talked till almost midnight, when the waiters were hovering with anxious looks on their faces. They wanted to close the restaurant, romance or no romance. When Orsini's closed for good, seven years later, the waiters gave me one of those flowered cups—a remembrance, they said, of that first night, when even they could see we were in love.

We both eyed the bill when it came, but he reached out for it before me. I nodded my thanks. He took my elbow as we left, walking out into the saunalike heat on Fifty-sixth Street. "Let's put you in a cab," he said. Again, my heart sank. For a moment I was sure he was sending me, not taking me, home. He stood out in the traffic, waving for a cab. I even liked the way he waved and stood. Everything about him was right—as though he had been sent from heaven.

When the cab arrived, he helped me in, then got in beside me. We drove uptown through the park, talking all the way. I felt I had only begun to say the things I wanted to say to him.

"Will you come upstairs?" I asked. He said he would be delighted. I filled two huge Lutèce glasses full of Perrier for us, and we sat down together on the couch, as close to each other as we had been in the restaurant. We talked for another hour.

"This apartment is huge and wonderful," he said, "and you are lucky you can see the river from the dining room."

"I would like to have two rooms with a view of the river on all sides," I said from somewhere. Actually, I'd never thought about that before.

When Louis got up to leave, we stood at the door, and then he kissed me. We kissed each other, I should say. It was wonderful. I went to bed in a daze.

The next day, flowers arrived. Big, beautiful lilies, yellow suns on green stalks. The note said, "2 RM. Riv Vu. It was wonderful last night. I'll call you as soon as I return." We saw each other the following weekend, and after our second date I asked him if he was free to become entangled with me. We were driving back into the city from Manhasset, where we had spent the day on the sailboat.

"There is someone I have been seeing, or rather, we have been in a relationship that is mostly off." I was crestfallen. But within a few days, Louis no longer had another relationship, and he and I were well into the beginning of ours."

Ever since that night at Orsini's, I found that I could talk to Louis about everything. We soon began spending all of our time together. At first, we talked about getting married but by now marriage seems to be something for other people. We both have been married before, and I like the idea that by not being married, though we are totally committed to each other, we serve in some way to balance the world a little.

"I wonder how we might do it if we did it?" he often asks after we have been to the wedding of one of our friends. "Perhaps Paris, on a boat on the Seine? Or at a ski lodge in the winter in Maine? Or perhaps we could be married at the top of the continental divide.''

Our first trip to the continental divide was at the end of that first summer. We flew to Denver, where my family was having a reunion. We all met at my mother's house.

"Louis, I'd like you to meet my brother David,'' I said. David's face was tan under his blond hair. He is still as towheaded as he was as a baby, I thought. I've known this beautiful, kind, sweet man since he was an infant. Patiently, he taught me how to ski, leading me down Ajax Mountain's steep slopes at Aspen as I followed his elegant form, which made it look so, so easy. David has listened to my tales of triumph and woe through the years. Today he has just come from racing his Formula V cars down in southwest Colorado, to my mother's horror, which he still does when he is not constructing houses. His hands are big and familiar, his eyes blue like my own. I felt my heart melt, and as I put my arms around him I had the familiar feeling of wanting to protect him from the world. Strange feeling, to want to protect a solid, tough, grown-up man from the world. But I have always felt that about Dave. Although he has been through many harsh times, he is in a way too gentle to bear the world's bitterness.

"Pleased to meet you,'' he said, putting out a hand to Louis.

"I feel I already know you, David,'' Louis said. The handshake became a bear hug, my brother's arms wrapped around Louis. It was the same with Michael, who arrived with his son, Matthew, and his wife, Susan. They had flown in from Madison, Wisconsin. In his work as a doctor of speech therapy, Michael has concentrated on patients suffering from aphasia as a result of stroke and also on Vietnam veterans whose head injuries left them with speech problems. His gentleness as a child has carried into adulthood.

"Meet my brother the doctor,'' I said to Louis. Michael's handsome face broke into a wide smile.

"You look like the rest of the family,'' Louis said.

"Welcome. Judy has told us about you.''

Denver John and his fiancée, Allison, came in from New York, where his career as a cameraman was going well. I hugged him. I still think of him as my baby brother—always the youngest even as he matures. Holly and Jim Keach arrived with little Kalen, then a year and a half old.

"Holly, this is Louis." I had told Holly every detail about our meeting and how I felt about him. She went to Louis, her arms open in an embrace.

"Are you overwhelmed by everyone?" she asked. "This is a huge crowd to meet all at once."

"I think I've got the names right," Louis looked like a kid in a candy store. He was surrounded by my family—my mother and stepfather, Robert, as well as my brothers and sister—and he looked like he belonged. He never did have any trouble with the names.

The next day we all piled into cars and went to the mountains. With our packs and boots, our shorts and canteens, we made the hike to Fern Lake. There was talk of the missing man—my father.

"Charlie sounds like a character. Everyone in your family has this vision of him as a bigger-than-life person," Louis said to me. I wish they had met, the Irishman and the Norwegian. I think they would have liked each other.

❧❧❧

In 1978, I started work on my seventeenth album. It had been two years since I had recorded and I was looking for a new producer. David Braun, my friend and former lawyer, suggested I talk to Charles Koppelman.

I had never met Charles, but his name had been familiar to me for years. He was John Sebastian's publisher and had worked with the Lovin' Spoonful and many songwriters. He had also become a producer and formed the Entertainment Company, with Sam Lefrak. Using Gary Klein as his line producer, he had produced albums with Barabra Streisand and had just released Dolly Parton's *Here You Come Again*, also with Gary.

Charles and I sat in my office in the old General Motors building on Fifty-seventh Street, the sun streaming into the room. We talked about the material I wanted to record, a song by a writer I had recently found, Hugh Prestwood. Prestwood is a good, solid country/city writer with a sweet melodic line and strong lyrics. His song "Hard Times for Lovers" would be the title cut. I also planned to record the great Eagles song "Desperado." "Where or When" would be on the album because it had been one of my father's favorites, and I would record Sondheim's "I Remember Sky."

In late August of 1978, I went to Los Angeles to make the record. Gary Klein produced it, and Armin Steiner was the engineer. This was my first experience in many years of making a record without alcohol between me and reality. There was no "reward" at the end of the sessions, at the end of the day. I felt raw and exposed.

"Can we do that vocal again?"

I saw Gary's lean, brown face next to Armin's in the studio.

"Judy, that sounded fine." A duet of mouths moved together.

"Just one more, for me." I said. I was unsure of the sound of my voice still, feeling my way back, or forward, to who I was. I had to learn that life is its own reward.

Back in New York, I remixed *Hard Times for Lovers* and started work on the cover. I wanted to reflect the new feeling I had about my body. I had spent the first thirty-eight years of my life trying to control my weight and I had always wanted to look different than I did. When I had to go to the West Coast in the sixties, one of the things I dreaded most was the trips to Mendocino, where everyone promptly took off their clothes at any time of the day or night and jumped naked into the hot tub together. Everyone thought you were impossibly "square" if you didn't join in. I usually had an excuse, "I must be going." The sackcloth I wore singing didn't work in the hot water of the group baths.

When I couldn't escape the ritual, I breathed in the scent of the eucalyptus and closed my eyes, praying everyone else was too stoned to notice I had no breasts. Sometimes on these trips I went to Big Sur, and at the baths at Esalen I saw thin, beautiful bodies doing yoga in the sunlight while I hid under the hot water and reached for the towel to cover myself.

From the baths at Big Sur, I found my way to yoga classes on West End Avenue in New York. I didn't look bad in a leotard. The yoga was taught by robed, calm, vegetarian young men and women who looked happy. They ate nuts and fruit and drank herbal tea. In the class, I felt an unusual calmness.

My life had changed a great deal by the time I was ready to take the pictures for the cover of *Hard Times for Lovers*. I had lost twenty-five pounds. My diet was now healthy and I'd made progress recovering from my eating disorder. Even my concert rider reflected the difference. Every performer has a long list of items called the rider that concert promoters must provide. Before I quit drinking, I asked for fresh fruit, coffee, a quart of vodka, a bottle of white wine, a case of beer for the crew, and dinner for twelve. It's still dinner for twelve, but now I request homemade chicken soup with no salt, quarts of Perrier, soft drinks, plenty of spring water. Change was difficult, but no one had said it would be easy, and I was getting better.

I called Francesco Scavullo, whom I had come to know when he photographed me for the cover of *Judith*.

"Francesco, would you take some nude photographs of me for a record cover?"

He laughed. "I'd even take pictures of you with your clothes on!"

At his brownstone the next day, among the vivid paintings that reminded me of my own, we drank herbal tea and talked about nudity.

"It is an unusual idea for you to do this. I am surprised that the girl of wildflowers and protest lines and marches wants to take off her clothes. It is quite an idea, and if you don't change your mind"—he stopped and looked at me, then smiled and continued—"it will be a classic cover. I'll have Way Bandy do your makeup again. I know you work well with him."

I had done pictures with Way for my *Judith* cover and thought he was a genius at what he did. His makeup was always soft and looked natural.

"Way is the best makeup artist there is," I said. Two days later we did the pictures. Francesco made it so easy. I was at my most relaxed. It felt very much as though I were having baby pictures taken; he didn't make me feel "looked at" or judged in any way.

At the end of the session, Francesco asked me to turn my back to him, hold my hair up off my neck—he wanted to take that classic photo of the nude that is in every culture, in every century throughout history. The cover was the first photograph of me in my new life, and the picture of the girl with her back to the camera is not only me, but all women, holding their hair off their backs, stretching their arms high above their heads, celebrating sensuality, celebrating life.

When the album was released, word came back that it was a controversial cover. My record company would not publish the whole breast and cropped me on the upper chest, but the nude back portrait is intact. I wanted to tell other women that they were all right, too, as I had come to realize I was. I think of those pictures as a celebration.

Hard Times for Lovers did well. Joe Smith, the new president of Elektra, was enthusiastic about it. It had good radio play and we sold a lot of albums.

After its release, I went on tour in the spring of 1979. Singing in concert was another first—I had to learn to do that all over again as well. Gary Klein came to the first concert on the tour and afterward, in the dressing room, he told me he had been shocked.

"You are singing better than ever," he said. "Better even than on the record. Your voice is in wonderful shape." The strange thing was that after the surgery, my voice did seem to have gained a strength it never had before. People noticed something new. In my lessons with Max, I suddenly understood more about phrasing, and things we had been talking about for years took hold. The years of training had taken me to a new plateau; not only was I singing better than I ever had in my life, but also critics began to write about it. My friends told me it was uncanny, and finally even I knew it. Stephen Holden in the *New York Times* said I had achieved a new level of singing. Reviews took notice of a voice "silvery" and newly strong.

That spring, Louis was able to meet up with me at many concerts because his business allowed him to crisscross the country.

"You can walk around while you sing, you don't have to stand still on every song," he said. It was a great relief that I was able to turn to Louis for help in finding a way to do things differently on-stage.

"You can trust yourself to move, to smile, to take in your audience, and to work with that positive energy they're giving you. You remember what we've said about exploration and raw instinct?" he said. "Here's a place where you can use both."

I put the guitar down on some songs, moved the microphone from center stage. The new space was vast and frightening. We decided to plot out and choreograph each song—how I would move, how the lighting would change. I memorized the moves, and afterward he and I would talk about the concert. This was all in order to make me comfortable with moving on the stage without a guitar. It was a new world.

I worked at Harrah's in Reno in September for eleven days

straight. My fans were there, faithful as ever—those beautiful faces that had witnessed all my adventures stood in the rain, sat in the sun, bought my records, and followed me from one end of the country to the other. I began to have production meetings before every show to discuss the order of songs, change of pace, light cues, to connect with my group before a concert. The details of the production, the amount of the check for the night's work, the "bottom line," are all things I learned to understand anew. Now every time I went out to do concerts, the process that had been slow and painful before was now exciting and fresh.

In February I did the *Tonight* show in Los Angeles, in March the *Today* show in New York, *Donahue* in Chicago. In May I ended the tour of two dozen cities in Alaska and came home to New York.

In August 1979, Denver John was married in Colorado to Allison Henske. I had not been able to write songs for three years. That source and resource, surely as everything else, had dried up. Now the desert bloomed, and songs began to pour out of me again. I wrote "The Wedding Song" and sang it at my brother's wedding. By the end of the year it was on another new album, *Running for My Life*; the lead song was also one of my own compositions. At the end of nine months I had written two dozen songs, more than the total of everything I had written before that. My writing block had vanished.

I felt better physically than I had in years; I had a new lease on life. In 1979, when my record contract with Elektra was up for renewal, I thought I would take the chance to move to Polygram Records when my old friend David Braun became the president of its United States company.

Feeling on top of the world, I went to lunch with David Horowitz, who had become a friend over the years at Warner's, the parent company of Elektra. David was on the board of directors at Warner's and I wanted to tell him my plans. We dined on arugula salad and Dover sole in the dizzy heights of the executive dining room atop Seventy-five Rockefeller Plaza, with show business executives at the tables around us.

"We would like you to stay with the company," said David. "You have been with us a long time."

"That's very flattering, David, but I don't feel I belong with Elektra the way it is run now." Joe Smith had been its president since 1977, and the promotional campaign on my recent albums had been disappointing.

"We are considering a move at Elektra that could be absolutely wonderful for you," said David. "Bruce Lundvall is coming on as president."

Bruce had been at Columbia Records for years; I had met him socially, and he was man of integrity—a man I had long wanted to work with. He lived in New York, and Horowitz told me Elektra was moving back to the East Coast after having been in Los Angeles for ten years. I was convinced part of the problem with my communication with Elektra was the distance. I liked Bruce and he said he liked my music. We would be in the same city and could talk about material, make records, like the old days.

I went home terribly excited to tell Louis about the news.

"I know this will be terrific, but I hope you realize there are no men on white horses at Elektra. You can only do the best work you know how to do."

I knew he was right, but somehow I wanted to believe what David Horowitz had told me. It sounded perfect. I should have known you can't go back.

Elektra made a generous financial offer for my renewal. In spite of my friendship with David Braun, I decided that since I'd had great successes with Elektra, and since they were bringing on Lundvall, I would stay.

When Bruce came on board, I was finishing *Times of Our Lives*. He seemed pleased with the record, and we got along well. He called me the day before I finished mixing the album.

"Judy, I've just come back from England, and I brought you the cast album of a new show that has a great song that would be good for you." I listened to "Memory," from *Cats*, and agreed.

"I want you to go into the studio with an orchestra and do the song. It should go on this album."

"But I've spent all my recording advance, there's nothing left. A session with a big orchestra would be expensive."

"Don't worry, just do it. Elektra will foot the bill." Bill Braun did a beautiful arrangement, and on October 8, 1982, we recorded "Memory" at A&R Studios, with Lew Hahn engineering, in the same room where I had recorded "Send In the Clowns." A lot of the players were the same—cellists, violists—

and Margaret, the harp player. As it happened, that night was Louis's forty-fifth birthday. The musicians played "Happy Birthday" for him fully orchestrated—another working celebration.

The album was well reviewed, but again, there was no support from Elektra. For some reason Lundvall hadn't been able to change things. There was still no promotion.

A record is commercial if it is treated commercially. It's a Catch-22; it's a Möbius strip. Within a few months, Bruce was replaced by Bob Krasnow. I still had another record in my contract.

I realized that part of my problem with getting Elektra to pay attention to my records was that for the past eleven years I had been managing myself, so in 1983 I started interviewing managers. I went to California to see Freddy DeMann. I had always like him when he was in the record promotion business. Ten years earlier, he left the record business to become a personal manager. Gladys Knight and the Pips were among his first clients; he managed the Jackson Five for a few years, and the year I signed my contract with him he had just supervised the release of the third single from *Thriller*, Michael Jackson's incredibly successful album. I always knew he was a brilliant record man, and now he was proving that he knew what he was doing in management as well. A few weeks after we started working together, he signed Madonna.

In the spring, we met with Bruce Lundvall, who was now vice-president of Elektra. We had breakfast at Bob Krasnow's Fifty-first Street apartment. We sat at an oval marble table and talked about the making of what was to be *Home Again*.

"Doesn't this sound incredible?" The Cleveland Orchestra was playing Mahler on Krasnow's new compact disc player. We all nodded in agreement. I looked out the window at the true believers going into St. Patrick's Cathedral, one of the few refuges in midtown Manhattan. I had knelt before the glass in the chapel before I came, praying for calm. It had ceased to bother me that I wasn't a Catholic. I would pray anywhere at any time.

"We have talked to Dave Grusin, and he is eager to produce Judy's new album," said Freddy.

"Dave Grusin is a great producer, I think he's a good choice." Krasnow smiled, the blessing had been bestowed. The Mahler still boomed through the room. We talked about the material we had chosen.

"This is a very commercial album, lots of up-tempo things mixed in with some strong ballads," Freddy said. "We've got an Elton John song called 'Sweethearts on Parade,' and Judy's song about handguns, 'Shoot First,' written with Dave Grusin, and Amanda McBroom's new ballad, 'From Where I Stand.' " (Amanda wrote "The Rose," and is one of the best writers in the business.)

Freddy was enthusiastic and seemed confident that the material on the album would make a record that was indeed commercial.

"I think 'Only You' could be a hit again, as it was for the Yaz in England. We'll do it pure rock-and-roll; it's very Judy and very solid upbeat radio." The meeting ended, and Bob Krasnow seemed happy with the choice of producers. I left feeling good about the whole project. Freddy went back to California and I went to work in the studio.

Dave Grusin and I recorded *Home Again* and finished the mixes in late August and early September of 1983. Stevie Phillips, Stacy's former agent, was married to Dave Grusin at that time, and during the making of *Home Again*, Stevie, Dave, Louis, and I had some wonderful times. The sessions went well and we were excited about the record.

Later in September, Freddy and I went to Elektra's offices for a meeting about promotion. There had been enthusiastic response from Elektra all the way through the making of the album, and now that it was finished we had to think about the video, the ads, the radio, all the things that are part of a good promotional package for a record. I was looking forward to a solid, supportive team working with me.

Bob Krasnow met me at the door to his office, then went back to the leather swivel chair behind his white marble desk. Bruce Lundvall joined us, and we all shook hands and exchanged small talk amid the chrome and glass and marble. We sipped our coffee and settled down to do business.

Bob Krasnow cleared his throat and looked at Freddy as he avoided my eyes. "We don't think this is an album we can sell," he said. "We don't think there is a hit single." Then he looked me straight in the eye. I must have looked sick.

Freddy said, "What happened here? You were all for it a month ago."

"I'm fresh out of suggestions," Krasnow said.

Freddy was a blank, no comment, no reaction, but his face registered the shock I was feeling.

So far Elektra had spent a great deal of money on the album. Didn't they want to recoup their investment? They said they didn't care. It was already spent. They didn't want to spend more money on it.

"I'll tell you what I'll do," said Bob. "I'll give you the album. You can have it as a gift."

I was too stunned to say thank you. It would mean a new and perhaps a very creative rethinking of my whole recording business. At the moment I couldn't absorb it.

Freddy and I left the meeting, putting on our winter coats. In spite of the sun, it was cold outside. Freddy was wearing his white wool coat. I remember being glad he wasn't wearing an endangered animal.

"I'll talk to him tomorrow. I can't imagine what else to do." We embraced, and I found my numb way home to the Upper West Side. Freddy went back to California. I tried to absorb what had happened.

A few weeks later, Louis and I went to Europe for ten days. We visited Virginia Dwan in Eze, France, and then rode the train to Rome, learning Italian phrases. I threw my neck out and spent the entire time with hot packs on my shoulder, for the pain, and looking through the phrase book trying to find out how to say "What the hell happened?" in Italian. When we came home, Louis said I had to give up being mad and angry and accept it.

"You can't do a thing about this. Why don't you take Krasnow's offer and start your own record company, distribute the thing yourself?"

Before I could think about it, I got a call from Bruce Lundvall. "I've found a great song for you, Judy. It's a Michael Masser song. If you like it, it could be the single, and we'll put it on the album."

Good for Bruce, he was still rooting for me.

"It's a good record, Judy. We'll see if we can find the right single to get this company off its ass. Motivate them, as they say."

A few days before Christmas, Michael Masser came to my apartment and sang me "Home Again." It *was* a beautiful song, and a few months later I recorded it as a duet with T.G. Sheppard, a country singer. He put it on his latest album, and it was the lead cut on mine. All recording costs can ultimately be recouped from artists' royalties, but the cost of the recording sessions was now expensive; Elektra paid. I had asked Louis to design the artwork on this album. He had already done beautiful work on the cover and now he changed it, redid the mechanical to include the new song. The total cost of *Home Again* was now very high. In the summer, Elektra released the single of "Home Again."

And let it die.

I couldn't believe it.

"But why would they do that, Freddy?" It made no sense. The reviews were good, and Elektra still didn't push the record.

"Politics," he said.

I hired my own public relations firm. I spent more money on promotion and tried releasing another single, "Shoot First," the song Dave Grusin and I had written together, one of the songs I love the most. It has a wonderful synthesizer arrangement and was very "state of the art" musically. In 1984, "Home Again" was on T.G.'s album and sold a lot of copies. But mine wouldn't budge. Nothing helped. After so much time on a project I loved, it was hard to accept that nothing was happening.

Freddy was as baffled and perplexed as I.

"I hate to take your money when I can't help you," he said. I told him I thought he was a brilliant manager and that I was sorry we didn't make a connection. Somehow I thought if I could just hold out long enough, Freddy would be able to save the day—but Louis was right, the men riding in on white horses are all gone.

There are no shortcuts; there are no heroes. It doesn't matter about the past, and still I cannot stop wanting. Why is the lesson so hard?

An old Chinese proverb comes to mind this morning: "Expect nothing and all will be velvet."

Friday, June 21, 1985 / Eze, France

We left wet and wretched London and flew to Nice, where we've spent ten days with Virginia at her chateau in nearby Eze, a medieval village on the south coast of France. Our stay has been a contemplative time. I found myself staring out at the sea, my inner visions moving, but my body still. It was such a pleasure not to have to be anywhere, do anything. It has been a gift of quiet in which I don't feel I have to compete. I usually have felt that I do, just in order to survive. With myself. And especially with my lovers.

Until I met Louis, I felt I had to perform successfully to have the right to any love. If I were manifesting gold records, awards, praise, public triumph, I was lovable; if not, I wasn't. From the beginning, my relationship with him was different from those I had had with other men. There was a calmness about it; it was not erratic, plunging up and down with every mood and nuance. It held its course, it stayed where you put it. If you should look for it in the place you had left it, it would still be there.

With many men in my life, beginning with my father, I felt I had to prove myself constantly in order to be good enough to be lovable. I thought my father didn't love me unless I was expressing "success." If I was in a creative trough, one of those times that must come with every creative effort, I felt I was failing. With Louis I know it doesn't matter if I am on *Entertainment Tonight* or sitting in the hot tub. I am who I am, warts and all, as they say. I don't feel I must constantly prove myself to gain his love.

It's eleven at night, and quiet here in the chateau. I've come out of a hot bath, my skin is warm, my body tired. I feel exhausted emotionally but relief has come finally. I feel the past slipping away—Freddy and Elektra and worn-out fantasies, crumbling and falling from my body, like dead dreams flying away. There is nothing I can do about the past but turn and face the present. Life is what happens next.

Tomorrow we return to New York, and the day after tomorrow the touring begins again when I sing with the Atlanta Symphony. I'm ready to go home, back to my own work and my own wars.

Tuesday, July 2, 1985 / New York

Long talk with Peter Yarrow, who called about Peter, Paul and Mary's reunion at the Bitter End next week. Of course, I wouldn't miss it.

"It's time for us to get going again, the war in Nicaragua is heating up, we are needed," he says. Peter's familiar face, thin and worried behind his glasses, looks determined. He has kept on with his political work, as I have, for many years, while he, Paul, and Mary each worked at their individual careers. He gives me a hug and holds me at arm's length.

"We are just the same, aren't we?" We both laugh, "This is the old war again," he says, sighing, and I nod my head in agreement. "Don't we ever learn? We have to go out again, and we are good at this, we have done it for so long." I do not tell Peter that this is not enough for my internal Nazi. Through it all, the voice (which is really my voice) says, It doesn't matter. It is not enough, you should have been invited to be on Live Aid at Philadelphia.

After I moved to New York in 1963, I became involved with organizations to register black voters in the South, and in 1964 I packed my guitar and my bags and went to Jackson, Mississippi. I met up with Barbara Dane, a songwriter and singer of blues-oriented songs. We checked into the Holiday Inn in Jackson for the briefing before we started on the road to cities throughout the state. I spent my first days at the Conference of Federated Organizations (COFO) headquarters for voter registration, in the black neighborhood on Lynch Street. Frequently during the next two weeks I was sent to sing at churches and private homes in Jackson, and at night I went back to the motel. Among the whites who gathered around the swimming pool in the evening, you could hear the long Southern drawls and the whispered words "Northerners" and "Communists." We watched people's eyes looking at us and not looking at us. They looked through us, just as they must have looked through the suffragettes who struggled to win their right, and my right, to vote.

After a few days, we were grouped into small bands, four or

five to a car, and began traveling through Mississippi to sing at voter registration centers around the state.

At the COFO office we got our marching orders. There were doctors and lawyers as well as students who had come to help in the effort. People in the movement were getting arrested, but a new group came to Mississippi every day, and from there fanned out into the other Southern states. Everyone was especially frightened since James Chaney, Michael Schwerner, and Andrew Goodman had been missing for weeks by then.

"We don't say it, but we fear the worst," Bob Cohen, the director of the Jackson center, told us. "We have to assume they have been murdered. You should never travel integrated. There is to be no integrated mingling in public spots, with the exception of one or two places in Jackson." Jackson was still a racist city by northern standards, but loose by the standards of most of the South. I would be traveling with the East Gate Singers from Chicago.

In this war zone the rules had to be strictly followed. The Jackson COFO office directed the activities of the whole Mississippi project, and each day every Freedom School office in in the state was called by the main office three times as a standard security practice. When you left one office, you estimated your time of arrival at the next stop, and when you arrived you called your original base to let them know you were safe. If you didn't call within the prescribed time, the office would begin calling hospitals and jails in the area where you were traveling.

My first stop with the East Gate Singers was Greenville. On the way, every pickup truck that passed by on the road carried a double gun rack in the back window. We drove under the speed limit. The kids in Greenville went to school in hot, poorly equipped buildings all summer because they had to be free to pick cotton in the fall. In the 100-degree heat they sang with their bright, hopeful voices, ". . . ain't gonna let nobody turn me 'round. . . ." They were surrounded by white policemen who stared at their black faces with hard, grim expressions. Everywhere we went, the police encircled our freedom rallies, stood with their arms folded on their stomachs, their billy clubs poking out from their belts; they shouted into their bullhorns, warning people not to come out to register, but the people came anyway.

Fannie Lou Hamer traveled with me for a few days. I would sit with her in the Volkswagen, changing the strings on my guitar to keep my hands from trembling. I was terrified, and I found the only way to calm my inner fears was to keep busy and to sing. I thought Ms. Hamer must have felt fear as well, and I asked her.

"Yes, and I pray, so I won't be afraid, and I trust my God," she said.

One night, at the Freedom School offices in Ruleville, a white man came to the door. It was very late. The lights were low; the ceiling fan turned slowly, vainly moving the air around. He had come on a bicycle and was dressed in an Orlon shirt and Bermuda shorts. He introduced himself as Mr. Smith and took the seat offered to him. The heat was unbearable; sweat dripped from every face, black and white alike. Mr. Smith asked questions for four hours and the COFO workers answered every one, without giving any indication of tiring or wanting him to go. He wanted to know why we were here, in his state. How could outside agitators possibly know what the problems were?

"Do you want to intermarry, is that it?"

He had come to the Freedom School knowing that if his neighbors in town found out, he would be persecuted, blackballed, perhaps killed. He kept saying, "I think you people are sincere, you seem sincere, but why do you think you are needed here?"

Next morning, twelve ladies from the North came to listen to the workers and the Mississippi Freedom Democratic Party representatives talk about the problems in the state. These women belonged to the Wednesday in Mississippi Project. They would come and listen and learn, then go back to raise money to send down to Mississippi. I listened, too. We drank hot coffee and ate bread and heard Fannie Lou Hamer, who was brilliant talking to those women. I had grown to love her. She and I were different but not because she was black and I was white. We were different because I had no spiritual faith and I could see in her face that she did. I heard it in her words, I heard it in her singing.

The morning I was leaving Mississippi, they found the bodies of the missing boys, murdered, buried under a newly constructed dam. Chaney, Schwerner, and Goodman had become martyrs. No one was surprised that they had been killed, yet a stunned pall hung over the entire country, perhaps the world.

Outside the office, the morning I was leaving to go back to

New York, a pickup truck rolled to a stop and idled, the engine purring. The driver was a familiar face in town, the white man who had threatened to kill Lafayette, one of the black organizers. We all stood and sang "It Isn't Nice" right at him—the song by Barbara and Malvina.

Afterward we went to the church for a rally. It ended late, and we all went home with no voices left. That was the way I had to end it; it was the only thing I had to give, my voice. Fannie Lou Hamer had her faith, and I had none. Conviction, but not faith. I didn't know then, as Fannie Lou knew, that faith was in me, and I could call on it anytime. One night, at a rally where everyone was frightened and gathering strength from one another, she smiled at me and said, "I believe, help thou my disbelief. I have faith, God help my faithlessness." In her darkest hour, when no music came from her lips, she stood with her faith and her freedom.

After I came home from Mississippi, and long after Fannie Lou was dead, I found strength in her courage and spirit. I will never forget her.

Monday, July 8, 1985 / Connecticut

A call from John Martin in London. An English recording company is interested in doing a record. The idea of working with a new company is very appealing, but I have reservations. They want me to choose the songs, a group of songs of hope, the idea we talked about in London last month. The record will be with players from the Royal Philharmonic and the London Symphony. They want to do it in September, which means I'll put all the material together, the arrangements that I have already and six new ones that will be done by a very good composer, Tony Britten.

If the old ways are falling off like old skin, what is going to replace my raw flesh? There is no burn center for victims of change, except by putting one foot in front of another, going through the flames.

Saturday, August 3, 1985 / Newport

Blue moon. Yesterday was a full moon and today as well. It only happens once every seven years that the full moon falls twice in the same month. They say it brings luck.

First day of the Newport Folk Festival revival at Fort Adams State Park, a magnificent setting overlooking the boats, the sea, and the bridges. It has been fourteen years since the last one. The festival closed because of huge crowds that became so unruly, the little town couldn't contain the people or the energy.

Louis and I are here together, as though I'm showing him a scene from my past.

"I don't remember you as a folk singer. To me you will always be a singer who defies categories." I laugh because I'm still uncomfortable about being categorized at all.

We are all here this weekend, performers who played the mountain fiddle and the ones who appear on television, the ones who make commercial music and the ones who keep faith with a folk tradition. I wondered for years if I belong among a group called folk singers, as if in the name there might be some contradiction, but today I find it no longer matters. We are all so different. In other times, I might be called a troubadour, in other countries a chanteuse or a singer-speaker. I might dress in silk or leather, but still I would sing these songs I choose from the world of music and story, whether written by anonymous folk or Broadway lyricists. I know I do belong.

Many newspapers and national magazines are here to cover the event, and in the grassy quadrangle behind the stage, I join a group under an elm tree, posing for photographs.

"Can you hold it, just like that, thanks." Dave Gahr's camera is snapping every few seconds.

"On the count of three, cross your eyes," says Mimi, and giggles. The Baez clan, Mimi and Big Joan and Joanie, along with me, are immortalized with our eyeballs looking in every direction but toward the camera. Dave Gahr has photographed many festivals. Though his hair is now gray he looks the same, and his smile of pleasure is familiar. He always looks pleased to be at the right place at the right time, and his enthusiasm makes you feel you are, as well.

"Put your arms around each other, and look at me without crossing your eyes, girls," Dave says. We smile, serious business. Mimi and Joan both do their sets in the afternoon, and at the end of Joanie's she asks us all onto the stage and we sing "Amazing Grace" together, with Taj Mahal, Dave Bromberg, Tom Paxton, Bonnie Raitt, and Dave Van Ronk joining us. From the stage, I see bridges looping into the air over the blue water and the audience spread out on the lawn, dressed in every color of the rainbow, babies and slim, long-haired mothers and bearded older men who used to be flower children. And teen-agers, the new banner bearers, sunburned and dancing to the music.

We go back to our rooms at the Viking Hotel for a bath and dinner. In the dining room, the Baez family is at a table looking as though they just stepped out of a Henry James novel. They have an easy beauty that is not learned; they were born with it. After dinner there is a party in one of the big downstairs rooms, with many drinks and much nostalgia.

In a corner of the room, I find my old friend Dave Van Ronk. Dave and I haven't seen each other for years. He still looks like a big bear, and he sang this afternoon, doing his own songs and those of other singers. He has a beautiful rendition of "Both Sides Now," which he sings with his smoky, whiskey voice. Dave and I talk about our musical tryst so many years ago.

In the winter of 1961 Van Ronk and I were on the same bill together, singing at the Laughing Buddha in Oklahoma City. We were both put up in the wooden house owned by the club.

"I slept downstairs by the heater while you had the floor above," I say to Dave. It was deep-freeze February weather in the Midwest.

"The place was a block from the club, remember? They gave us the place for free, along with our paycheck from the club."

I remember those nights. We would come home from the club, walking together through the cold streets of Oklahoma City, and I would huddle under the covers, drinking Scotch to keep warm.

"You always told me stories and sang me songs till I fell asleep," I say.

"Those were my best stories, about the time I was in the Merchant Marine, before I became a folk singer. You always wanted me to keep telling the stories, even when you could hardly keep awake." I was comforted in that Oklahoma flat country, so far from home, far from my baby and my husband in the farmhouse in Connecticut.

"Oh Dave," I say, "were we ever that young?"

There is a fraternity one feels with the warriors of that road, a real kinship with the soldiers of misfortune and fortune whose days were spent spinning yarns in song, drinking nights away, and touring from one town to another.

I remember other clubs across the country, and Dave and I swap stories of the places we have worked in and the bizarre things that happened during our "work day."

"There was a hotel I used to stay at in Chicago, called the Cass," I say.

"I remember the Cass. I stayed there often on the road," Dave says. "It was a real dump!"

"Yes, even worse than the Oklahoma City house we stayed in! I often didn't finish working till late, and was afraid to walk the Chicago streets alone. Bob Booth gave me his handgun one night, 'just in case.' I put it in my pocket, sure I would know what to do with it. Back in the hotel room, as I stood in front of the open window, the gun went off. I lay in bed thinking I had probably shot someone down in the street, waiting for the cops to come and get me. In the morning I found that the bullet had hit the window bar, ricocheted back into the room, and fallen on the floor near the spot where I had been standing. I returned the gun to Bob that afternoon, and told him what had happened.

" 'You just don't know how to do that,' " he said, pointing it away from me. It went off again, the bullet plunging deep into the side of the door.

Dave shakes his head. "It's amazing any of us is alive," he says.

We talk about the early Newport festivals. The memory is hazy. I don't remember it as a clear, legible line, but as a fog of music and people I knew and loved. Son House's face, beaming while he sang; standing around with the Charles River Valley Boys from Boston, Val and John Cooke, listening to Lightnin' Hopkins play all night till day broke; in the hot sun, standing with Ralph Rinzler, watching a man from Nova Scotia make engravings in whalebone out on the lawn at one of the crafts workshops; hugging Mary Travers around the waist, and her hugging me back, after one of the first appearances she did with

Peter and Paul; being in the dressing room with Buffy Sainte-Marie and Maria Muldaur, putting flowers in our hair before we went on stage for the finale one Saturday night and laughing like schoolgirls; staying up all night trying to comfort a young man who was on a bad acid trip with Leonard Cohen in the same room practicing "Hey, That's No Way to Say Goodbye," with me joining in on the choruses; the feeling at the big finales after the last concert, where Joan Baez sang, and Pete Seeger and Mike Seeger, and Theo Bikel and Odetta: joining them on-stage at the end of one night when we all had the feeling we could change the world.

Dave Van Ronk is older and looks tired. When his refill comes, he drinks deep and launches into another story, one of his arms still looped around my shoulder. His cheeks are rounder and he is much taller than I remember. Suddenly, I must leave. The ice in my Perrier has melted, drops of water run down into my sleeves, and I am aware that I have no tolerance anymore for long hours and old stories. There is something terribly lonely about drinking a Perrier when everyone else is fueled for the night and just getting started. It is like an amputated limb that buzzes, still registering pain and pleasure, though the part itself is long gone. I feel enormously sad for a moment. It's not that I want a drink; perhaps my sadness is for all the years I've lost. I head upstairs to a good night's sleep thinking how far we have all come, how much we have changed, and how much we are really the same.

Sunday, August 4, 1985 / Newport

This afternoon I did my set, closing the second day of the festival at Newport. I went on late in the afternoon, singing for ten thousand people who believe they have a chance to be heard again.

Backstage, Mr. Bones is sitting in a blue canvas chair. He is white and old, and the bones between his fingers dance, though I cannot hear the sound. His body's whiteness and the white bones move in time to the music as I watch him across the grass. The day is almost over, everyone is tired and happy, the crowd is leaving the grassy lawn, the performers are milling, laughing, listening to Mr. Bones, talking about old times.

"People seem ready to get back into the swing of 'social commitment,' and this was sort of a shot in the arm to everyone," someone says. The crowds begin to stream off the green lawn, heading toward their cars, heading home. Do they know their power? They just raised a hundred million dollars to feed the hungry, they are the same people who marched in Atlanta and went to jail on the picket lines for equal rights and votes. They stopped the Vietnam war machine. They were tired and are going to wake up now after having had a rest; they are going to pick themselves up and do it again in Nicaragua, as they did it in Vietnam.

On the water, boats and bridges under blue sky. Newport at her best, coming home.

Tuesday evening, September 3, 1985 / Grosvenor House, London

I flew to London to make a record with a symphony orchestra that will be distributed by RCA in the United Kingdom. Staying at the Grosvenor House, I am remembering my trip to England in 1977, to do *The Muppet Show.* I was here at the same hotel, even the same room. Every day I went swimming in the pool, with the exotic paintings of Oriental women on the walls; sometimes Edward Heath, the former prime minister, would swim beside me. Though there were great successes in my career—hit records, glad tidings—I was in misery. But now, inside me, where the garden had been dead, there are flowers blooming. Peace of mind, the priceless thing that eluded me and that I thought I could find outside myself, is mine today.

James Bond walks past my room, down my hallway, in the middle of the night. Agent 007 in the flesh, Sean Connery. Dressed in a pink silk robe, I was pulling my dinner cart into the hall when a handsome man stopped, looked right at me, and said, "May I help you?"

"Oh, yes," I said, "yes, you can help me move this thing into the hall." He is much more handsome in person than in the movies. "Thank you," I said. He has a ready smile and looks intelligent—a nice, stable man. Solid. I wanted to tell him about reading St. Augustine and watching *Octopussy* in a Fargo motel room. He looked like the sort of person who would understand the situation.

I retreat to my room and unpack, buzzing with the feeling that happens when the movies come to life. Tomorrow I will meet Tony Britten, who will be producing this album.

Saturday night, September 7, 1985 / London

Today I spent eight hours at the Abbey Road Studio, where the Beatles made so many records. This is not the project I came to London to do, but another: two songs for a collection of Andrew Lloyd Webber songs. I am one of a number of singers who will work with Andrew Powell on this album. I am working on a song called "Another Suitcase in Another Hall," a song I only heard this week.

I was nervous about Andrew Powell, who is a new name to me. He is producing this collection, and I haven't met him until today, though he comes highly recommended. That old familiar fear of having a man's hands around my throat comes over me.

"That's just great, Judy," he says, and with his English accent he could be saying anything at all. I'm on the floor of the studio, my head encased by earphones, my music stand in front of me. We have just heard the playback of the last take on the song.

"I'd like to repeat that last line," I say, trying to get my voice to sound civil. That's the thing about the voice—if you are upset about singing something right and say it, it sounds tense, and I don't mean it to be tense. The musicians who are playing are very good, and the song sounds fine, but my perfectionism will not let anything rest.

"Fine, it's your version of the song, do it as many times as you'd like," says Andrew into the earphones. I can see him in the booth behind the glass, a full floor above me. To get to the booth from the floor of this studio, you must walk up an entire flight of stairs. Andrew's tea, white, with one lump, is getting cold; he would like to pack this in and get on to another song. I wind up doing it half a dozen times and then feel upset—I think I sang too much, maybe strained my voice. Back up in the booth a fresh cup of tea is in Andrew's hands. We do a rough mix, listening to the takes we have just done, and watch the video screens above us, where the configuration of my voice appears in dancing colors, circles and loops, crossing each other.

"You have a very pretty configuration, if you don't mind my

saying so," says Andrew. Every mix, every song, is life and death, none of the technology has changed that. I won't be around for a final mix or the mastering, and ultimately I am at the mercy of the producer, whom I may not see again this year.

"Andrew, this sounds like me, this take. I am very happy about this whole thing. Is there some way you can mark down the equalization, the level to the instruments, so that it will maintain that quality?"

"This equipment will do anything. We just find your configuration on the video screen digitally, touch a dial with these numbers on them, and it will always be thus, as you like it." I don't really believe him, but I have no choice.

"How great, no need for the singer to do anything but sing, what?"

"That's right," says Andrew. He sips his tea. We say good-bye. I shake his hand in parting with a prayer that he will be able to remember my configuration in the final mix, when it counts. On Tuesday I begin the project I actually came to London to do. It will be another producer and a new crowd of people; I am coproducing and will inflict, most assuredly, my will and purpose upon it.

Monday, September 9, 1985 / Grosvenor House, London

How hard it is to have a relationship with anybody who is constantly at a distance. Louis at one end of the telephone, the connection is terrible.

"What time is it in New York?"

I think of the whales and fish swimming between our voices.

"It's raining, I love you, I love you," I say, barely able to hear him, my own voice echoing in the ocean. There must be shipwrecks and mermaids, around which our words wiggle and plunge.

"I can barely hear you, it is sunny and bright," I hear his voice three times, crackling, breaking apart. It is pointless to go on. Not even a thought is complete on this lousy connection.

"Wish I were with you. I love you. Sleep well. God bless you. Good-bye, good-bye, I miss you."

Through the sound of submarines having an underwater race, I think I hear anger and unhappiness in his voice.

Before I met Louis, I needed a loophole through which I might, if I chose, fall and break my neck, or my heart. With him the loophole is sealed at last. But sometimes I feel the effort that is required to be deeply involved with the "creative" process is just as threatening as another lover might be. Maybe more so. And I remember his words when we met, that he didn't know if he could take it again, another love affair of separation and tours and telephones. I have been on the road for more than two months. Months since I have been with him to his house in the country, where he loves to go and where I love to go as well. He is feeling lonely, I know. So am I.

Tuesday, September 10, 1985 / London

A sore throat, the serious, heavy kind! I couldn't believe it last night, when I felt it coming on. I hoped it was some kind of nervous anxiety about the recording sessions that begin today. But there it was, in the middle of the night, a painful, deeply sore throat. All night I woke every two hours, drank bitter lemon, the only thing in the mini bar that looked as if it might be fortified with vitamin C, and prayed. And laughed. This is ridiculous.

Aspirin, liquids, a humidifier ordered from Harrods, gargling with salt and eating salt so I won't get dehydrated. I'll get through today, tomorrow I have off, so I will get in bed and stay for a day, with the steamer, learning lyrics, and drinking lots and lots of chicken soup.

Evening of the Unicorn, September 10, 1985 / London

I am working in the Olympic Studio, a sister studio to the one where I first recorded here in London, when Mark Abramson and I came over in 1966 to make *In My Life*.

Keith Grant, the engineer I am working with, is very good. He has made records with Barbara Streisand, Tony Bennett, Ella Fitzgerald, and many symphonies in Europe and the United States. His hands are magic; he knows the right microphone, the old model, a Neumann U 47. Neumann doesn't make it anymore, but it makes my voice sound like me. In New York I rent the Neumann microphones from David Smith, who has a priceless half dozen. Keith has three, plus the old Pultec echo chamber, no longer in production, that adds just the right amount of sweetness to the sound of the voice, complimenting the natural sound of this room where we are recording, a huge room made of wood, with a high ceiling; it's like the old A&R Studio in New York where I recorded "Send In the Clowns," only Olympic is ten times the size of A&R. It is personal, built for singers.

Deciding who is going to engineer and produce my records has always been difficult because I, like all singers, am at the mercy of the producer if he has an agenda that does not include hearing the lyric. I have struggled to make the lyric understandable from the beginning. At first, it was nothing one had to fight over. You listened to the song, the singer, the story. But as "productions" became more complicated and rock-and-roll dominated the technical aspects of the music business, finding an engineer who knew how to record a singer and not embed the voice deep among the sounds of strings, drums, horns, and whatever else was handy became a real problem.

A big orchestration doesn't necessarily mean too much sound; it can be just the thing that's needed to flatter the singer and set up the lyric. But I always have my heart in my mouth if I don't know a producer, because it can mean heartache, fights, short tempers, and ultimately that I am not happy with the final product; I can't afford to let things go that far wrong.

I am always amazed when I listen to the Doors that, contrary to later rock and roll, you can always understand every word Jim Morrison is singing. It was true for Elvis, for the Beatles, the Everly Brothers, even the Mamas and the Papas and Crosby, Stills, Nash and Young. But for many years during the seventies and into the eighties, you might have thought it was a crime for anybody to know what the story was in most pop music. I suppose the producers' theory was that if so much money was being spent on the musicians, then they should be heard.

I remember one story about Leonard Cohen and Phil Spector, who was famous for a very successful style of recording that was known as the "wall of sound." For some reason, Leonard was given Spector as a producer by his recording company, Columbia. Phil was so determined that Leonard should have no say in the final mixes that he kept the master tapes from Leonard at gunpoint.

It really feels like a matter of life and death, and I must always make sure an engineer or a producer is right for me. Paul Simon sent me to Phil Ramone. Phil understands how to record the voice, and in making records with him I have come to trust him. Phil says that Keith Grant is one of the best engineers and producers of all kinds of music in the world.

Phil is right about Keith. The level of voice to track is right. I can relax and sing. In spite of my sore throat, we record five songs. They sound good, the orchestra is divine.

Through the park in a London taxi, past the streetlamps that light the park, back to the Grosvenor House, exhausted. Lots of chicken soup and a long, good night's sleep.

Thursday night, September 12, 1985 / London

It is all going so well and I am so ill! The problem is time. I am on such a tight schedule. I must record and mix sixteen songs in three weeks and be back in the States on the twenty-fourth of September for a concert with the Atlanta Symphony. Three more songs with the orchestra, and this evening three more, but the ones tonight are without vocals. I am feeling wretched, very ill. I've got two days off now, and Sunday we begin again. I'll spend the next two days in bed, praying for calm, for health.

Making a record is like living in a black hole. I spent a twelve-hour day yesterday, working at the studio. We added the chorus of singers, the little boys from the Trinity choir.

Sixteen songs done, and most of the final vocals. I'm much better, just a bit worn out, tired in the voice. Coming up for air, eating, sleeping, making a phone call, pressing on now to get this album done in the next two or three days. Everyone seems to think ''Jerusalem'' is a single.

Wednesday, September 18, 1985 / Olympic Studio, London

Louis came for the weekend on the way to Sweden for a business trip. They want his ideas for a new transportation system in Copenhagen. Though I know he wanted to talk about a thousand things, I spent the entire time in bed, resting, trying to get over the flu, and not wanting to talk much. I was so sick I didn't have any energy to give. I hope he wasn't sorry he came. He did go out with me to the recording studio. After hearing what we had done, he looked at me in amazement.

"You can hardly speak on the phone, but you're singing fine." We both smiled. By now he has seen me in every conceivable situation and his being here helps me get through the day.

It's just before noon on Wednesday. Keith Grant is at the board, his black hair so curly it stands out straight from his head. His hands are on the computerized board, his fingers jumping, pushing, moving, pressing; buttons, channels, red and green lights, rows of red knobs, each one a different channel. Strings. Drums. Guitars. Horns. When Keith sits behind the console during a take of a song, his body moves almost as if he were dancing.

I thought that was a good take yesterday. I hear the voice raw this morning, no echo, sounds hoarse, troubled, choppy, no air, no ambiance, as stark as a bruised knee. The flu is there, the voice is not doing what I call on it to do. I suppress a desire to scream, and take another sip of black studio coffee. Keith's hands on the wheels and dials throw a switch, the echo is on and there I am, round, smooth, the voice I recognize as my own.

Late in the evening

An early night—I only worked fourteen hours today! Back at the hotel at 11:30 P.M. and sleep late! Till 8:30 A.M.

Saturday, 1:10 p.m., September 21, 1985 / London

The computer goes down. Having made an incredible mix, voice sounding strong, the big lighted machine, full of knobs and switches, begins to beep and flash "#59" on its digital readout. Keith pulls out a big fat book and goes to #59—"bad initial input." He does another pass at the mix and punches "Keep." As some lights flash, he picks up the phone and calls maintenance.

"Do you remember the old quarter-inch tape? Cutting the

song on the block, with a razor?'' he asks. Mark Abramson and I would sit together over the ribbons of tape he had cut—so many brown ribbon streamers, my life—and stuck on the tape deck so that they hung over the edges. My heart was always in my mouth, fearing he would lose one or put them back in the wrong order; they were like strips of my own skin. But Mark was a great producer.

Each year I made another album, and the complexity of the technology increased. There were more tracks, wider tape, more microphones, dials and switches, massive rooms filled with blinking machines whose dials spun around. More and more time was spent on the mix, putting the final levels of voice to instruments; I know people who moved into the studio for weeks and months to mix. Sometimes it seemed as if the singer were a tourist, passing through to add the notes, then passing out of the process, like a phantom.

I refuse to become a phantom.

Now—red lights off, we have gone back to the previous mix. The computer seems happy. It bleeps "OK" and takes the mix.

It's late, I'm tired, but not weary to the marrow with fighting, as I have been in the past with some producers. I'm safe with Keith. With him I haven't had that feeling of my throat being laid naked across the editing block—waiting for cold sharp steel to slice across my cords, splitting the white skin open and laying bloody white muscles out in the air. When I tell him to bring out a word, a phrase, he does not look at me as though I am certifiable, he just twists a knob or two, and lo, there is the lyric.

The live mixes were great; now, we go for perfection.

"You have to be a perfectionist, nobody else cares," Keith says. "It's not my name they look at on the album, it's yours."

Sunday morning, September 22, 1985 / London

I am sitting in front of the window, looking out on the courtyard. The sky is a scuddy blue and white, clouds and sun. London at the end of September. I have on my pink robe with the blue silk bird on the back, my tray with coffee and the last of my cereal is sitting beside me. I am listening to the completed record of *Amazing Grace*, an album of songs of hope—it was finished yesterday, when we did the last three mixes and the sequence. I have done the whole album, from beginning to end with the orchestra, in twelve days. The twelve days of Christmas, which is when it will be released in England. There are big risks that worked on this album, a performance of "Amazing Grace" that is original and flawed, not as perfect and therefore perhaps better than I would have done if I could have.

The sky is very blue now, all blue.

I wish Louis were here, too. It is a good finish. Today, finally, I am over the flu, just in time to pack up the record and go home.

Thursday, September 26, 1985 / En route,
Kalamazoo to Minneapolis

Back from England, and out on the road again. The hotel in Kalamazoo was drab, and that fleeting road depression hit me coming into the room last night and going out this morning. How did I, a girl who loves quiet, get this job of a wandering minstrel?

"Ms. Collins, let me take your things," says the driver of our limousine, meeting me at the door of the hotel, guiding me toward the sleek stretch Cadillac. I decline, grasping my shoulder bags to my sides; they're the only things that seem really mine on these long trips. Maria gives me a good-morning hug.

"How are you, did you sleep well?" She looks bright and fresh, her makeup on, a purple wool cape thrown over her shoulders. It's chilly, really autumn here.

"I feel good; nothing like a night in Kalamazoo to set you up."

When I told Holly yesterday how long I still have to travel in the next six weeks, which is all of the time, she said it would be surprising if Louis didn't kill me.

There has been more traveling this year than last. I'm up to sixty concerts already, there are twenty to go. I am away so much right now, and it has been a tough year, with so much distance. I reach out to him more, try to let him know I am there in spirit even when I am away on a plane and know what we really need is a few days in the country, together, making love, talking, being.

Tuesday evening as we ate dinner at Frieda's, he told me he feels I am "apart."

I don't feel the distance. Am I being insensitive? Maybe I don't tell him often enough how much he means to me, how wonderful he is, how handsome, how kind, how amazing as a friend and as a companion. As a lover. I tell him tonight. Back at home after dinner, we are alone, and the lights are low, and the candles are burning, and our peace is returning. We'll make it through this year, I know it. Then, when it is over, I can rest.

But at dinner I felt rage, the desire to weep, to isolate, to get up and throw the table over. It lasted about ten minutes while I sat glaring over my tomatoes and mozzarella, my appetite gone.

That feeling is very seductive. I would have liked, with all the old familiarity it brings, to have stayed in it for a while. Drama. Fire. Argument. Recrimination. Scenes that begin with "How can you say such a thing to me, you are being unsupportive and awful, just when I need love and tenderness and understanding!" and end with "I'm leaving" and the door that slams, such a feeling of triumph, of fleeting satisfaction that is so sweet because it is so brief. The hangdog return must follow, the bitter reproaches eaten without the salt of satisfaction, for there was never any satisfaction in these scenes I played so many times. Such a scene flared and evaporated into the air when his hand reached over and held mine on the table.

"You're here now, and I do love you."

The territory of the torn, ragged, wounded, howling lover is forbidden. I did it once too often.

The man I was seeing before I met Louis, a man I'll call Samuel, was someone with whom I acted out many of those scenes. We did not check our words but let fly, intending to wound. The last time I saw him was over seven years ago.

On March 2, 1978, Samuel announced he was ending our three-and-a-half-year relationship. It had never been completely successful, but it was as close as I got to intimacy in those days. He called me on a morning after we had spent what I thought was a good weekend together. He said he would not be coming back.

"I'm tired of having two of everything, one at your place, one at mine," he said. Along with his toothbrush, I wondered if he also had another lover at his apartment.

I was in a state of shock and asked him if we could see each other to talk it over—wasn't there some mistake? There had to be. He agreed to come by late that afternoon to see me one last time. A kind gesture.

When he arrived we sat on opposite couches and he said nothing. I asked him why he was leaving. He had no answer except that the time had come to move on. I had done this so many times that I recognized the script. Here is where he stands up as I had done. I knew the ending; I had often been on the other end of the scene. There was no discussion. His eyes kept wandering to the glass in my hand. The ice had melted and the play was over.

After he left, I called a messenger service to pick up his bicycle and typewriter and the pages of his partly finished novel and take them back downtown to his apartment. I sent him one white rose and a note that said, "I can't live like this." I didn't see how he could walk away from what we had had with not even a glance back. I have never seen him since. So much for therapy, maturity, friendship, and love.

At first, I sifted the memory of that day back and forth, trying to make it come out some other way. I dreamed a thousand endings and thought any one of them would have been an improvement. I wanted it any way but the way it was. Now every cell in my body is replaced. I have entirely new ears and eyes and my nose is new and my nipples and toes and my navel are all brand new. My liver is new and my small intestine. My gall bladder and spleen are mint fresh, as are my blood and some of my brain cells. My heart is new. I've heard it said that when you lose something, you make way for something better to come. Soon after, my life with Louis began, and has led me so far away from that dark time.

Friday, September 27, 1985 / En route, Minneapolis to Columbus

Last night I saw my friend Susan Rice. She is a writer whose screenplays have been optioned by Jane Fonda, Louise Lasser, Robert Redford, and Marlo Thomas, among others. Her comedy about chimpanzees is currently being filmed in New Mexico. I always call Susan to play her my latest song and she gives me her latest screenplay to read.

"I love the new play," I say. It's called *Enough Rope* and is about sisters who discover a murderer living in their condominium.

"Do you like it better than the other one?" she asks, making a sad face. Like many comedy writers, Susan seldom indulges in a conversation without humor that is aimed at herself.

"I love all of your plays equally," I say.

"It's impossible to love all your children the same. Just don't tell the one who's getting the short end." As yet, Susan's only children are her plays.

A visit with Clark. He is so much a cutout of his dad, it makes me gasp. He walked into the dressing room with the granola and coffee beans I had asked for ("Horsefeed with raisins!"— he laughed), and his face, always, is still my own—the eyes and the cheekbones, which are not as etched as they were, but are now looking fuller since he has put on weight. His red hair is very, very short—the tiny strand down the back, punk style, is strawberry. He looks happy, normal, well. That pale thin wraith, the ghost of whom was still there when I saw him in February, is going, chased off by the sun and by the sanity that has come with health. He still seemed like a fragile child last spring. Last night when he walked through the door, I saw my son, a man, no longer a child.

After Clark returned to New York in 1974, we spent the next three years in a strange dance of truth and lies. He went to St. Ann's in Brooklyn, graduating within a year. At home, we maneuvered around each other's habits and had our daily hassles. I was tense and short-tempered. In the mornings he would give me a look that sent a spasm of guilt through my body. There is nothing quite like having your own child know the truth—that your life is unmanageable.

As my life changed, Clark's own career in school moved him from Brooklyn to a short semester at Sarah Lawrence, to a year at the New School in New York, two years at the Rhode Island School of Design, and three semesters at Columbia, where he studied Mandarin Chinese and semiology. When he was twenty-four, he began to find himself. He went out to St. Paul, where he started school, got his life together, and now, happy and healthy, lives on his own.

He has made a life I respect and admire out there in the far regions of the Midwest. He has lost that waif look and become healthy. He will graduate, finally, soon.

Home to the warm, empty apartment. Louis is up at the house in Connecticut, where a big limb from the willow tree was blown down, and the electricity is off. I haven't been to the country place for a long time, and won't get there, I should think, till November. By that time the hot tub will be in and working, the record in England will be out.

Though I am alone here, I am not alone. The Buddhists and Thomas Merton say that when you are meditating, you bring the forces of evil and good into balance in your own life, and doing this for yourself is to do it for the planet, for the universe. In that sense I suppose that prayer and meditation are political actions as much as any march or demonstration may be. Emmet Fox wrote, "Prayer is the only real action in the full sense of the word, because prayer is the only thing that changes one's character." He also said that prayer actually changes the physical makeup of people, places, and things; that it is not an illusion, but a reality. When I am able to meditate, the pain leaves, the tide turns.

Trust Your Heart

Tuesday, October 1, 1985 / New York

A fall day, crisp air, bright light; the Hudson is shining blue beyond the trees on Riverside Drive. Yesterday I ran into my former sister-in-law, Minky Goodman, walking briskly along Madison Avenue with a glazed look about her blue eyes.

"Minky, hello."

For a moment she looks beyond me, her face concentrated.

"You have mountains and far pavilions in your eyes!" I say. She hugs me, laughing, wrapping me in blue angora, a tight hug.

"Honestly, I was trying to decide what to wear to a party tonight, for which I am now late already," she says, out of breath. "How are you?"

Minky and I, along with all of my ex-husband's side of the family, became alienated during my divorce and the custody fight over Clark. I saw her across the courtroom in Rockland County with Peter's family, and I hated her and them. Her husband, my former brother-in-law, Gary, was no longer on my side. How life catches up with us and teaches us to love and forgive each other.

Minky and I have met in New York during these years. We made our peace and now spend time talking about our sons. We are so different and so much alike—a lace-curtain Irish girl and one from Westchester County, trying to solve the problems of living, being grown women, mothers, lovers, friends. When her own time came, Minky was ill prepared for divorce as I had been, with children running amok, the image of the good Catholic family broken after fifteen years.

"Judy, I'm graduating from social work school in a few months, at last," she says. She went back to school after her divorce. "Maybe after all the things I've gone through, I can help somebody a little bit. It would be nice to have all this life experience to do some good!"

"Congratulations! That's wonderful. How are your sons?" She tells me all but one are out of the house. "Adam is all teenager, either trouble or triumph. But I can't complain, they are well. How is Clark?"

The cousins have remained close friends, and I tell Minky that Clark is great, looking healthy and living in Minnesota. The look I remember in Minky's eyes when we were young is there again: the same questions burn in her eyes, the ones we talked about in Denver when her hair was black and she came to conquer her lover's family, before the babies and the diapers and adolescent boys' problems. She is young again, intense, a girl again. I never thought I would wish her well, but I do.

Wednesday, October 2, 1985 / New York

Reading Thomas Merton's secular diary this morning, I find this quote: ". . . people began to get self-conscious about the fact that their misconducted lives were going to pieces; so, instead of ceasing to do the things that made them ashamed and unhappy, they made it a new rule that they must never be ashamed of the things they did. There was to be only one capital sin: to be ashamed."

I call Max today to see how he is. He likes me to be well prepared and is upset that the recording was so rushed.

"Max, it went well, and I want you to hear the songs." I am nervous, but he sounds happy to hear from me.

"Fine, come on over, we'll listen." I am relieved, glad I am going to see him. I cannot bear to be distanced from him.

Yesterday, out of the blue, I get a call from Steve Harris, who was the top record promotion man at Elektra for ten years, in its early days. He worked on many of the songs that became hit singles for me, among them "Amazing Grace" in 1972 and "Send In the Clowns" in 1974, the first time it was on the charts. Now he is working for Norman Kurtz, who manages Rupert Holmes.

"Judy, I have some news for you. Rupert Holmes wants to go into the studio with you as soon as possible to make a record of "Moonfall," the love song from *The Mystery of Edwin Drood*. We're opening the show on Broadway in December, and we would record early next year. Are you interested?"

I resist yelling out loud.

"It's a wonderful song, Steve. I'd love to do it. Bruce Lundvall gave me a tape of it this summer, and I saw the Shakespeare in the Park production. Of course I'll do it!"

"Rupert will arrange and produce it with an orchestra early next year. What do you think?"

I think it is uncanny. In the morning, not an hour before Steve called, I had put the tape Bruce had given me on the cassette player and was listening to "Moonfall," learning it.

Monday, snowed in, October 7, 1985 / Butte, Montana

Last night Butte was as bare as an old bone when I arrived in the late afternoon, not even a splendid sunset to put color in her cheeks. She looked sallow and washed out, finished with summer, but not a sign yet of snow anywhere except on the tops of the low mountains. We are looking for a location to do a video for the English recording. The producer in London wants snow, and the location scout, Gary Hanson, looks as if he stepped out from a Marlboro ad. He knows where the best snow will be tomorrow. At my motel room, as I closed the curtain, I saw the snow beginning to fall outside my window. It was falling hard by the time I went to sleep, and this morning the ground is white, the snowdrifts up to the roofs. I thought we would go high into the mountains, but we are going nowhere. We are snowbound.

In spite of all my best-laid plans, I am going to be away from Louis on his birthday tomorrow. From the moment we began to plan for this snow scene I was worried about it, and tried to put it ahead by doing it last week; but here I am, and the snow is so heavy I cannot get out the door. Louis said on the phone that he is upset I will not be with him on his birthday tomorrow. I'm angry at the weather, but what am I to do.

I think of the fact that God not only comforts the afflicted, but also afflicts the comfortable.

Tuesday, October 8, 1985 / Butte, Montana

This morning I call Louis to wish him a happy birthday, guilt dialing the number. He is not in the office. I drive to the site with the crew feeling half present. I know he will be furious.

Going on location a long way to get a cover shot, and a video for an album, is not unusual. I've been photographed for covers in Spain, the Rocky Mountains, Staten Island, and Los Angeles's Griffith Park. But this time I feel the weather has informed against me. Getting a cover is not worth losing a relationship.

I feel uncomfortable as we drive to a church, twenty miles from Butte. There is snow on the wooden fences and trees along the river and up along the far mountain ranges. The sun is bright and the church looks like a snowman, with the windows and the door as its button eyes and mouth, its bell tower like a cap upon its innocent face. I am dressed in plums and pinks and wander down the road, beside the fences next to the highway, looking at mountains, looking at cows, carrying a single rose in my hand. It is freezing.

In the four-wheel-drive Silverado and the Winnebago, the crew and I chase the sun in and out of mountain passes all day, getting more footage for the video. Susan, the combination makeup girl-gaffer-driver-gofer, is disorganized and very young. Somehow, as we traipse in the snow from eight in the morning to nearly eight at night, we manage to have nothing to eat but a handful of oatmeal cookies. I'm very good at being flexible when I'm hungry and I have no choice.

Flying out from the Butte airport the next day, I remember we don't always get what we want, but sometimes we get what we need. Isn't that the thing to remember?—courtesy of the Rolling Stones.

Friday, October 11, 1985 / New York

Home for a few days, hoping it will ease the difficulties of separation from Louis. Whirling through my apartment, wielding my scissors like a scimitar, I cut back the plants today, pruning most of them to the roots. The ones that are left have a freshly butchered look. The windows are now unobstructed as I look out into the gray October day, as cold and damp as my mood.

I had hoped cutting the plants might lead me to some inner cleansing, some gardening of the weeds that clutter and tangle and choke my thoughts this afternoon. I am really not sure what this fight with Louis is about, but I know it is sapping my energy and spoiling my mood. Louis says that I have been emotionally unavailable lately, and perhaps he is right. Certainly I have been traveling a lot.

But God, it is good to be home even for a few days! People in New York are amazing, dressed in everything from junk clothes to haute couture, and they all look as if they belong together.

When I returned home, I found that my friend Martha Schlamme had died. Martha was making records when I began. She did European songs, Brecht and Weill, and fifteen years ago she began studying acting with Alvin Epstein in New Haven. Max has told me for years that I should study with him, but New Haven seemed far off. Martha herself became a fine acting teacher. I had planned to take her class this fall. She just had a big success in New York in a show of Brecht and Weill songs at Playwrights Horizon with Alvin Epstein. The night she suffered her fatal stroke, she was on stage, singing a concert in Jamestown, New York. It is what we all want, to die with our boots on, in our stride.

Monday night, October 14, 1985 / San Francisco

I open tonight at the Fairmont. Flowers came this afternoon, a glorious bouquet with a note that says, "I love you more with each passing day." Louis called this morning to tell me how sorry he was for being so mad at me for being away on his birthday, and how sorry he is that we have been having a difficult time. Could our recent trouble be like a vaccination, like a smallpox shot, the antitoxin to forever cure lovers' quarrels?

Friday, October 18, 1985 / San Francisco

John Denver came to the show last night, and we sang a duet together of the Beatles' song "Here, There, and Everywhere." We learned it in Colorado twenty years ago, and sang it as though not a day had gone by.

I come off stage tonight to a standing ovation, a full house. Tony Bennett is in the audience as well. He is appreciative, glowing, handsome. We embrace after my set and he tells me how wonderful I am. He tells me he is going to make a record with Keith Grant in London, and we talk about how good Keith is. Tony is a generous audience, and he makes the night.

Performers are generous as a rule, because they know better than anybody what it takes to get out and do it, whether you feel like it or not. There's a song by Noel Coward called "Why Must the Show Go On?" But it must. Other performers understand my feelings that I have never done enough, will never be enough. There are days when all the applause, all the good I could ever do, will not budge a conviction that though I am going as fast as I can and doing as much as I can, it is not enough. I often can appreciate the sadness in the lives of other performers, whose hearts must be sustained and lifted by the applause, and on some nights I can even see my own need. The need is very deep and the sense of worthiness is very shallow on those nights when we must depend on the lift that comes from a great show and the applause that follows it. We develop skin as tough as tissue paper. Some nights applause is all that saves your life.

Benefit concert this afternoon for Bread and Roses, Mimi Baez Fariña's foundation that puts on entertainment for people in hospitals, jails, old peoples's homes and institutions in the San Francisco area. Today's show is at Laguna Honda Hospital. To perform for people who need to hear the music is one of the most satisfying feelings I know. I love my audiences, they are faithful and give me so much but this group of people is particularly special—hundreds of paralyzed, wheelchair-bound people of all ages and the volunteers who wheel them into a huge auditorium full of balloons, flowers like faces and faces like flowers, victims of stroke and senility, birth defects, motorcycle accidents, everyone singing "Amazing Grace."

This is my last day here in San Francisco at the Fairmont. Twenty-two shows down and two to go. I will be going home tomorrow. There is packing to do. The whole wardrobe of clothes, most of which I haven't worn, must be put back into the suitcases. And I am bone weary.

Monday, November 4, 1985 / New York

Saturday night, Louis and I went to hear Cynthia Macdonald reading from her new book of poetry at the Ninety-second Street Y. Cynthia has been a friend for many years. She began her career as an opera singer after attending Bennington and lived in many cities in the world, following her husband's career with Shell Oil. She found her life constantly disrupted by these moves, and twenty years ago she changed careers and became a poet. Her latest book, from which she read, is called *Alternate Means of Transport.* Our friendship has been very close and at one point, when our children were away at school, we spent a year as roommates in New York. She now runs the poetry and literature department at the University of Houston.

At the party afterward I see Helen Frankenthaler, an old friend of Cynthia's from Bennington, and my friend Andrée Hayum and Jennifer Macdonald, Cynthia's daughter. We all talk about the press, and fans.

"Does it bother you when you are recognized at a party, or dinner, when people tell you how much they enjoy your work?" asks a young poet.

"I think most performers are very shy outside of their work, off-stage, out of the recording studio," I say.

"If someone thanks me for the pleasure my poetry has given them, I'm thrilled. I know it is genuine, or at least tell myself I know," says Cynthia. A writer once told me that writers don't get the kind of fans that singers get. "Fans of painters and poets are different from fans of pop singers," he said. "Fans of singers want a piece of your clothing, a piece of your equipment, a photograph of you; fans of poets want a piece of your soul, they want you to read their manuscripts and poems."

"Did you ever have groupies follow you around, like the rock groups?" asks Jennifer. She is a painter, very talented.

"Sometimes. Music is a powerful psychic phenomenon, and sometimes it creates confusion in the mind of a listener. I have had a couple of people write me letters full of implications that we are brother and sister, or that I am a close friend who has somehow become misplaced and whom they have found again in my being. Once a woman insisted that I had had a sex change and then wanted to meet me, to get back together, certain that we had been lovers in some previous life."

For a number of years I had a fan who sent me bouquets at Carnegie Hall and Symphony Hall and the Greek Theatre every year—huge, extravagant, exotic arrangements that must have cost a mint. They would arrive, lush as flowerbeds, stuffed birds among the stems, violets and orchids, peat moss and tangles of roses woven into fabulous creations. At last I thanked him myself in a personal note. I thought, This fan has simply lost his mind with appreciation. It was a man, I'll call him Paul, and he answered my brief thank-you note with a long and complimentary letter, and endeared himself to my secretary at the time, and to me, as I read with pleasure the letters that followed. For many years, every time I played in a city near him, he would sent the bouquets, and they became a familiar presence, although we had never met.

When he finally did come backstage to a concert in Los Angeles, he proved to be a tall, good-looking man, with a sensitive and intelligent face. I only met him that once, but the flowers continued to arrive. Two years later, my secretary came into my studio holding a copy of the *Daily News*.

"Isn't this our Paul?" she asked. His picture was plastered over the front page.

"Yes, that's our flower child," I said. The headlines blazed in two-inch-high letters that our Paul had been arrested for the murder of a young woman out in the West. The night of the murder he turned himself in and confessed everything. The trial was a cut-and-dried affair, in which his past mental illness was explored.

There was a call from a Los Angeles reporter a few months ago, asking if I would talk to him about Paul. It seems that on the night of the murder, my office telephone number was dialed from the scene of the crime. No one was at the office, so I don't know if the call came before or after the murder.

Paul wrote to me recently from the prison hospital to ask if I'd heard about what happened to him back in 1983 and to say that he'd been diagnosed as having AIDS. He closed by asking me to send a picture, with something special written to him, to give him some encouragement.

I sent the photo, and my heart goes out to him. However distantly we were connected, he had become a fan. I was someone Paul thought of as part of his life, part of his family.

Friday night, November 8, 1985 / Connecticut

"It's a gorgeous day, Louis," I say, as though he had hung each leaf, stretched each shaft of light between the trees. I am wrapped in the silver Jaguar, doing sixty up the Saw Mill River Parkway, headed for the house in the country. It is the first time I have been able to do this in months. No wonder he has been feeling neglected and left alone. He has been.

The lake is low, and as we turn into the gravel road to the house, the birds fly away, bound up in tangled groups. A hemlock planted in the spring this year is doing well, looking like a stout green dwarf on the hill amid the fallen leaves.

The transformation of the house is nearly complete. Louis designed this place himself and cares about every doorway and floorboard. The shingles are stained a color close to mica and granite, the hot tub's round form juts out from the new terrace, the new outer buildings settle into the ground. The basement is finished off, the heat works, the spiral staircase is bolted in, the paint nearly perfect in the whole house. Tomorrow the piano will be moved in. Dust and piles of broken wood are gone, the new awning stretches out toward the lake where we will sit to get out of the rain and watch the swans and the ducks after we soak in the hot tub, languid and satisfied.

The house is changed, changing, as I am, my new roots finding their way. Everything seems to have fallen into place as my life is falling into place, rearranging itself into another configuration. There are new songs in the air, the music of birds that are migrating.

The cardinal flaps up from the willow with his sweet, lonely whistle. Geese call on the lake, darkness is falling. The sky is the color of blue slate and fleece, fading to black, bells ringing in the trees. Night in the country, home with Louis, happily, finally, together.

Thursday, November 14, 1985 / New York

Last night I went to a party for Bob Dylan at the Whitney Museum. In my jeweled black velvet jacket I stood with Dylan for the photographers, with one of his arms around me and one around Billy Joel. Bob is giggling. I have never seen him do that before. Billy Joel's wife, Christie Brinkley, is wearing a gold lamé shirt and she is very pregnant. She looks ready to have the baby at any minute.

There is so much of show business in what used to be thought of as folk music. Dylan would have roared with disbelief if he had been told in 1962 that he would be the establishment, revered at the Whitney Museum by the president of Columbia Records and a gathering of his friends in the music business. He probably would have written a funny song at the mere thought of it. But tonight, with his millions of records, his twenty-five years on Columbia (with a brief hiatus) being celebrated, and the added worship of the title of most influential man in pop music, he seems to be taking it all very calmly.

Dylan has a new album out, and you can hear the words. You could always hear the words to Bob's songs in the first records, and he was saying things we all wanted to hear. His lyrics had been buried in a number of records in recent years, lost in the kind of "contemporary mix" that is so fashionable, which really means you hear lots of bass and lots of track and little or no voice. That doesn't work for a singer for whom the lyric is essential. On his new album he has mixed the tracks himself, so that we can hear the words again. Hallelujah, for there are songs there that we still want to hear.

Tonight he seems happy. He is gracious, talking to everyone from behind his dark glasses and his mass of long, curly hair. He is wearing a soft white leather jacket and pants, a pair of boots. I told him I had seen him on *20/20*.

"I particularly like when you were so honest in discussing the trouble you had singing the lyrics to 'We Are the World.' " He had told the interviewer, sitting in the yard of his home over-looking the Pacific Ocean, that he disliked the lyrics to the song. Stevie Wonder showed Dylan how to sing the part of Dylan: "Do it like Bobby would do it," said Stevie, and leaned back from the piano and sang the words in the old Dylan style.

A lot of the young men who were Dylan's contemporaries are middle-aged now, as we used to call our parents when they were the same age. But they have an elusive quality, an ageless look about them. I don't think it is the hair or the things they wear. I think it is that Dylan and his contemporaries changed the way we think about their age. Their lyrics, daring because they talked about feelings, seeped into the thinking of the world. The dream of the sixties, which gave us another way of looking at sex, and race, and war, is not over; it is sealed beneath the skin. It is no longer possible to grow old; the writers challenged the order of death by defying it in their lyrics, in that musical drama that found its way from the Village coffee shops to the covers of *Time* and *Life* and the variety shows on television, and finally to the top-ten record charts, replacing Dorothy Collins and Snooky Lanson to become contemporary rock-and-roll and folk. Many of these writers are at Dylan's party tonight. They will never grow old.

Roger McGuinn is here, who changed his name from Jim McGuinn. I met him when he played for Bobby Darin in Las Vegas. He did the arrangements on my third album, in 1963. Roger started the Byrds, and put Dylan on the charts for the first time with an arrangement of "Mr. Tambourine Man," which he and I had first performed on my fifth album. Roy Orbison, Pete Townshend, Arlo Guthrie, and I stand together for more photographs. Billy Joel puts his arm around me, the other around Dylan, winks at the camera.

"We famous singers and songwriters do this all the time," he says. Dylan goes over to the table to talk to Arlo, who has been sitting all night, watching the party whirl by him. He, too, is one of those ageless men of folk music, a child of the sixties.

"It takes me a week to get over one of these parties," he says.

I have known Arlo since he was young, when I went into Harold Leventhal's office as a client in 1963. I sang at Arlo's wedding in Stockbridge when he married Jackie, the mother of his four children.

"It was your singing that kept us together," he tells me now, smiling. I worry about his health. Hungtington's disease is genetically transmitted, and children of Huntington's victims have a fifty-fifty chance of getting the disease. But he looks well and healthy tonight. Arlo was one of the first of the group with whom I found I could talk comfortably about anything. He is very intelligent and easygoing. I sit down for a while, and the talk turns to songwriting.

"Most of the songs I have written," I say, "are about my family—Mother, Father, my son, my siblings. It seems the easiest way for me to connect with my feelings."

"I couldn't write anything personal for about forty years," says Arlo. "I was brought up in the arm's-length school of writing, since I learned from Pete Seeger and Woody. They wrote about the world 'out there,' the masses, the ideas of life. I had to go through a lot of personal pain before it could come out in my writing and I could talk about my own feelings, my own emotions."

"And I found it easy to do autobiographical writing," I say. "That came the easiest for me."

"I have to shut myself up in a room for days at a time to get anything good done," Arlo says. "After about three days I come out, and if I'm lucky, I've got a song. If I'm not, I've got a problem, 'cause I just have to go back until I do get one."

I think a lot about those songs tonight. I've recorded many of Dylan's songs, and they hum through my head as the stars come and go, during the speeches, while the hors d'oeuvres are served—"Masters of War," "Just Like Tom Thumb's Blues," "Mr. Tambourine Man," "Daddy, You've Been on My Mind," and the one I always wanted to record and didn't, "Just Like a Rolling Stone." Their presence is like an unquestioned value in my conscience, like knowing gravity is for everybody and doesn't suspend itself when a famous person jumps out a window. They are tried and true, like laughter.

Later in the evening Louis and I sit down at a table with Harold Leventhal, who, although he hasn't managed me since 1972, has remained my friend. His wife, Natalie, is here with Toshi Seeger, without Pete. He couldn't come; he is up in the country, between benefits, resting.

"Pete chops wood to keep in shape," says Toshi.

"I'm glad. I can't imagine Pete Seeger going to the New York Health and Racquet Club. It wouldn't be right." Pete, with his

hair getting whiter, is the youngest of all the young men. I ask
Toshi what she has been doing lately.

"I'm running the Clearwater Festival up on the Hudson, with
eleven stages and twenty acts and ten thousand people attending
every year. I'll bet you never thought of me as capable of that;
you thought I always just washed Pete's socks," she says. This
is said not to me in particular but to the room. As a matter of
fact, I don't think Pete could function without Toshi, whether
she washes his socks or not. I have always thought of her as a
powerful woman.

"I'll bet you chop wood and he washes your socks as well,"
I say. Toshi is Japanese, and gives the impression of someone
who has won many of her battles and is ready to take on whatever comes next. I met Toshi and Pete in 1963. Sometimes Pete
would come in from a particularly tough touring schedule, and
I would find him sleeping behind a couch or on the floor behind
a desk in Harold's office when I came for business meetings. He
would be resting before he took the train up to Beacon, where
he lives. He always looked very tall and very exhausted, like a
long-necked banjo stretched out on the floor. His songs are of
the youth of the spirit and the spirit of peace in the world.

"He is nearly seventy, he's got to cut back on the touring,"
Toshi says. Harold always says that Pete still takes every job that
comes his way, especially if it's for free. He also takes more
than one date a night, sometimes in different cities, which drives
Harold crazy.

"But if he didn't he wouldn't be Pete," says Harold. I'm sorry
he isn't here tonight. Dylan claims Pete and Woody Guthrie
were the men who inspired him and gave him his direction for
his music. I guess Pete doesn't have to be here—he's already
here, inspiring what has come to be known as contemporary
music.

Walter Yetnikoff, the president of Columbia, is in the corner
talking to my old friend David Braun. Yoko Ono and David
Bowie make their star-studded entrance, turning heads as they
speed through the room, their entourage flying in V formation
behind them. Someone reaches out to Bowie as he slips away
like quicksilver, with a wave of his elegant arm, headed for
Entertainment Tonight.

All night the forty-eight television screens set up on the main
floor of the Whitney, above the party, play Dylan footage of

concerts, videos. His young face moves forty-eight times in agreement. Everyone is glad he has continued to make music. Dylan at the Whitney, living art.

Saturday, November 23, 1985 / Providence, Rhode Island

Water pouring from my trench coat, my boots dripping, we check into the Marriott in Providence. We flew up on a twenty-passenger twin-engine plane.

Maria and I arrive at the backstage door of the old Performing Arts Center, hauling our bags into the dressing rooms, trying to figure out which of the rooms is going to be the most comfortable. We choose one; there is a water bug in the bathroom, climbing the wall, and a mouse comes out of his hole and takes a walk three feet from me while I sit meditating. Wildlife.

I check the calls on my answering machine—messages from Jac Holzman offering to license *Amazing Grace* in the States, telling me it's the "best thing you have done in twenty-five years, dear." It is coming out any day now in London. Rupert Holmes is getting ready for our recording of "Moonfall," writing the arrangement, talking to me about keys and players. That song will be on Polygram. Danny Goldberg wants to distribute the English album in the United States as well, on his new label, Gold Castle. I suggest to Danny that I put my two latest songs about meditation on the album and call it *Trust Your Heart* in the States, after one of my new songs. I'd also like to have "Moonfall" on it, so that all of these songs can be together, and possibly Polygram could distribute it for Gold Castle. Danny Goldberg says this is impossible because he is going to make his distribution deal with MCA, where he has his other label. It is a far-off dream, but why not dream?

My head spins. Why can't I wheel and deal with ease? I am managing myself again, as I did for eleven years after I left Harold and before my short fling with Freddy. It may not be the way I want it, but it's the way it is. I must accept that nobody knows everything, and that managing myself, hassles and all, is what I have to do now. I just have to remember to smile while my heart is pounding, keep saying the words like a sensible adult while my pulse is throbbing and my face is red. It just takes practice, that's all. Keep in the moment, keep balanced, pretend to be sane.

I call my sister. It's midnight in Providence. She answers the phone in Santa Monica; she sounds very near.

"Holly, I feel out of control, as though I don't know what I'm doing. Maybe I don't. I'm searching for the right thing, but it all feels scary again."

"I was feeling much the same this week," she says, "and I suddenly thought, it says in the Bible, 'Seek ye first the Kingdom of God.' It doesn't say, 'Find ye first the Kingdom of God.' "

We laugh, relief.

"I didn't know Bob Dylan wrote a song for you," she says. "I heard someone on the radio reading the notes from Dylan's new collection, and it says that he wrote 'I'll Keep It With Mine' for you. Did you know that?"

I didn't know. Dylan, man of mystery, put it in his notes for the world to read, but didn't tell me.

Thursday, December 5, 1985 / New York

Avery Fisher Hall. My annual New York concert. It's usually at Carnegie Hall, but this year Carnegie is closed for renovations.

"I need a choir of angels," I say to my friend Tom Bogdan. Tom is a crystal-clear tenor who often performs his own solo concerts. He sang backup for me on my tour after *Hard Times for Lovers* was released and he knows all the singers in New York.

"I know just the voices to give you a heavenly backup," he says. He arranges to have the New York City Children's Choir sing the hymn "Jerusalem" from *Chariots of Fire* with me. While I sing the encore, the children walk on stage, humming "When You Wish Upon a Star" behind me. Giggles, sighs, murmurs from the audience. Then "Jerusalem," with that glorious descant, high and angelic, and the ending, "Amazing Grace." It is thrilling. I think I enjoy it more than anyone else, my present to myself, my gift to New York, my adopted town.

Sunday, December 8, 1985 / New York

I arrive at the Mayflower Hotel in an elegant suit from Givenchy and high heels, my hair up under a cranberry red felt hat. My makeup is carefully done, I carry a new purse from an Italian shop on Madison Avenue. I am looking my best for this special occasion. I go into the lobby to pick up Dr. Brico for our annual lunch at the Russian Tea Room. She comes to New York once a year from Denver.

"You look wonderful. I am so glad you put your hair up; you look like a grown-up."

I can't contain my pleasure that she noticed—quite a difference from that first meeting, so many years ago, when she saw a girl with pigtails, scruffy oxfords, dog-eared music.

At the Tea Room, we order borscht and lamb. The maître d', Richard Baron, knows us both. He embraces us and shows us to our table.

"No onions, no celery, no pork," says Dr. Brico, shaking her head vehemently at Richard, who is smiling.

"You know there is never any pork or celery or onions in our borscht," he says.

"Here," she says to him before he can go off to get our order, "take our picture, will you?" She thrusts a camera into Richard's hands. "Just push that button." Richard clicks the camera. Antonia and I are immortalized together at the Tea Room, smiling into the bright flash.

After our lunch, I take Antonia to a rehearsal of the National Dance Institute's event that is coming up in a few months. I have a part in it, singing some of the songs I wrote and serving as our mistress of ceremonies. She was thrilled to see the children dancing, and afterward she said to me, "You know how I never could forgive you for giving up and not becoming a great pianist?"

I'll say I remember. How can I forget? For many years I would invite Dr. Brico to hear me sing, in Denver, or in New York, at Carnegie, with symphonies. I always introduced her from the stage as my beloved teacher, and she would come backstage afterward, take my hands in hers, and look at me with a deep sigh.

"You really could have gone places, little Judy," she would

say. I could never get a response to what I was doing rather than to what she thought I should be doing.

"Well, I finally got over that," she says to me today. I cannot believe my ears.

And she talks about the songs I have just done for this rehearsal at the Felt Forum.

I still don't believe I've heard her correctly.

"Oh, they were just some little songs," I say.

"No," she says. "You are marvelous."

I walk as if in a dream, as if under water. For thirty years I have longed for these words. But I never thought it possible. I'm exuberant. A circle is completed; my friend, my mentor, my nemesis, my imperfect and perfectly beloved teacher Antonia.

Tuesday, December 10, 1985 / New York

Yesterday the new album, *Amazing Grace*, arrived from London. The cover looks good—our trip to Butte paid off—and the album sounds wonderful. My heart only plummeted once, during one song, on a line that was remixed by Keith Grant and Tony Britten after I had left London. Otherwise, the sixteen songs really stand up. The album has gone on the pop record charts in London, the advertising is good, they expect to sell a lot of records. The Andrew Lloyd Webber album, with my version of "I Know Him So Well" from *Chess* and "Another Suitcase," is doing very well.

I'm working on "Moonfall," learning it to record. It's a difficult song, and I'm not sure it is accessible without many hearings. I fell in love with it on the spot, but it needs to be studied—it has big intervals, difficult entrances. The singer must be like a swan gliding on the surface, feet paddling like mad beneath the water. There should be no strain in the lyrics, the eyes, the mouth, or the muscles of the neck. Only beneath the chest bones, where the power goes deep down to the pelvis, are the muscles hard at work—a solid, breathing, secure structure, invisible and invincible.

I must swim many times a week to keep my lungs in shape to make breathing choices in maximum condition, and I must work with Max as often as I can.

The dates have been set for recording "Moonfall," in mid-January, when I return from the Virgin Islands. The cast album of the show has been placed with Polygram. I will do the single, and when it is out and being played, Polygram will want to release an album.

My friends were probably right, I should have left Elecktra long ago. I wonder what I was suppose to learn by staying all those years.

It's a nice feeling to be wanted.

Thursday, December 12, 1985 / Connecticut

Louis and I have been having a close and loving time together for the past few weeks. Again our moods are compatible and our time a pleasure. At the point of least resistance, in all my previous relationships, I have run or been run from. Louis and I have stayed together, neither of us has run, and we are stronger together.

I don't slam the doors anymore. I used to. During one fight we had here at the lake, I threw a plate across the room after Louis left by the door. The plate smashed into a million pieces. Slammed phones, slammed doors, screaming fights. We have had them. Not today. I knock wood and think about luck and time.

Whatever was happening between us was like a cyclone speeding through some town in Kansas; it seemed to clear out the corners and clean up the air.

Tuesday, December 17, 1985 / New York

I've spent all day wrapping presents for my family and friends. The Andrew Lloyd Webber collection is on the charts at thirty-nine today and my *Amazing Grace* is at thirty-six. Who would have guessed it a year ago?

Ribbons and silver paper, red shining surfaces and glittery Santa Claus cards sprinkling their sparkling dust everywhere. I'm giving most of my friends copies of the album from England, Louis gets a first edition of Churchill's *History of the English-Speaking Peoples* and a pair of glass swans.

The last time I saw my father was Christmas of 1967 in Colorado. The whole family climbed into two cars and rolled up into the mountains, into the clean blue and white air of the Rockies. There were my parents, Holly, Mike and his wife, Susan, Denver John, and I. My brother David was living and teaching skiing in Winter Park, Colorado, so we rented a cabin nearby, settled in, and spent the snowy night of Christmas Eve together. *In My Life* had gone gold that year, I had started to make money, and I wanted to give my parents something special, something that would show them tangibly that their little girl had, finally, made it. I had bought them two round-trip tickets to Hawaii, all expenses paid—first class all the way. The tickets were wrapped in shiny green paper with silver bows and Santa Claus on the card, shiny flakes of tinsel falling from Santa's bag. I knew they would be thrilled.

My father sat on the far side of the room from me, his back to the fire. His smile was wooden, his face somber and dark. He was not in a jovial mood. He didn't exclaim over every fur mitten, or the shiny surface of a new wallet, or the texture of his new sheepskin coat. He was quiet, his attention divided. I know now that he was thinking not of the spirit of Christmas, but of his own death.

When we had opened all our presents, eaten dinner, sat around the stripped tree, and burned all the red and gold and green wrapping paper in the crackling fireplace, we put on our coats and drove up the mountain to see our friend Kay Bradley, whose house sat on the breast of the longest ski slope at Winter Park. I put my arm through my father's as we walked on the slick ice to the car. He left my hand looped through his elbow. I should have known then. He got into the car beside me, subdued. I asked him if he liked my gift—the promise of two weeks of sun and swimming and rest. He said he thought he could use a rest.

Below the Bradley's house the cars were parked in stacks, and the road was slick with ice. Our three carfuls had to park down the hill, and by the time we found spaces we were back near the main road. Instead of taking the winding road up to the lighted house on the hill, I suggested the route straight up, through the snow.

Again my father took my arm. The rest of the gang straggled uphill, Denver John and Mike and Susan leading the way, David and Mother moving right along. I walked more slowly. My father was panting, his breathing fierce and heavy.

When we made it to the house, which had twinkled before us all the way up, I realized I had been frightened my father would fall dead before we got there, in front of the sparkling house in the snow. It was freezing outside, but in the house he was pale, sweat stood out on his forehead. Everyone said, "Charlie, you should have gone back down." Kay made him a drink, and his face slowly returned to its normal color. He smiled and the sadness almost left his face—his blue glass eyes opened wide, and he began to take in the party, the house, Kay Bradley, as though he could see. That night was the last time I saw him alive.

He and my mother did go to Hawaii. He became ill there and, in terrible pain, went to the hospital for extensive testing. Mother spent the two weeks between the beach at Waikki and the hospital room. They put him through every battery of tests they knew, but the doctors couldn't find anything wrong. When they came back he went into the hospital in Denver, where the specialists continued to find nothing wrong and he continued to scream in pain.

They sent him home and he tried to get dressed and go to work, sweating through his suit. Back in the hospital he moaned and called for medication, while on the other end of the telephone I repeated what the doctors had told me. "They can't find anything wrong with you, Daddy." The doctors said not to worry.

I went to England to work, reassured. My father died on May 4, 1968, of a blood vessel bursting near his spine.

My godfather, Holden, was the last to see Daddy alive. He was there late at night, having insisted on staying long after visiting hours were over. Daddy was very ill, he said, and as he leaned over the bed, trying to be appropriately soothing, Daddy squeezed his hand. The two friends had had a wager for years on who would be the first to die.

"Well, old buddy, I guess I won, didn't I?" Holden said he knew when he left the hospital that night that he wouldn't see Chuck again.

My mother said, "Don't bring any black clothes. I don't want any black. He would have wanted his funeral in living color."

He was cremated, as he had wished. In July, when the snow

melted from the high passes, Michael and Denver and David took our father's ashes to Rocky Mountain National Park and scattered them over Fern Lake.

The Christmases since, all seventeen of them, have been lonely without him.

Saturday, December 21, 1985 / Connecticut

At the house, snow is covering the lake, lighting up the air with sparkles; snow is falling through the wind chimes.

It seems to me that all my life I dreamed of being here, among the snowflakes that fall through the bells in these trees. The life I led, with its surface of sin as deep as I could imagine or manage, was something I ran through blindly to get to this place. Often, from my windows on the Upper West Side of Manhattan, I watched the Hudson River, sludged with frozen ice or plodding as it shone in the summer heat. I often felt as if I were being circled by prey and longed to be out of where I was, but I didn't know how to get to this.

The boys, children of our neighbors here in the country, are still skating on the lake. The sun, behind a row of pines on the other side of the lake, is tipping the edge of the trees. Light shatters on the lake, spilling gold and white on the snowy surfaces. Perhaps I'll take the shovel out and clear a space for skating in front of the house. There is light enough for that now, light enough for many things.

Monday, December 23, 1985 / New York

The Three Wise Men followed a star that some say was Halley's Comet, which flies in the sky tonight. The Christmas tree stands as tall as the very high ceilings, and it is fat enough so that its arms reach out just the right distance into the room. We will trim it with ribbons of white with gold embroidery, the ribbons I used to get from a Rumanian shop in the Village—Rumanian dream ribbon, ribbon to make wishes on. An angel on the treetop, the finishing touch.

On the mantel of each of the houses I lived in when I was growing up—in Los Angeles, at 11572 Mississippi Avenue, and in Denver, on Willow, on Oneida, on Emerson, on Marion, on Fulton—was the figure of a Buddah. His body was dark wood; his stomach, folding many times over in front of him, was shiny and glowed with a rich finish. He was laughing, a wide grin on his dark face. Under him was a twisted, gnarled, wooden stand, carved for him to sit on out of the same dark shiny wood. I have no idea where he came from. Perhaps from a relative of ours who was a missionary in China, my mother's Aunt Belle's husband, Harry. The Buddha was the only icon in our house.

In each house he took a prominent position, watching over our chaos and our games. I think now that he must have been of Korean or Malay origin, from someplace where the deity is a carouser, a humorist. The shiny black laughing Buddha on our mantelpiece was somehow like our family—black sheep banded together outside the herd, black for different, black for out of the ordinary. He looked a little like my father.

Nearly all the packages for my family are wrapped and sent— earrings for Mom, a golf video for my stepfather, Robert, slippers for David, books for Michael, a sweater for Denver, a silk blouse for Holly, presents for husbands and wives, nieces and nephews. Though Denver's family will join us for our Christmas party, I wish we could all be together this year. The plates and glasses have arrived for the party on Christmas Day, stacked high in the utility rooms. I've been shopping for the finishing touches—the mousse cakes that are the best, the pfeffernuss without which it would not seem like Christmas. We have, I think, invited everyone we want to see and most of them are going to be here. But not Susie, she and Joe are going to Ireland; nor Susan Rice, she is in Detroit for the holiday; Patricia Elliott is doing a play in England; and Florence and Harold Rome will be in Japan.

Thursday, December 26, 1985 / New York

On Christmas Eve Louis and I went to St. Thomas's to hear the Evensong and the story of Christmas as told to the little children around the crèche. The little boys' voices in the descants were angelic, the ritual telling of the old story was as fresh as though Christ had been born that evening, laid in the manger of the little crèche, found by the Wise Men, and heralded by the angels. Children's voices, little babies and tots, shouted and made a commotion through some of the service, while everyone in their Christmas Eve best looked pleased. This was the children's service, and I felt it was exactly where I belonged.

Louis was raised a Lutheran, and I was raised as a sort of milquetoast Methodist. Louis once told me about teaching Sunday school to Lutheran children.

"I fell away from the church after a Sunday service where the pastor gave a sermon saying from the pulpit that we 'must not marry outside of our racial community.' That day a parishioner had come home to Queens with his Japanese wife. The couple stood up and walked out of the church. I left soon afterward myself. If this was a principle of Christianity, then I didn't want to have anything to do with it. I could no longer listen to a pastor who was a racist. It was many years before I found my way back to a spiritual life."

Since I met Louis, he and I have shared many experiences of going to holy places—temples, churches, and chapels. In Jerusalem we made our wishes at the Wailing Wall, and we prayed together in Matisse's chapel at Vence, France.

This year we went to a Seder at the Brauns' home, where David's grandmother and I sang the songs in the Haggadah—I from a book, she by heart. The ceremonies that mark the essentials of life, the "outer signs of inner grace," mark our lives, and it is good to participate in them, the weddings, the funerals, the shared meditations. As I wrote years ago in my song "Secret Gardens," they are passages of the body through the changes of the heart.

> *But most of all, it is me that has changed,*
> *And yet still I'm the same.*
> *That's me at the weddings, that's me at the graves*
> *Dressed like the people who once looked so grown-up and brave.*
> *I look in the mirror*
> *Through the eyes of the child that was me.*
> *I see willows bending, the season is spring,*
> *And the silverblue sailing birds fly with the sun on their wings.*
> *Secret gardens of the heart*
> *Where the seasons change forever.*
> *I see you shining through the night*
> *In the ice and snow of winter.*

It was warm outside, and after the service at St. Thomas's, we roamed down Fifth Avenue, taking our time, our eyes looking at the lights, the stores wrapped in the glittering magic that is Christmas in New York—Cartier in a ribbon the size of the store, glittering trees stacked on the corners of the Trump Tower, the Salvation Army's red buckets swinging under the voices of the volunteers, who rang their bells for all they were worth. In front of St. Patrick's the crowds were so dense that Louis said, "Do you think they will let us in?" I said, "Yes, they can't tell we're not real Catholics, we could easily pass." Inside, the television lights were already being set up for midnight mass, the poinsettias overflowed the altar, the bigger-than-life crèche was still missing the baby Jesus. Christ was born at St. Thomas's earlier.

We left money in the boxes for the poor and went across the street to the crowds swarming under the big tree at Rockefeller Center, at the end of the line of white wire angels blowing bugles. On the rink, the skaters drifted over the ice, and the tree above seemed enormous.

At home, Louis and I unwrapped the presents we had for each other under the tree and the ones from our families and friends. It is our eighth Christmas together, and it's so good to have him to myself, to have this quiet time. I feel at peace, filled with the spirit of this night.

Saturday, December 28, 1985 / Connecticut

"Something shocking occurs to me, that I may not want to be a singer anymore."

Louis and I are sitting in the hot tub, our bodies submerged. The moon is full, the lake is white under its light, a sheen of silk on the snow-covered trees, the snow-covered lake. Undeniable. The feeling is quite painful.

Where is it coming from? Louis leans his head back onto the tub, looking at me, his naked body visible under the water.

"Have you ever had this thought before?"

"When you begin to learn the piano at such an early age, no one asks you what you are going to be, what you are going to do. Whether you make plans for it or not, it is assumed that you are going to give back the thing that you have been given, give it to the world. The world owns you in a way that it doesn't own other people.''

Perhaps my early training made me feel I had to perform in order to survive. Performing was as ingrained in my being as the mark of a tattoo is ingrained in the skin—a scar carried for life. A wound that nourishes. I was always told I had to show my "gift," that it would bring joy to others and, finally, would never let me down.

"You're in the slip now, the wind has dropped. You're just having the chance to look at things from another perspective in a safe harbor," says Louis.

His moustache is covered with very fine mist from the hot tub, and the cold in the air is freezing it into tiny drops around his lips.

I sink into the tub and let the steam come into my lungs. Perhaps Louis is right. This meandering question of what I might want to do with my life is allowed, at least on the twenty-eighth of December, up to my nose in the hot water, holding my lover's hand.

Tuesday, December 31, 1985 / New York

I awoke early on this last day of the year, got up, and fed the cat, Ruffles, who purred and rubbed his face against my leg, making that wonderful *ruffles* sound that is a cross between a roar and a meow. Sunlight slanted into the kitchen through blue glass, making a pattern across the floor and on my silk gown as I passed through its shivering brilliance. I brought Louis his coffee, and he woke, stretching and smiling that wonderful smile. We embraced, sharing the ecstasy of the morning together.

"Happy last day of the year," he said.

Tomorrow we pack our snorkel gear and toothpaste in that indisputable intimacy with the man I love enough to share everything. Elena Poniatowska, the Mexican writer, has said that everything essential is invisible. It is true. We hold on to air, we breathe fantasy, we are made of thought. Things appear to be the same as they were a year ago—the sunlight, Louis's embrace, my own eyes reflected in the mirror, the schedule to be kept, the songs to be sung. Yet there is an inner difference. I've heard it said that what separates men and women from the beasts is that men and women must tell their stories. Our stories unite us with nature and the primitive, bonding us with our own beauty and our own beast.

My story belongs to no one else, and yet our stories, yours and mine, are the same under the skin, beyond the facts, beyond the names and dates. Only the heart speaks to the heart, and in my journal this year I have written what I know. I needed to tell you my story as I need to hear yours, so that we may share our secrets and trust our hearts.

The promise, as old as flame, as new as sunrise, is coming through. I feel grateful for the view of the spirit that this year's journey has provided. There is nothing in the promise that says the bird that flies out of the ashes will always fly a perfect course; only that she will rise from the ashes on new wings.

Epilogue

Wednesday, April 1, 1987 / New York

Clark was married on the twenty-eighth of March, last weekend. I went to St. Paul for his wedding to Alyson Sinclair Lloyd, a woman of twenty-five who is beautiful and blessed to have come along at the right moment. Louis and I went to the wedding together. We celebrated for two days with my family and Alyson's. Clark's father, Peter, my ex-husband, was there. It had probably been ten years since we had said more than a few words to each other, twenty since we spent two days together. I sang "Amazing Grace" during the ceremony, managing to get through the song without crying only by thinking of toothpaste. Every other face had tears on it, and mine did as well, later—tears, and aching muscles in my face from all the smiling.

The years of struggle for Clark are in the past, the dark times and the heartbreak. Our paths have merged and paralleled. Today is a new beginning.

> *Amazing grace, how sweet the sound*
> *That saved a wretch like me.*
> *I once was lost, but now am found*
> *Was blind, but now I see.*

Discography

A Maid of Constant Sorrow   October 15, 1961

MAID OF CONSTANT SORROW • THE PRICKILIE BUSH • WILD MOUN-
TAIN THYME • TIM EVANS • SAILOR'S LIFE • BOLD FENIAN MEN
• WARS OF GERMANY • O DADDY BE GAY • I KNOW WHERE I'M
GOING • JOHN RILEY • PRETTY SARO • THE RISING OF THE MOON

The Golden Apples of the Sun   Mid-1962

GOLDEN APPLES OF THE SUN • BONNIE SHIP THE DIAMOND • LIT-
TLE BROWN DOG • TWELVE GATES TO THE CITY • CHRIST CHILD
LULLABY • GREAT SELCHIE OF SHULE SKERRY • TELL ME WHO I'LL
MARRY • FANNERIO • CROW ON THE CRADLE • LARK IN THE
MORNING • SING HALLELUJAH • SHULE AROON

Judy Collins #3   March/April 1964

ANATHEA • BULLGINE RUN • FAREWELL • HEY, NELLY, NELLY
• TEN O'CLOCK ALL IS WELL • THE DOVE • MASTERS OF WAR •
IN THE HILLS OF SHILOH • THE BELLS OF RHYMNEY • DEPORTEE
• SETTLE DOWN • COME AWAY MELINDA • TURN! TURN! TURN!

The Judy Collins Concert   October 1964

WINTER SKY • THE LAST THING ON MY MIND • TEAR DOWN THE WALLS • BONNIE BOY IS YOUNG • ME AND MY UNCLE • WILD RIPPLING WATER • THE LONESOME DEATH OF HATTIE CARROLL • MY RAMBLIN' BOY • RED-WINGED BLACKBIRD • COAL TATTOO • CRUEL MOTHER • BOTTLE OF WINE • MEDGAR EVERS LULLABY • HEY, NELLY, NELLY

Judy Collins Fifth Album   November 1965

PACK UP YOUR SORROWS • THE COMING OF THE ROADS • SO EARLY, EARLY IN THE SPRING • TOMORROW IS A LONG TIME • DADDY YOU'VE BEEN ON MY MIND • THIRSTY BOOTS • MR. TAMBOURINE MAN • LORD GREGORY • IN THE HEAT OF THE SUMMER • EARLY MORNING RAIN • CARRY IT ON • IT ISN'T NICE

In My Life   November 1966   Certified Gold, December 21, 1970

TOM THUMB'S BLUES • HARD LOVIN' LOSER • PIRATE JENNY • SUZANNE • LA COLOMBE • MARAT/SADE • I THINK IT'S GOING TO RAIN TODAY • SUNNY GOODGE STREET • LIVERPOOL LULLABY • DRESS REHEARSAL RAG • IN MY LIFE

Wildflowers   November 1967   Certified Gold, January 20, 1969

MICHAEL FROM MOUNTAINS • SINCE YOU ASKED • SISTERS OF MERCY • PRIESTS • A BALLATA OF FRANCESCO LANDINI: LASSO! DI DONNA • BOTH SIDES NOW • LA CHANSON DES VIEUX AMANTS • SKY FELL • ALBATROSS • HEY, THAT'S NO WAY TO SAY GOODBYE

Who Knows Where the Time Goes   November 1968   Certified Gold, October 8, 1969

HELLO, HORRAY • STORY OF ISAAC • MY FATHER • SOMEDAY SOON • WHO KNOWS WHERE THE TIME GOES • POOR IMMIGRANT • FIRST BOY I LOVED • BIRD ON THE WIRE • PRETTY POLLY

Recollections   *July 1969*

PACK UP YOUR SORROWS • TOMORROW IS A LONG TIME • EARLY
MORNING RAIN • ANATHEA • TURN! TURN! TURN! • DADDY
YOU'VE BEEN ON MY MIND • MR. TAMBOURINE MAN • WINTER
SKY • THE LAST THING ON MY MIND • THE BELLS OF RHYMNEY •
FAREWELL

Whales and Nightingales   *November 12, 1970*   *Certified Gold,
April 6, 1971*

SONG   FOR   DAVID • SONS   OF • THE   PATRIOT   GAME •
PROTHALAMIUM • OH, HAD I A GOLDEN THREAD • GENE'S SONG
• FAREWELL TO TARWATHIE • TIME PASSES SLOWLY • MARIEKE •
NIGHTINGALE I • NIGHTINGALE II • SIMPLE GIFTS • AMAZING
GRACE

Living   *November 2, 1972*

JOAN OF ARC • 4 STRONG WINDS • VIETNAM LOVE SONG •
INNISFREE • SONG FOR JUDITH (OPEN THE DOOR) • ALL THINGS ARE
QUITE   SILENT • EASY   TIMES • CHELSEA   MORNING • BLUE
RAINCOAT • JUST LIKE TOM THUMB'S BLUES

Colors of the Day: The Best Of   *May 8, 1972*   *Certified Gold,
January 22, 1974*

SOMEDAY SOON • SINCE YOU ASKED • BOTH SIDES NOW • SONS
OF • SUZANNE • FAREWELL TO TARWATHIE • WHO KNOWS WHERE
THE TIME GOES • SUNNY GOODGE STREET • MY FATHER •
ALBATROSS • IN MY LIFE • AMAZING GRACE

True Stories and Other Dreams   *January 18, 1973*

COOK WITH HONEY • SO BEGINS THE TASK • FISHERMEN SONG •
THE DEALER (DOWN AND LOSIN') • SECRET GARDENS • HOLLY
ANN • THE HOSTAGE • SONG FOR MARTIN • CHE

Judith   March 24, 1975   Certified Gold, November 19, 1975

THE MOON IS A HARSH MISTRESS • ANGEL, SPREAD YOUR WINGS • HOUSES • THE LOVIN' OF THE GAME • SONG FOR DUKE • SEND IN THE CLOWNS • SALT OF THE EARTH • BROTHER, CAN YOU SPARE A DIME • CITY OF NEW ORLEANS • I'LL BE SEEING YOU • PIRATE SHIPS • BORN TO THE BREED

Bread and Roses   August 25, 1976

BREAD AND ROSES • EVERYTHING MUST CHANGE • SPECIAL DELIVERY • OUT OF CONTROL • PLEGARIA A UN LABRADOR • COME DOWN IN TIME • SPANISH IS THE LOVING TONGUE • I DIDN'T KNOW ABOUT YOU • TAKE THIS LONGING • LOVE HURTS • MARJORIE • KING DAVID

So Early in the Spring   July 19, 1977

PRETTY POLLY • SO EARLY, EARLY IN THE SPRING • PRETTY SARO • GOLDEN APPLES OF THE SUN • BONNIE SHIP THE DIAMOND • FAREWELL TO TARWATHIE • THE HOSTAGE • LA COLOMBE • COAL TATTOO • CARRY IT ON • BREAD AND ROSES • MARAT/SADE • SPECIAL DELIVERY • THE LOVIN' OF THE GAME • BOTH SIDES NOW • MARIEKE • SEND IN THE CLOWNS • BIRD ON THE WIRE • SINCE YOU'VE ASKED • BORN TO THE BREED • MY FATHER • HOLLY ANN • HOUSES • SECRET GARDENS

Hard Times for Lovers   February 20, 1979

HARD TIMES FOR LOVERS • MARIE • HAPPY END • DESPERADO • I REMEMBER SKY • STARMAKER • DOROTHY • I'LL NEVER SAY "GOODBYE" (THEME FROM *THE PROMISE*) • THROUGH THE EYES OF LOVE (THEME FROM *ICE CASTLES*) • WHERE OR WHEN

Running for My Life   March 28, 1980

RUNNING FOR MY LIFE • BRIGHT MORNING STAR • GREEN FINCH AND LINNET BIRD • MARIEKE • PRETTY WOMEN • ALMOST FREE • I COULD REALLY SHOW YOU AROUND • I'VE DONE ENOUGH DYIN' TODAY • ANYONE WOULD LOVE YOU • THE RAINBOW CONNECTION • THIS IS THE DAY • WEDDING SONG

Time of Our Lives   January 22, 1982

GREAT EXPECTATIONS • THE REST OF YOUR LIFE • GRANDADDY • IT'S GONNA BE ONE OF THOSE NIGHTS • MEMORY • SUN SON • MAMA MAMA • DRINK A ROUND TO IRELAND • ANGEL ON MY SIDE • DON'T SAY GOODBYE LOVE

Home Again   1984

ONLY YOU • SWEETHEART ON PARADE • EVERYBODY WORKS IN CHINA • YELLOW KIMONO • FROM WHERE I STAND • HOME AGAIN • SHOOT FIRST • DON'T SAY LOVE • DREAM ON • THE BEST IS YET TO COME

Amazing Grace   1985 (English release only)

AMAZING GRACE • DAY BY DAY • BRIDGE OVER TROUBLED WATER • I DON'T KNOW HOW TO LOVE HIM • BOTH SIDES NOW • ABIDE WITH ME • JUST A CLOSER WALK WITH THEE • WHEN YOU WISH UPON A STAR • WHEN A CHILD IS BORN • THE ROSE • ONE DAY AT A TIME • OH HAPPY DAY • MORNING HAS BROKEN • SEND IN THE CLOWNS • THE LORD IS MY SHEPHERD • JERUSALEM

Trust Your Heart   April 13, 1987

TRUST YOUR HEART • AMAZING GRACE • JERUSALEM • DAY BY DAY • THE LIFE YOU DREAM • THE ROSE • MOONFALL • MORNING HAS BROKEN • WHEN A CHILD IS BORN • WHEN YOU WISH UPON A STAR

About the Author

JUDY COLLINS was born on May 1, 1939, in Seattle, Washington. She began recording with Elektra Records in 1961. The release of the album ''Trust Your Heart'' brings to twenty-two the number of albums in Ms. Collins prolific career, including six gold albums. Over the years many of her interpretations have become world famous. ''Both Sides Now,'' ''Amazing Grace,'' ''Send In The Clowns,'' ''Someday Soon,'' and ''Suzanne'' are just some of the songs that have placed Judy Collins's personal stamp on popular music. Judy Collins has lived in New York since 1963.